# THE EMERGING SCENARIO OF ETHICS

# THE EMERGING SCENARIO OF ETHICS
## Based Governance in India

**Habibur Rehman**

GYAN

ISBN : 978-81-212-1241-0

Price: ₹ 790

First Published, 2015

*Published by*

Gyan Publishing House
23, Main Ansari Road, Darya Ganj,
New Delhi-110002
Ph. : 23282060, 23261060
Fax: 011-23285914
E-mail: books@gyanbooks.com

*Laser Typesetting* : Sanya Computers, Delhi
*Printed at* : G. Print Process, Delhi

**Cataloging in Publication Data—DK**
Courtesy: D.K. Agencies (P) Ltd. <docinfo@dkagencies.com>

**Rehman, Habibur.**
The emerging scenario ethics : based governance in India / Habibur Rehman.
p. cm.
Includes index.
ISBN 9788121212410

1. Political ethics—India. 2. India—Politics and government—21st century. 3. Social ethics—India. 4. Parent and child—India. 5. Parenting—India. 6. India—Economic conditions—1991- I. Title.

DDC 172.0954 23

# Contents

# Preface

So long as we remained under dogmatic slumber, passive of events and playthings of others we could not change our destiny and miserably failed to mould our future. The initiation came to us only after 1947, and we decided to make the history of our choice and build India of our dreams. We dreamt of an independent India in which every citizen possessed an equal place and full opportunity of growth and service, where inequality in wealth and status did not exist and where the vital impulses of men were directed to creative and co-operative endeavours. What we aimed to achieve through independence was not just a change of masters from white to brown but a really democratic administration, a rule by *Aam Aadmi* and a welfare state in true sense.

So long as the stewardship of the country remained in the hands of those great men, who were utterly incapable of doing any wrong and harm to the people, the country prospered. So long as people remained committed to their vibrant social customs, time-tested cultural norms, sterling values, moral perceptions, spiritual guidelines and golden heritage the nation moved towards the path of progress and peaceful coexistence. So long wealth satisfied their material, biological and economic needs, happiness contented them mentally and emotionally, virtues provided support to their rational, social and moral perceptions and the *Dharma* controlled their instincts, appetites, desires and greed by reason and faith, the people did not deviate from principles.

However, when selfishness, aversion, delusion, lust, fear, anger, grief, hatred, envy, personal interest, egoism, pride, boastfulness and hypocrisy overtook men, the whole system derailed. In the quest for more and more, in the lure of worldly charms and under the demonstration and high-mass consumption affects many of our people lost the sense of direction. To get success by hook or crook, to become quickly rich and to be called big and famous they became rootless. Under the impact of money, muscle, *mafia,* media and tongue powers they made compromises and lost their fighting powers. When the storm of western culture, tornado of alien ways of living, hurricane of materialism and the cyclone of New World Order impacted them they became dumb-founded.

My Countrymen! having seen the bit by bit fall of the glorious past of our beloved country and the frustration of Indian masses, the author could not remain silent as his patience ran out. He took his pen and portrayed the feelings, ambitions, aspirations and expectations which the *Aam Aadmi* had when India became free and tried to show what they got during the last six decades. He highlighted different kinds of efforts which were made by various segments of the society to salvage the condition of the country through legislations. He also warned that merely the Acts, Statutes and Ordinances would not succeed without changing the mind-set of the people. He exhibited how Indians had divorced their sterling qualities which had distinguished them from rest of the people, how they had abandoned their dynamic institutional framework which sustained them for so long and how they were becoming the victim of the New World Order which was detrimental to their culture, ethos and civilisation. He pointed out how the Indian economy was not benefitting common man, how inflation, adulteration, weak infrastructure, shaky health-care system, inequalities in income and reckless entry of multi-national companies and the FDIs in consumer sectors have broken the backbone of Indian masses.

He analysed the undemocratic activities of some of the elected representatives, examined the degenerated democratic nature of the country, highlighted the indecisiveness of the governing structure and pinpointed the impact of rampant corruption on the growth and development of the country.

Lastly, he cautioned the men at the helm of affairs that *Aam Aadmi* had become frustrated and bore the brunt due to unbridled corruption, and he cannot wait any more. He has decided to come in the forefront and the days are not too far when the country would be witnessing the uprising by the conscientious *Aam Aadmi* with potentials to change the destiny of the people and the future of the country. In the end, he made it clear that the ball was now in their court and if they failed to play it nicely, the posterity would never forgive them.

**Habibur Rehman**

## Acknowledgements

I am immensely grateful to Dr. K.L Gupta, Mrs. Padmini U.Nair, Eng. Kaleem Ahmed, Eng S.V. Subramanyam, Mr. Syed Farookh Ahmed and all eminent personalities whose contributions, suggestions and assistance helped me to undertake this work.

I am also extremely thankful to my wife Mrs.Masarrat Habib, daughter Dr. Sitwat Khan, son Eng. Bilal Habib, son-in-law Dr. Jamshedur Rehman Khan, Daughter-in-law Dr. Reshma Mukhtar, Grand son-in-law Dr. Danish Kazmi, Grandson Mr. Basil Habib Khan, and Grand-daughters Dr. Areeba Kazmi Khan, Eng. Abeer Khan, Ms. Rahma Habib Khan and Ms Rifa Habib Khan and all other well wishers who came to my rescue in giving shape to this venture.

**Habibur Rehman**

# 1 Why Am I Addressing My Beloved Countrymen?

Oh! my dearest countrymen. With most profound and sincere apology I would like to submit that I am addressing my countrymen on behalf of *Aam Aadmi*, who has been affected most by the ills and maladies of the country. His anger is reflected in the form of *Aam Aadmi* movement in India. If I have faltered in my endeavour in truly representing his sentiments, grievances, aspirations and ambitions I am sure you will be gracious enough to forgive me for which I shall always feel highly obliged and grateful. My dear brothers and sisters, all of us know that there is a limit to everything. When water approaches beyond the nose or when one is pushed back to the wall, reaction is inevitable. Some suffocate silently, many agitate openly, a few discuss privately and the multitude grumbles widely. Being the citizen of a great country like India it became impossible for me like millions of countrymen to remain silent and unaffected especially when I saw that, things were not going in the right direction. Compelled by circumstances, I am venturing to point out some of the slips and lapses of our meaningful countrymen on behalf of *Aam Aadmi* which I rightly or wrongly found to be detrimental to the interest of our country and which have affected all of us beyond redemption.

At the very outset, I wish to remind my brethren that I am not ignorant of the contribution of our nation. I confess that our country has made tremendous progress in various areas both at the national as well as international levels which has kept our heads high among the nations of the world. However, there are some advertent or inadvertent omissions and commissions on the part of our countrymen that have compelled me to ask many uncomfortable questions which I am sure would raise several eyebrows of the vested interests and the critics.

Knowing it fully well that many would react pro-actively and a few would lament upon my common sense I did not bother about the consequences since I was determined to let people know what the masses of India felt, what was happening around them and hence took the risk of cajoling our people in the larger interest of our country and the countrymen. One can genuinely ask a pertinent question to me as to why am I doing all that? Am I a political personality of some significance? Am I a social or political reformer? Am I a philosopher and thinker? Am I a far-sighted genius and statesman? Have I proved my credentials before my people? Have my countrymen chosen me to speak on their behalf? The reply is definitely in absolute no since nobody has deputed me but I have myself felt strongly to describe the ideas of *Aam Aadmi* in my own words just merely in the interest of the nation.

**Merely in the Interest of the Nation**

My loved ones! The one and the only one answer that can be given of my efforts in this context is that it is basically the national interest, the same interest of the country which constrained millions of Indians to sacrifice their lives under gallows or die unsung on the battle grounds.

Plato has rightly said;

> *"There can be no affinity nearer than our own country".*

When I observed things around me, I too came under utter strain like so many distinguished Indians from every political party, every section of the society and every socio-economic background who stood up and focussed the attention of the Indians on the fact that all was not well with the affairs of the country as well as with the mind-sets of many countrymen. I too mustered the required courage to say in my own humble way what I found to be prejudicial to the interest of the nation. I also felt like millions of learned and respected Indians that slowly and slowly the country was drifting towards bewilderment and confusion, little by little the rich heritage of the country was being throttled, gradually and gradually the country's well-tested institutions were slipping towards decadence and drop by drop the old and time-honoured values of the nation were being systematically and tactfully replaced by new values most of which were detrimental to the ethos, customs, traditions and heritage of the country.

It is a fact that for many countries, groups and individuals, the matters concerning cultures, conduct, traditions and civilisations are not very special to their social dynamics, political trigonometry, economic calculus, moral values, ethical sanctions and spiritual piety. Many of these nations are essentially pragmatic in nature and they consider only those deeds desirable and acceptable which are practicable and useful, irrespective of the fact whether they are morally and ethically sound or not. They are highly impressed by the western culture and Epicurean ways of living. The mighty wind of change from America and Europe proved to be a God- given gift for them as it provided them ample opportunities for physical, material and economic development. They whole-heartedly supported the materialistic philosophy based on economic democracy, enlightenment, *Laissez Faire,* gender parity and individual freedom.

However, for Oriental countries and especially those nations whose roots were grafted in their golden past, brilliant heritage, Holy Scriptures and sacred authority, it was difficult to swallow the pill of value—neutrality and ethical anarchy. History is witness to the fact that many intellectuals and geniuses from traditional countries and societies have stood up against the unwanted changes that are flattening their cultures, norms and traditions.

**Question of Conscience**

My Fellow brothers! Having observed the adverse events occurring around us, any Indian who has a slightest respect for his country can never remain silent. I too could not be the exception. My friends! Experience tells us that there comes a time in one's transitory life when one reaches the fag end of life when the body joints start cracking, ambitions begin to shatter, worldly charms, attractions, distinctions and titles appear trivial, repulsive and very small. One looks at the other end of the tunnel where one gets ready to perform the last and final journey in the infinite silence, eternal calm and perfect obscurity to finally sleep in the gracious lap of the Lord. It is the time when one should not falter in telling the truth, one should not hesitate in calling a spade a spade and one should never fail in expressing what one honestly and sincerely feels to be true. If one fails to act according to the voice of his conscience at the last phase of one's life, one falls in one's own eyes.

Channing has aptly remarked;

*"It is far more important to me to preserve an unblemished conscience than to compass any object however great".*

In the words of Stanislaus;

*"Conscience warns us as a friend before it punishes us as judge".*

In the words of Sophocles;

*"There is no witness so terrible—no accuser so powerful as conscience which dwells within us".*

The sages have said;

*If you notice any evil happening anywhere, stop it by force, if you can, else denounce it by words of mouth. If you fail in both, consider it at least wrong in your heart, though it would reflect the weakness of your conscience.*

Fortunately, there are millions of distinguished people in the country whose insight is absolutely pure and they are at the fag ends of their lives and they have no hesitation in denouncing the falsehood and calling a *Brutus a Brutus.* Besides, there are thousands of gifted legislators, pious saints, distinguished jurists, eminent bureaucrats, famous teachers, renowned legal luminaries, intelligent media persons, competent technocrats, efficient professionals, successful businessmen and countless well-wishers of the country who are equally upset and are raising their voices in every corner of the country against what is happening around them. Not only this, there are numberless ordinary people and commoners who are not vocal but expressing their disgust about the lapses of their higher ups silently. There is no dearth of writers, poets and critics who have dared not to pen down their views in *black and white* and the multitude from among the masses are not lagging behind in the process to become the part of the whole show.

So, it is not necessary that my views and the views of my countrymen may resemble with each other in all respects but it certainly gives me some consolation and solace that I am not thinking on the wrong lines and I am not alone in the mêlée. I am confident that, without doubting my intentions and integrity, the geniuses of the country would certainly understand my pain and anxiety and condone me for my inadvertent misadventures, if there are any.

**No Blame Game**

Oh! my loving brothers, I want to assure you with all sincerity at my back that by drawing your attention towards certain detrimental facts about the country, I never wish to blame any political party, cultural organisation, social group or men in power or personnel in the governing structure for I believe that in one way or the other all of us are somewhat responsible for what is happening in the country. My intention is neither to praise any political party, glorify any movement, adore any segment nor to challenge the intentions of any section, doubt the deeds of any society or condemn the activities of any religious organisation, I simply want to coax the conscience of each and every Indian, so that he or she may look at his or her balance sheet and judge where he or she faltered and make necessary corrections accordingly.

I know that it is not too late. Things can be improved, provided we have will and vision. I am convinced that many of our people are more knowledgeable and farsighted than me but the difference between them and me is that they have means to express their feelings in proper forums aptly and nicely. They have ample resources to convey their well-thought out views to those whom they deem fit and they can afford to tell their heart-felt secrets to a select few who are important and meaningful, but my problem is that, unfortunately I am not that much resourceful and fortunate. Being under constraints, I have been left with no alternatives but to do what I am doing.

**Aware of India's Glorious Heritage**

Do not think for a moment that I am raising my fingers unmindful and ignorant of our glorious heritage, wonderful cultural milieu, exceptional behaviour pattern and memorable hospitality. Actually, it is our brilliant past, splendid place in history and the majestic historical legacy which have compelled me to remind us as to what we are doing. I have not forgotten our good olden days, our conquests, our victories and our triumphant advances. I am also fully aware of our unparallel tolerance, unprecedented broad-mindedness, unforgettable endurance and unique forbearance. I love every inch of our beautiful land, I admire every beauty spot of our motherland, I adore every act of faithfulness and sacrifice of our people and I am proud of being a part and parcel of our country. I praise our countrymen, I cherish the flora and fauna of the nation, I read the history of our bygone days with compassion, I recite the folklore of the country with admiration and I admire the cultural heritage of our nation with intense love and sincerity. The people are my heart, the natural endowments of the country are my body, the national ideology is my brain and India is my soul. I can never dream to dent national dignity, honour and grace.

Nobody denies that our country is the wonderful gift of nature. We have immeasurable things of beauty and joys for which we can raise our heads in grace and dignity. Our shining snowy peaks, shifting sand dunes, vast-sea shores and deep valleys are matchless. Surely our mighty dust storms, hovering clouds and nerve-cracking deserts are awe inspiring. Definitely our heavenly Ganges, pious Yamuna, serpentine Indus and mighty Brahmaputra are splendid. Undoubtedly, our picturesque Ajanta, antiqued Ellora, wonderful Taj Mahal, glittering Golden Temple and towering Qutub Minar are magnificent. Certainly there is a divine beauty in our ancient Hastinapur, piety in renowned Ayodhya, and grace in reputed Patliputra, magnificence in well-known Sanchi and exalted beauty in pious *Char Dhams.* The beautiful Dal Lake, scenic Kanyakumari, sacred Gangotri, artistic Chopati and pictorial Eastern and Western Ghats impress every eye. We have classical Kolkata, historical Delhi, religious Banaras, entertaining Mumbai and pious *Sangam.* Our National Anthem is melodious and inspiring, our National song is heartening and reassuring and our National Flag is enchanting and mesmerising. Our lotus flower is pious, our mango fruit is juicy, our peacock is marvelous, our tiger is gracious and our banyan tree is wonderful. We can talk for hours about our Kashmiri *vazvan,* Hyderabadi *Biryani,* Punjabi *Lassi*, Mumbai's *Bhelpuri,* Jodhpur's *Dalbati*, Lucknow's *Kebab* and Tamil Nadu's *Idli Dosa.* We never tire praising our Rajasthani folk songs, South Indian *Kathakali* and Luckhnowi *Mujra.* We relish discussing the intricacies of *Tabla* played by master artist Allah Rakha, melodies of *Shehnai* generated by Ustad Bismillah Khan, piercing tunes on *Sarod* produced by talented Ustad Amjad Ali Khan, captivating melody initiated from the flute of Chaurasia and miracles of sitar produced by gracious Ravi Shankar.

Our sentiments are worth seen when we communicate on the artistic qualities of Raj Kapoor, glamorous acting of

Dilip Kumar, angry young man's aspect of Amitabh Bachan, kingly behaviour of Shahrukh Khan, admirable beauty of Madhubala and captivating charms of Nargis. Similarly, when we speak about Master Sachin Tendulkar, agile Dhyan Chand, brainy Viswanathan Anand, strong Milkha Singh or gifted P.T. Usha, grace is reflected from our faces.

My sincere countrymen! I also know that our head is raised in grace and dignity when one talks in admirable manners about our pious saints like Ramkrishna Param Hansa, Kabir, Yoga Guru Baba Ramdev and Art of Living Guru Sri Sri Ravi Shankar. We are flattered when we are reminded of our Far-sighted geniuses like Pandit Nehru, Maulana Azad , Indira Gandhi, Sardar Vallabhbhai Patel and Atal Bihari Vajpayee. We feel proud of our eminent intellectuals like Tagore and Raman, famous artists like M.F. Hussain and Gujral and exemplary humanists like Rajaji and Zakir Husain. We take pride in gracious Rama, legendary Krishna, calm Gautama and pious Mahavira. We feel flattered when Vedas, Gita, Quran, Bible, Old Testament and Granth Sahib are mentioned before us with piety and devotion. We rejoice when we hear *Gurbani* from Gurdwara, ringing of bells from the churches and chanting of hymns from the temples and *azan* from the mosque. We enjoy most profoundly our glamorous *Diwali,* robust *Holi,* sacred *Eid* and memorable Republic Day.

I know that we have learned and brainy *Brahmans* who have guided our governing structure since time immemorial. I am conscious of brave and proud Rajputs, bold and dauntless Sikhs; gallant and fearless Marathas; heroic and mighty Pathans' dashing and dynamic Jats; agile and aggressive Yadavas; hardy and courageous *Ahirs* and industrious and mighty *Kurmis* who have defended the country since unknown times. I have not forgotten the knowledgeable and far-sighted *Kshatriyas,* simple and innocent *dalits*; hard-working and patient *harijans,* who came to the rescue of the country when the country needed them most. I always remember the intelligent and wise Bengalis, smart and pious Assamese; sharp and tactful

Malayalis; dashing and brilliant Tamils who have contributed tremendously in the growth and the development of the country. I have deepest respect for the alert and aesthetic Oriyas; sagacious and conscientious Biharis; smart and sharp-witted Kashmiris and pioneering and rational Guajarati's who have played a significant role in shaping the destiny of the country. I also can never ignore the tolerant and peaceful artisans; innocent and clean-hearted farmers, Marginalised and depressed workers and innumerable unsung heroes and activists who have sharpened the rainbow of the country with their magnificent colours and splendid brilliance. I feel immense pleasure when I look from Kashmir to Kanyakumari or Amritsar to Kolkata and notice the beauty, grace and grandeur of India's geniuses of all communities, all castes and all segments. My head is raised high when I read the stories of their sacrifices, the tales of their bravery, and the accounts of their courage and the narrations of their loyalty. I miserably fail to control my emotions when I see them sacrificing their lives on the gallows, on the battle fields and on our borders.

I confess that our country is full of beautiful and chaste women for which no parallel can be given. They are the symbols of families, pillars of the societies and builders of the nation. They are renowned for their sacrifices, remembered for their commitments and adored for their loyalties. With their charming eyes, saffron colour, captivating smile, shining teeth, enchanting hair-locks and shapely figures they can conquer every heart. We have read the intensely passionate love stories of these dignified and most beautiful women of our country. We have seen these gracious and dignified women burning in blazing flames to save their chastity. We have observed swords in the beautiful and majestic hands of these brave and dauntless women to save the country. We have not forgotten that they have sacrificed willingly and smilingly their sons, husbands, brothers and fathers on the borders of the country. We do remember that they are the mothers, sisters, daughters and wives of our great scientists, philosophers, thinkers and the geniuses. We know people search heaven under their feet, compassion in their lapses, contentment under their arms and love near their bosoms. Alas! We have no brush to portrait their beauties, no words to express their sacrifices and no hammer to chisel their statues.

My well-wishers! We also know that the stately tombs of our mighty kings and the strong mausoleums of our emperors convinced each and everybody beyond any shred of doubt that our ancestors ruled the waves. The battle dresses of our warriors, the variety of our war beguiles and the heavy columns of our fire emitting cannons exhibited the strength of our army which deterred our enemy beyond imagination. Our victory towers are the testimony of our might and grace; our fort and fortresses tell the stories of our valour and triumphs; our ancient towns and cities sing the songs of our grace and glory. The world knows that our country has produced righteous Swami Vivekananda, Channakya, wise Kalidasa, chivalrous Rana Pratap, courageous Chatrapati Shivaji, magnanimous Asoka, just Vikramaditya and farsighted Akbar. Nobody is in doubt about our brilliant past, wonderful contribution and matchless achievements but the question arises for how long we can survive on our splendid past and historical legacy. The world simply wants to know what were our expectations when we were fighting for our freedom and what have we achieved after securing our independence from British?

**Expectations of Indians from Free India**

My dearest countrymen! When we got independence I was a lad of eighteen years and to the best of my knowledge, we were completely shattered by the divide and rule policy of the British, exhausted by the exploitative economic policies of the alien rulers and broken from the loss of our genuine rights. Our country became free in 1947 and unfortunately it was divided into Bharat and Pakistan. There was large scale migration across the borders and the economy and socio-political structure of the country was severely affected by communal riots, arsons, looting and bloodshed. Our agriculture, industry and trade got severe beating and there prevailed a climate of mistrust, hatred and disgust. Our *Dalits* were the victims of untouchability, the *Zamindari* system had broken the back bone of the farmers and poverty, diseases, hunger and ignorance were impacting India in every sphere. Our landless-labourers were mostly bonded slaves, artisans were at the mercy of the money-lenders, and petty shop-keepers and the hawkers were penniless. Country's raw material was being used in the factories of London, Manchester and Liverpool, Indian literates were mostly *babus* and clerks and our leaders were frustrated, confused and confounded. Agricultural sector was left stagnated, industry was ruined and the infrastructure was shabby. The families were constrained by archaic customs, people were superstitious and there were geological layers in the society. Famines, unemployment and starvation were part and parcel of life, illiteracy and blind faith prevailed on large-scale and ghettos, broken roads and heaps of dirt were significant part of our destiny.

In such a situation we wanted smiles in the eyes of the *Dalits,* hope in the hearts of the bonded labourers and confidence on the faces of the farmers. We desired to wipe out the tears of the hawkers, frustration from the artisans and relieve the petty shop-keepers from the agony of pennilessness. We wished to revitalise Indian agriculture, modernise industry and trade and improve the infrastructure. We hoped to honour our youths with the robes of excellent education, decent jobs and purposeful married life. We intended to decorate our aged, unemployed, sick and disabled with the titles of pension, social security and health care. We expected to reduce the agonies of the widows, pains of the divorcees and the frustrations of the separated. We were certain to assure food to every hungry, clothes to each pauper and shelter to each homeless. We wanted to modernise our family system, rationalise our customs and ethos, impose our cultural values and improve our image. We believed in providing love to each child, grace to every elder, and respect to each citizen and prosperity to every civilian.

We desired to see happiness and grace on every face, courage and patience in each heart and compassion and sweetness on every tongue. It was our earnest desire to see large-hearted tolerance and forbearance in each individual, pride and self-respect in each entity and physical fitness and cleanliness in everybody. We longed to see energy and confidence in every limb, wisdom and intelligence in every mind and piety and compassion in every soul. We wanted every Indian as an embodiment of harmony and peaceful co-existence, each citizen an example of dignified and enlightened personality, every resident a model of a leader and a pioneer; every subject an industrious and diligent; each civilian calm and conscientious; everybody expert and skillful; each individual a torch-bearer of peace and prosperity; every man an image of bravery and gallantry; each woman a portrait of elegance and dignity and every child a figure of charm and beauty.

Our people wanted that India faced no hostile neighbours and its boundaries were well-protected and well-guarded from all sides by its mighty armed forces. Logistically, we desired that no country could dare to attack our oceans, skies and fleets and the country had enough deterrent power to dent the enemies. Internationally we wished India to be called a superpower and an emerging and dynamic nation. Politically we aspired that India's foreign policy was so designed that it could suit the interests of the country as well as its immediate neighbours and the humanity at large. Economically, we expected its balance of payment position in an extremely sound position, its currency to be treated as the standard currency of the world and its products to be demanded in every corner of the world. We were longing for renowned scientific academies, rich knowledge parks and pioneering investigating agencies and famous *yoga* centers. We also desired Noble Laureates, famous literary figures and eminent statesmen in significant number. We aspired for poets, writers, cartoonists and journalist of world fame in plenty. We had a special liking for glamorous actors, wonderful artists, master architects, expert musicians, melodious singers and agile sportsmen.

We wanted to glorify our respected teachers, revered preachers, pious saints and men of sound moral code of conducts.

We longed for enough stock of food stuffs in the Godowns of the state, stable and affordable prices of the necessities and comforts, plenty of vegetables, pulses and fruits in the grocery of the country and no shortage of milk, butter, meat and other eatables. Besides, we stressed that the country produced sufficient material for its food joints, branded cloth market, health and education sectors and industrial and agricultural segments. We wanted to see ample strength and vigour in the backbone of the farmers so that they could plough well, enough might and zeal in the limbs of the labourers so that they could strike the spades faster and deeper. We also hoped that the artisans' piercing eyes would tug neatly and beautifully, the grocery of the petty shop-keepers would be fruitfully sold, the youths would find comfortable employment in the job market and there would be an adequate social security system for old, sick, unemployed and handicapped. It was also our expectation that the hawkers were to return home with pockets full of money before sun set; there was enough shine on the faces of the cobblers after they had finished their works and there was sufficient cooking material in domestic kitchens. We also thought that the security agencies were capable and alert and the fifth columnists were conspicuous by absence.

We wished that every child born in India completed his life cycle from womb to tomb comfortably and conscientiously, no issue was aborted before birth and every new born was delivered in proper health care centre. It was also our expectation that no infant died of mal-nutrition, no baby suffered from polio, tetanus and whooping cough and every child was looked after by mother or baby sitter. It was upper most in our minds that there was a nearby nursery school for every kid, there were sufficient playing grounds for the little ones and no boy or girl looked towards others' toys with helplessness. We coveted that no child felt ashamed of his dress, every child slept with belly full of adequate calories and no orphan or step child was the victim of child labour. It was our firm belief that the sons and daughters were not considered burden, there was no foul play with the offspring, heir or descendents and even the illegitimate and urchin too were treated with care and compassion. We aspired that every youth got fullest opportunities to develop his personality, the youngsters were not throttled due to paucity of funds, the young ones were not debarred from colleges and universities due to lack of fees and seats, adolescents were not subject to discrimination and exploitation and the younglings did not pine for what was naught. It was also our conviction that the infant girls were not aborted before birth; brides were not burnt alive for not bringing dowry, the girls were not divorced on slightest suspicions, the maids were not sold for money and the destitute were not thrown in the brothels.

My Countrymen! There was nothing abnormal in expecting much from the mighty and resourceful country like India which was bestowed with costly natural resources and which possessed tremendous talents and potentials .The fault of the countrymen was that they were not fully prepared to face the stewardship of a great country like India. Many people took the freedom lightly and they made no efforts to transform it into a dynamic and progressive nation. Besides, no proper homework was done to revitalise its various institutions and constituents through movements like Renaissance, Reformation and Counter Reformation. The people at the helm of affairs did not learn much from Enlightenment type movement, Industrial, French and Glorious revolutions that could convert Indians into a bunch of matured, responsible, enlightened and far-sighted citizens. Over and above this, the country gave over emphasis to economic development through Five Year Plan without simultaneously reforming countries social, cultural, political, moral and spiritual lives of the people. The result of too much emphasis on material progress was that, the quest for material prosperity and the physical well-being accompanied by greed, lust and selfishness made people hungry for wealth, power, name and fame.

We know that physical and material prosperity too is necessary for the grace of every nation but the dignity of the nation cannot be enhanced merely by material forces because history does not record the quantum of bricks and mortar or yards of clothes and hectors of lands. It also gives merely the lip service to roads, buildings, mighty forts, victory towers and means of comforts and luxury for these things are transitory and passing in nature. They vanish with the time and are destroyed by the vagaries of seasons, changes in climates and wear and tear. People are remembered by their strength of character, generosity of their moral fiber, richness of their conducts, soundness of their behaviour pattern and quality of their visions and missions. The vitality of the social systems, eternality of cultural values, depth of the national heritage, viability of the political structure, beauty of the aesthetical patterns, soundness of moral and ethical norms and spiritual connotations leave unforgettable imprints on the pages of history. Similarly, the compassion of heart, sanity of mind and purity of soul of the commoners, courage and large-hearted forbearance of the mediocre and the magnanimity and compassion of the high ups distinguish the nationals of a civilised country from the residents of the wicked and nasty nations.

We have several developed and civilised nations that have surpassed all nations in material prosperity. The misfortune of such nations is that they appear great in stature only but within their showy structure they are hollow. They have killed millions of innocent people merely at the instance of their egos, they have butchered thousands of children merely due to their fear-psychosis and they have made innumerable widows just to increase the sale of their armaments. Their children are brought up routinely, their elders find no place in the homes of their children, their spouses resort to frequent divorces, their girls generally avoid pregnancy and their men prefer live-in-relationship. Their churches are deserted, their religious institutions have no takers and their scriptures are the grace of libraries only. They are the worshippers of wealth and faith has been practically vanished from their lands. They are rich and famous but discontented. They are prosperous and progressive but lonely. They are intelligent and competent but hungry for love and affection. Their objects of material prosperity such as splendid houses, gorgeous clothes, delicious foods, intoxicating drinks, shining cars, beautiful cities provide them mere conveniences and not satisfaction and happiness.

It has been rightly said;

*"Worldly wealth is the devil's bait; and those whose minds feed upon riches, recede in general from real happiness, in proportion as their stores increase; as the moon, when she is fullest of light, is farthest from the sun." — Burton*

*In the words of Bessie A Stonley;*

*"Satisfaction does not lie merely in material prosperity and physical well-being. It lies in giving to others what we have and sharing with others what we can. "It is the law of exact reciprocity, Joy increases as you give and diminishes as you try to keep for yourself."*

*"World has achieved success who has lived well-laughed often and loved much; who has gained the respect of intelligent men, the trust of pure women and the love of little children; who has nicked and accomplished his task; who has left the world better than he found it, whether an improved poppy, a perfect poem or a rescued soul; who has never lacked appreciation of earth's beauty or failed to express it, who has looked for the best in others and given them the best he had, whose memory is a benediction."*

A saint believes in giving it to others rather than taking anything from others. Hence, he gets the same satisfaction from the first rays of the sun which the Emperors get by conquering the world. A wise draws the same pleasure by reading the classical epic which the wealthy trader gets in counting coins of gold and silver. A genius is mesmerised by the smile of the child in the same way as one is hypnotised by hearing the news of one's elevation to one of the highest offices of the country. Thus, those Indians who were interested in exploring the genuine parameters of greatness, prosperity and success for India, made the mistake of exploring them in India's material and physical well-beings only instead of examine them in their totality of things covering physical, moral and spiritual aspects of life.

Oh my countrymen! After examining our expectations, we should ask us where are we after nearly six decades of self rule? We should ponder over it with cool mind and compassionate heart what have we achieved and what have we lost during this period? We should definitely keep one thing in mind that whatever might have been the expectations of our people, the world in general too was expecting many things from us. We are not an ordinary nation but a nation of millions of people with tremendous potentials and we were expected to compete with countries like America, China, Russia and others. It was expected from our intellectuals that they would come up with several inventions and discoveries in their credits to secure several noble prizes in science, technology and humanity and chair International bodies in their fields. Our younger ones would conquer virgin peaks, discover new territories and face the hazards of lava, hurricanes and deep seas. They would also sweep the tally of Gold Medals in world Olympics, get their achievements recorded in Guiness Book in multitude, roam in space crafts, land on far-flung planets and leave a lasting impact upon world history. The world also expected too much from our politicians, leaders and planners. Many smaller nations were sure that India would surely and certainly challenge the Super Powers for their international hegemony, check them from exploiting the weaker nations, stand in support of the aggrieved countries against their mighty aggressors, persuade the quarreling nations to desist from wars and Cold Wars and help in spreading peace, progress, prosperity and harmony among various segments of the humanity. The answers perhaps would be disheartening.

We should also ask ourselves whether any material difference occurred in the status of people at grassroots level after 1947. Are we really free from most of our wants, needs and necessities or our claim is merely in name sake? Are we immune from crimes, extortions, exploitation and persecutions? Are we not the victim of fear, hatred, prejudices and communal bias? Are we not afraid of terror attacks? Do we peacefully sleep in our homes without any fear to our life, honour and possessions? Do we give respect to each woman as we give to our daughters, sisters and mothers? Are there enough volunteers who come to the rescue of the girls and ladies in trouble in the buses, in railway compartments and on the roads? Do passersby disengage the quarrelling and entangled people on the roads? Do our far-fetched villages have plenty of clean water to drink? Have we succeeded in removing the worries of the nomadic tribes? Have we done anything to remove the *ghettos* from the cities? Have we established banks in each locality? Do we have post offices at convenient places in every village, bus stops near each settlement, all-weather roads connecting every helmet and electricity lighting every hut? Has our country provided reasonable sized land to every family free or at throw away prices to build a reasonable house within meager means? Have we done anything to provide *Pucca* house to every citizen of the country and job to every able-bodied? Are there toilets in the mud houses, gas connection in farmers and artisans kitchens? Does our child get birth under healthy conditions in government hospitals? Do we have enough hospitals and health centers equipped with qualified surgeons, physicians and technicians where the poor can get free or affordable treatment? Are there nice and low-cost government hotels in each of our cities for our middle and lower middle income groups? Do we have decent schools and qualified teachers to teach reading, writing and arithmetic to our children in the remote areas of the country? Do we have world class colleges, institutes and universities and renowned super specialty centers and research institutes of extraordinary excellence to provide scientific, engineering, medical, management, computer and professional education to our students throughout the country? Do we have clean and pollution-free cremation and burial grounds where we may pay last respects to our departed souls?

Have we succeeded in solving the river water problems between states completely? Are we not facing the problem of the creation of new states every now and then? Are the residents of different states not facing the problem of the sons of soils in various states of the country? Do we not find cries for reservations in jobs and services on the basis of castes, regions and religions? Do we not face farmers' protests on the issue of acquisition of farm lands? Do we not face student's unrest here and there? Do we not find a hidden tussle between the judiciary and the legislature? Have we prevailed in checking the brain drain? Have we triumphed in checking the students from going to foreign countries for higher education in ordinary institutions? Have we succeeded in controlling the dreaded diseases? We need not give the answer because the truth is already known to all of us.

**Good Works done during this Period**

Now, let us ask us what we have actually done after securing our treasured freedom so that the gap between expectations and realisation may be brought to the notice of our people. Let me tell that none can deny the good work done by our governments and the people after obtaining freedom. We admit that many memorable works have been done in free India through the process of Five Year Plans and the dedication of the Government of India, co-operation of State governments, and help of various agencies and the efforts of civil society. The Green Revolution initiated by Dr. M.S. Swaninathan in 1965 helped 400 to 500 million Indians to raise their living standards. The White Revolution pioneered by Dr. Verghese Kurien saved the skins of several million undernourished children, and The Telecom Revolution, the thought process of Sam Pitroda helped in linking Indian villages with one another. Similarly, the

Economic Reform of 1991 started by P.V. Narasimha Rao, Dr. Manmohan Singh, P.C. Chidambaram and Dr. Montek Singh Ahluwalia created a viable and healthy climate for industrial growth in the country. Prof. Yashpal's SITE provided television facilities to millions of Indians in the villages and the cities and the emergence of the world class media and the presence of eminent journalists like Arnav Goswami, Barkha Dutt, Rajdeep Sardesai, Shekhar Gupta and Sucheta Dalal and many more strengthened the 'Fourth Pillar' of democracy in the country. Likewise, the involvement of Dr. Homi J. Bhabha in India's nuclear science research and the participation of Dr. A.P.J. Abdul Kalam in Space Programme and N. Vittal's software technology and the related developments led to the immense growth and development in the country. We are proud of the fact that our Rakesh Sharma viewed the earth from the space and we can also boast of sending Robotic Mars probe to the Red Planet recently.

We built almost more than twenty lakh kms new roads, completed new complexes, constructed mighty dams and beautiful bridges and sent satellites and rockets in space. We multiplied steel production by 50 times, the cement production by twenty times and our IT-sector grew from US$ 100 million in 1992 to US$ 40 billion in 2007. In recent years our economy grew at the rate of nine per cent a year, our hard currency reserves were all-time high and they multiplied from US$ 1.5 billion in 1991 to US$ 220 billion in 2007. Moreover, our exports increased at the rate of twenty to 25 per cent per annum and touched the magic figure of US$ 79 billion in 2004. We added nine million phone lines a month and the internet covered nearly 450 million users and our FDI was nearly US$ 25 billion during 2007, which was five times what it was three years ago. Our global trade accounted for 25 per cent of the world's GDP, the numbers of our billionaires were highest in Asia and our stock markets were booming. On the basis of purchasing power, we are the fourth largest economy of the world next to the USA, China and Japan.

Over and above this, we have the third largest education system in the world next to China and the USA and we are the largest producer of engineers and the scientists in the world. By the end of 2003, our ninety per cent of population possessed primary school at a distance of one-km and 84 per cent of our people had upper primary school within the range of three-km and the Gross Enrollment Ratio (GER) in primary education rose from 82 per cent in 1991 to 95 per cent in 2003 and in upper primary from 54 per cent to 61 per cent in the same period.

During 2004 India had nearly 311 Universities, 15,600 Colleges but this number has skyrocketed after privatization of education in the country. Out of 10.5 million students attending universities 88.9 per cent enrolled for undergraduate's degrees and 9.4 per cent for postgraduate programmes. India produced 2.5 million graduates and 35,000 engineers every year. India's contribution in producing university graduates was 1.5 times the size of China and twice as large as USA. The number of degrees awarded by various educational institutions in India as well as engineering colleges increased from 70 per cent in 1990 to 90 per cent in 2004. These achievements are commendable by all standards in absolute terms but in relative terms the benefit of these various schemes and programmes has not percolated up to the grassroots level.

We find a strange India in the form of an oasis of prosperity within the vast desert of poverty. We find golden utensils, Italian furniture, Korean 3D Television sets and wonderful consumer durables at the mansions of highly privileged business houses; splendid pent houses, ultra-modern pickups, majestic ferry boats and fabulous racing cars of the neo rich; spacious gardens, fabulous parties, Western music and the presence of the celebrities at the gathering of the famous builders and commission agents, glass covered swimming pools and glittering toilets and beautiful court yards in the dwellings of some of the corrupt government servants. Our eyes are amazed when we see the wondrous sofa sets of the drawing rooms, spectacular chairs of the dining tables and legendary crockery of the kitchens of the renowned actors, television artists and the rich and famous. When we see the walls of some of the very rich cricketers and the galleries of the world fame tennis players being decorated by Husain's paintings, mythical antiques and golden frames, we are reminded of the rajas and the maharajas of yester years. We hear of glamorous marriage parties of the international bookies wherein people relish juices of several kinds, salads of every type, and food dishes of different nature. When we glance young girls dancing in ecstasy, youths drunk and elders rejoicing at the time of some of the election victories of the politicians, we are dumb-founded. When we happen to see the holiday resorts, rest houses and farm houses of the rich and famous soft- ware and hard-ware IT experts, we forget whether we are in India or in Europe. The stylish and branded clothes of the successful fashion designers, the American accent of the charming receptionists of the important nursing homes and sturdiness of the body guards of the owners of the a few private engineering, management and dental colleges impress each eye. The vicinities of the important hoteliers, the shopping complexes of the big franchise owners and the paraphernalia of the multi-national Indian companies compel us to think that we have made tremendous progress.

We are saddened when we observe that at one end the dogs of some of the rich and famous eat cakes and at nearby corner the children of the destitute aspire for a loaf of bread. Their few packs of foreign whisky cost more than the earnings of several have-nots. The equivalent of one night stay of these glamorous people in a seven-star hotel is enough to marry several orphan girls. The amount of wealth which they spend in a casino can feed many hungry and cloth several under privileged. The budget that the rich allot for their pleasure trips can build several hospitals, nursing homes, dormitories and lunatic asylums. The money that is drained from their pockets in watching entertainment shows, participating at race courses and enjoying beauty contests can bring smile on the faces of many widows, aged and handicapped. Every second year they tend to change the model of their cars, every month they try to visit America, Europe or Australia and at the slightest opportunity they do not hesitate in changing the entire design of their houses. They organise lavish birth day parties to show off their wealth, they pay hefty donations to some of the political parties to gain their favours and they help charitable organisations generally to attract public attention. Their resources automatically increase with the passing of each budget, their wealth multiplies with the rising in prices and their bank balances enhance due to accrual of interests. It is this minor segment of the rich politicians, famous leaders, big business magnets, IT experts, builders, commission agents, dishonest government officials, neo-rich farmers, fashion designers, antique sellers, owners of branded clothes, fast foods, nursing homes and private colleges and universities which is buying gold, diamonds and consumer durables and spending lavishly on extravagant consumption and show off. Having seen the rich, powerful and meaningful people in extreme luxury one is tempted to believe that India is shining and everything is well under control.

The story goes like this;

*On the suggestion of his mother the world fame sculpture made the statue of a most beautiful woman with a raised hand holding the bunch of grapes hanging towards her mouth ready to pluck from the mouth. The statue was placed before the general public for inspection. The people were amazed having seen the beauty of the lady and the charm of the bunch of grapes. It appeared as if all was natural. They were dumb-founded when they saw that the birds were rushing towards the bunch of grapes and it so appeared to them that they would take away the whole bunch from the hands of the beautiful lady. When the mother saw the scene she was immensely pleased by the expertise of her son. She embraced him and blessed him profusely upon which the son wept bitterly saying that he had succeeded merely partially but failed mostly. Mother could not understand what her son was saying. She demanded clarification. The son replied that the jumping of the birds towards the bunch of grapes showed that the grapes were real and that was his success but his greatest failure was that he could not sculpture the lady in realistic shape for if she looked real the birds would have never dared to rush towards the bunch of grapes as happens in real life.*

Our people too are under the illusion having seen the partial success. They are claiming that India is shining by just seeing a minor segment prospering, forgetting the fact that the major portion of the country is stagnating.

**The Grey Areas**

Despite our so many achievements if we look towards the Balance Sheet of the nation we find a gloomy picture. It is most unfortunate that we stand 127th in rank in the world in Human Development Index. Our productivity is 10 per cent of US level and the productivity of Chinese workers is 30 to 180 per cent higher than that of ours. The irony of fate of majority of the Indian population is that the purchasing power of rural population is very low because 65 per cent rural population adds 20 to 21 per cent in country's GDP which comes to rural per capita income to the extent of approximately Rs 11,000 per annum or little over Rs 30 per day which is not sufficient to meet the two ends of life. The poverty in India is 26 per cent compared to 11 per cent in China or in other words nearly 270 million Indians are struggling under poverty out of which 200 million live in the villages and 70 million in cities.

There are more than 300 million people in the country who are not free from hunger, diseases, ignorance and superstition. Besides, the condition of rural people is miserable as the rate of growth of agriculture is just merely two per cent which is absorbed by two per cent increase in the rural population and hence they remain where they are. The multi-dimensional Poverty Index shows that there are 81.4 per cent poor among Scheduled Tribes, 65.8 per cent in Scheduled Castes, 58.3 per cent in Other Backward Castes and 33.33 per cent in General Category.

Thousands of farmers are committing suicides every year due to bankruptcy, poverty, illness. Nearly 17,060 farmers ended their lives in 2006 and 16632 in 2007. Over and above this, about 250 to 300 million Indians or nearly 10 per cent Indian population is unemployed. 12 per cent of the 41 million unemployed are graduates or post-graduates. The country should create employment at the rate of 10 per cent per annum over the next five years to sustain the present unemployment rate but our capacity is limited to the extent of one per cent only. The problem becomes more difficult when we add 15 to 20 million new job seekers every year, 70 per cent of whom are illiterates aged between 18 and 25. Out of these new entrants the country can absorb only two to three million every year mostly in the private sector which provides 92 per cent jobs but where the salaries and wages are very low. Our 30.7 per cent workers are employed in household enterprises, 1.2 per cent as employers in household business, 24 per cent as unpaid family workers in household enterprises, 14.8 per cent in regular salaried jobs, 0.1 per cent as casual workers in public works and 29.2 per cent as casual labourers in other works. Most of the employees in Government sector work on lower positions such as nearly 98.7 per cent Indians are employed at lower positions in Indian Railways, 96.1 per cent in National security agencies and 98.6 per cent in post and Telegraphs. Country's 22.9 per cent population falls under lower income category which earns merely Rs. 20 per day, 69.8 per cent in middle income group which scarcely meets its socio-economic requirements and 7.3 per cent in higher income segment which is enjoying the luxurious life.

Our 39 per cent adults are illiterate and millions of children are out of schools. Our mean years of schooling of children aged 7-16 during 2001 was 3.95 for all, 4.18 for males and 3.69 for females. Our 16 per cent children aged 6-14 years never attended schools. Our 40 per cent downtrodden sections did not complete primary school, 59 per cent could not cross middle school and 76 per cent could not achieve their Metric certificate. We spend merely 1.9

per cent of our GDP on higher education which is the lowest in the world and we produce Ph.Ds. to the extent of one-tenth of the size of USA. Our share of Ph.Ds. in the computer science is around 25 compared to 88 in the USA and 2,500 in China and our 10 per cent engineers are only employable, and about 10 per cent students with degrees in humanities are globally competitive and India has only two universities in the top list of 500 while Japan has 34, China 18, South Korea seven and Brazil four.

It is quite disheartening to note that our approximately 320 million people do not have access to clean and safe drinking water and their demand exceeds supply by 30 per cent. More than 25 per cent of the residents in the country do not have approach to tap water, 630 million Indians have not enjoyed the benefits of reasonable sanitation conditions and 25 per cent live without sanitation facilities. Further 250 million do not have any reach to medical facilities, 51 per cent children are under nourished, 50 per cent fail to get life saving and essential drugs and about 200 people in the population of 100,000 suffer from malaria. Besides, there is tremendous traffic congestion in Indian cities which has reduced road transport efficiency by 50 per cent. Country's 40 per cent segment lacks all-weather access roads, 30 per cent does not have primary schools and 50 per cent villages are away by more than five km from the nearest health-care centre. We have 1.5 beds, 0.6 doctors, 0.8 nurses per 1000 people compared to six to eight beds, 12 doctors, and 26 nurses in developed countries. The housing shortage in Indian towns is to the extent of 22 million and 22 per cent of India's population lives in slums and by 2030 this percentage would go to the extent of 35 per cent. The coverage of health insurance is only two per cent and 80 per cent expenses are paid by the individuals themselves. It is expected that by 2030 more than 72 per cent India would be urbanised and the country would need 3.6 million houses in urban areas, 66,000 new primary schools and 3000 health centers every year. As per statistics in hand, there are thousands of small, medium and large villages with population less than 1000, between 1000 to 2000 and above

2000 in West Bengal, Uttar Pradesh, Bihar and Assam which are deficient in education, lack medical facilities and short of post offices, bus stops and proper approach roads.

**The Depressing Scenario**

Finally, I have no hesitation in concluding that the condition of the majority of the poor is miserable. Various segments from among the downtrodden are in terrible condition. We do not find the signs of bliss on the faces of the poor and depressed farmers that plough in the month of June in scorching heat. We miserably fail to see happiness in the surroundings of the shepherds moving along with their herds. We see no marks of cheer in the eyes of below poverty and illiterate people sitting with their heads between their knees. We perceive no symptoms of contentment on the factory labourers toiling under heavy machines. We conceive no delight in the *ghettos* of the poor and the destitute sleeping in the congested areas. We observe no ecstasy in the huts of the artisans and craftsmen being busy in their work with heavy optical on their eyes. We find no signs of happiness in the souls of the landless and bonded workers sitting aimless under the *Neem* trees. We miss joy from the innocent faces of the children and the youth looking towards the passersby. We notice the dearth of enjoyment in the environment of the ordinary Indians living in the deserted villages and the dirty cities. We witness no jubilation in the pessimistic looks of the elders and the hopelessness of the aged. We comprehend no happiness in the houses of those downtrodden who sleep on the payments and those have-nots who pass their nights on platforms and bus stops. We behold no marks of pleasure in the slums of the marginalised whose dwellings are burnt every year and the *Dalits,* who are very often compelled to do menial work. We view immense grief in the hearts of the unemployed youths who cannot find marriage partners and the underemployed who are refused work wherever they go. We comprehend extreme anxiety in the minds of the sick who cannot afford drugs and the weak, who are penniless. We notice no rejoicing in the inner most self of Indian people of all hue and colour. We come across thousands of widows crying for help, we find divorced wives struggling for livelihood and we glance aged, destitute and the handicapped begging. We observe an army of casual workers waiting for jobs, we comprehend a long queue trying to fetch water from municipal taps and we perceive passengers in long lines struggling for railway tickets. We notice platforms and bus stops occupied by destitute, sick and disabled. We see the wretched hands of the poor stretching for charity, depressed faces of orphans looking for help and the shabbily dressed maidens horribly covering their bodies. We find roads depleted and broken, vicinities dirty and congested and houses depleted and dim. We observe water supply polluted and in disarray, environment dirty and dark and electricity uninterrupted and uncertain. We see money-lenders chasing the indebted ones, rickshaw pullers toiling in noon and hawkers selling their groceries day and night. Neither have we found solace in the north nor contentment in the south nor relief in east nor consolation in the west. Everywhere save dissentions, conflicts, scuffles, strives, tussles and tensions, we witness nothing. Somewhere prejudices are weighty, elsewhere discrimination is the issue, many a time misuses of power becomes the bone of contention, and on several occasions emotional matters over rule all other considerations.

Wherever, we go people complain about the unfaithfulness and ungratefulness of their colleagues, niggardliness and selfishness of their friends, pride, ego and hot-headedness of their bosses and selfishness, dishonesty and treachery of their unfaithful leaders. They talk about inflation, adulteration and rising of prices. Whom ever we meet they raise the bogey of scams, black money in foreign banks and corruption in high offices. In each gathering we find people criticising the corrupt government officials for charging exorbitant bribes and diverting government funds towards their personal ends. In India, every tongue is critical of the bungling of the rogue politicians, every heart is grieved of the excesses of the irresponsible governing structure, each mind is perturbed from the manner in which justice is delivered in law courts and each soul is disgusted the way people are running after wealth breaking all the norms of justice, ethics, morality and good conducts. We find intellectuals perplexed from the mal practices of some of our leaders, conscientious people worried due to the erosion of cultural values, religious heads tormented because of distortions in religious norms.

### Is It the Dawn of Our Choice?

Having seen such a pitiable condition we naturally begin to wonder that certainly, it is not that cherished Independence for which we were longing for too long. We are sure that we never dreamt for this type of 'Free India' where people slept beneath the moon and basked under the sun, where they wanted to smile but had to sigh, where their funds were low and debts were high and where they thought they were near but were too far.

Certainly, it was not that dawn of our liking where destitute could not hope for good due to the risk of despair, where they could not try their best due to the danger of failure, where they could not show their love because of not being loved in return and where they could not live comfortably due to fear of dying in adversity.

Surely, it was not that night of joy in which people sowed the sacrifices but reaped the miseries, invested their destinies but became bankrupt, stood for the cause of the nation but broke their backbones and fought for whole life but got nothing. Admittedly, we can confirm that it was not that freedom which was to free us from all chains of ignorance, prejudices, poverty and diseases. It was not that *'Azadi'* for which many Indians sacrified their lives and it was not that Independence for which our leaders went to jails. Definitely it was not that liberty which prompted our martyrs to face the gallows willingly and smilingly, it was not the same *Swaraj* whose dream was seen by our freedom fighters and definitely it was not the same 'Ram Raj' of Mahatma Gandhi which was to provide prosperity, justice and happiness to every Indian.

Our freedom brought with it immense benefits but neither the rivers of prosperity and happiness flew in it nor India became a golden bird. Progress and harmony was also not seen in plenty. Unfortunately, the rich became richer and the poor became poorer, the country's fifty per cent wealth went in the hands of a few hundred families and the white rulers left the country but several browns became its masters. Save false propagandas, hollow promises and white lies people got nothing. Alas! It is not that India of our dreams and it is not that *Bharat* of our dreams. It is something entirely different from what we had perceived.

In the words of Faiz Ahmed Faiz;

*"Yeh Daagh Daagh ujala, Ye shabguzida Sehar, Woh intezar tha jiska, yeh woh sehar to nahi" (This black smeared light, this night ridden morning, that we had waited for, this is not that morning).*

Rahel has rightly said;

*"To have freedom is only to have that which is absolutely necessary to enable us to be what we ought to be, and to possess what we ought to possess."*

Goethe has also aptly remarked;

*"None are more hopelessly enslaved than those who falsely believe they are free."*

My Countrymen! The reality is that the *Aam Aadmi* is feeling cheated. He is convinced that the present system cannot solve his problems. Having tried several alternatives he came to the conclusion that it is futile to expect anything from the existing machinery because people manning the governing structure have become selfish and self-centered. They are blindly running after money, greed and name and fame and each one of them wants to achieve his objectives by hook or crook or even by crossing over others. The spirit of dedication, honesty, transparency and commitment which was the hall-mark of the people at the helm of affairs is completely missing.

Similarly, the inner voice and the voice of conscience which used to guide the result-oriented people to do what was right and avoid what was wrong have been badly dented. The complete mistrust in the political, economic, social and cultural environment has exhausted his tolerance level. He is desperately looking for some savior, who can provide him some solace and save the country from drifting to the lowest of the low.

# 2 We Want Change Simply Through Legislative Measures

My countrymen! Many of us strongly feel that our tolerance level for corruption and mismanagement has brought us to the wall and each one of us is now in search of some viable solution. Everyone of us is in search of a Messiah and each individual is hopelessly looking for a ray of light at the other end of the tunnel. The participation of masses at the rallies of their well-wishers in large number, their waving hands on the roads and shouting slogans in favour of their leaders and their enthusiastically facing the music at the hands of law enforcing agencies amply testify that people are not satisfied with what is happening around them. They wish to see silver lining in the clouded night of their country. Similarly, several leaders sitting on hunger fast and people of diverse hue coming on the roads in support of measures that can uproot corruption and other evils of the nation show that there is unrest in the public and the people in general intend to see the dawn of an ethic based prosperous and progressive India. In the same way, the daily news papers are full of news about black money in foreign banks and the television channels cover programmes in substantial details about the future strategies of those leaders who intend to create a mass movement against bad governance and misrule. The opposition too is not lagging behind. It is also crying foul and making every effort to bring the Government down. The ruling government on the other hand is not sitting silent. It is trying its best to convince the people that it has zero tolerance towards corruption and it is doing everything to rule it out from every sphere of the country. Besides, many enlightened citizens want that a Constitution based Lokpal Bill should be introduced in the

Parliament, several emphasize that government should take proactive part in bringing back the black money from the foreign banks and there is no dearth of people who want a Citizens' Charter, an Ombudsman Bill and a Code of Conduct for all the employees as well as political parties and a monitoring, evaluating and controlling body to assess the role of the governing structure. Over and above this, there are numberless citizens who aspire for electoral reforms, value base politics and control over inflation and improvement in infrastructure. Some suggest that the power at the centre should be decentralised by amending the Constitution and various functionaries such as Pradhans, mayors; MLA's and MP's should be given more powers to frame and execute policies suiting to the development of their respective areas. Others believe in replacing the Parliamentary type of democracy into Presidential form of government, many believe in *Ram Rajya* as enunciated by Mahatma Gandhi and a few insist that the country should follow globalisation in the earnest spirit and compete in the international markets as a viable, progressive and dynamic nation. It appears that there is a near unanimity among many of the participants that these objectives can easily be achieved if proper legislations and administrative reforms are brought in true letter and spirit in various segments of the country.

### Short Cuts

My Countrymen! We are living in the era of short cuts, instant satisfaction and quick fixes. The lottery business and *'Kaun Banega Crorepati'* type shows are flourishing because people want to become millionaires overnight. Instant coffee, readymade garments, fast foods and pills to sleep and tubes to join broken parts are the remedies that are in much vogue these days. People normally do not want to work hard despite the fact that they fully know that there is no substitute to hard work. They want instant satisfaction, instant happiness, instant answers and instant solutions without following permanent or everlasting cures. We can remove headache by swallowing a pill but cannot escape with its side effects. Similarly, we can suppress weeds by moving lawn movers but they reappear. In order to get cure from headache we have to take a complete course extending over several months and in the same way we have to sit for hours on the lawns to extract the weeds from their roots so that they may not reoccur in near future. Instant cures or one-minute solutions give temporary satisfaction. It has been rightly said that; *if you want to stay for a year, grow vegetables, if you have to go after five years plant trees and if you have to stay for whole life develop friends.* We know that in order to erect a mighty building we have to base it on the strongest foundation. On the same analogy it can be said that we cannot solve India's multidimensional problems merely by following short cuts. We have to adopt the holistic approach. Legislations are quick fixes. They would surely help the nation but not on permanent basis. Unless and until we change the mindset of the people and transform them into enlightened citizens the problems cannot be solved easily.

Some legislative measures have been suggested in the following sections in the hope that they would go a long way in improving the condition of the country. It has been rightly said that;

> *"Bad men cannot make good citizens... A vitiated state of morals, a corrupted public conscience, is incompatible with freedom. No free government, or the blessings of liberty can be preserved to any people but by a firm adherence to justice, moderation, temperance, frugality, and virtue, and by a frequent recurrence to fundamental principles."* *(Patrick Henry)*

See the daring nature of those who are caught in corrupt practices. They do not deny their role in corruption but bring the alibi that others are not immune from it. Whomsoever you ask, why are you taking or giving bribe or adulterating products he would say who is not doing it? When situation comes to this level, drastic measures are needed.

## Overhauling of Various Systems

My countrymen! We are happy that many eminent people have realised the gravity of the situation but we are pained to note that instead of giving a comprehensive solution they are coming up with their own partial solutions based on their own perceptions. For instance Some personalities of repute claim that they can solve the problems of the nation by empowering the general masses whereas others stress that the problems can be solved only when the reigns of the country are vested in the hands of honest, competent, dedicated and ethically sound people. The ruling government and the opposition are convinced that in a democracy the evils of the nationhood can be tackled constitutionally through bringing suitable legislations in the Parliament. The tragedy of the country is that there is no consensus among the various stakeholders. All the concerned people are perceiving the country's problems with their limited perceptions as the blinds perceive the elephant according to their own experiences. Those who catch hold of the legs of the elephant perceive the elephant like pillars, those that capture the tail treat it as a big groom and those who come in contact with the ear or teeth consider the elephant as a big fan or pointed stick. The fact, however, is that the elephant is all that but also none of them. Thus, without considering the country in its entirety no admirable solution can be given for the benefit of the country.

My countrymen! The first and the foremost requirement of the country is that there should be comprehensive overhauling of the whole administrative machinery, laws, practices, structures, and paraphernalia. The country became independent more than six decades ago and during this period many unwanted and unsocial elements have entered in the governing structure and many of them are still continuing. So long as they remain in the administration we can neither clean the system nor bring it back on the right track. As a first step all those employees who are corrupt or inefficient or not fit to work as government employees due to their unique mindset should be identified and shunted out by following suitable means. Besides, those employees against whom there is any case of corruption or who are known as corrupt officials should be dealt with immediately and firmly. Likewise, those politicians, civilians, professionals and business men who have unaccounted wealth should be subject to strict vigilance by the law enforcing agency. Besides black money from foreign banks and wherever it is, should be brought back in the country. It should be recovered and declared as national wealth and those who are responsible for plundering the national wealth should be brought to book. Similarly, those government servants and politicians including the retired ones who possess abnormal assets beyond their means too should not be spared. In addition to it, the Indian Penal code—IPC, Civil and criminal procedure Codes, Evidence Act, Police Act, Contract Act and other acts which were enacted during British times should be amended in the light of democratic spirit. Our Civil Service, Police department and other governing structures are not democratic in nature and content. They have the air of masterly arrogance of British times. Hence, all vital institutions as well as systems such as the mechanism of giving contracts, licences, permits, quotas, concessions, authorisations, rewards and awards which have, far reaching consequences should be democratized so as to make them compatible with democratic structure of our country. In the same way, our election rules need pruning so also we require stringent measures to check crimes against women and children and a comprehensive policy to control unwanted practices which are detrimental to the Indian society. Our main flaw has been that even after becoming independent we followed the archaic rules, regulations, practices, procedures and codes of conduct of British Raj and we did not streamline them in the true spirit of the Indian constitution. Consequently we failed to enjoy the fruits of democracy.

### The Lokpal Bill

It is the general consensus in the country that corruption starts from the top and percolates to the lower levels and hence the best option to control corruption is to bring the higher ups to book, if found guilty. This will not only deter the middle and lower staff but would also send a healthy signal to the public that no one is safe from the clutches of law. The best possible solution that is suggested in this regard is the establishment of a Lokpal to look after the crimes and omissions and commissions of the higher authorities. Importantly the difference of opinion lies in the fact that who would be covered under the act and what shall be the powers, jurisdictions and selection process of the Lokpal. A sizable segment of the society emphasise that all persons, who are associated with the governing structure such as the President and Vice-President of India, Prime Minister of the country, Governors, Ambassadors, Speaker of Lok Sabha, Members of Parliament, Chief Justice of India, Chief Election Officer, Chief Ministers of States, Members of Legislative Assemblies, Chief Justices of High Courts, Commanders of Army, Navy and Air Force, Accountant and Auditor General, Cabinet Secretary, Chief Secretaries and government officials of high rankings should come under the purview of the Lokpal. However, there are others who emphasise that we should also bring under the purview of Lokpal all the important NGO's and big contractors, license holders and beneficiaries who alleged to have wrongly benefitted from the state exchequer. There are some who suggest that the President and Vice-President of India, Prime Minister and Chief Justice of Supreme Court should not come under the purview of the Lokpal since they are the top most authorities of the country and chaos would occur if their integrities are doubted. It will not be out of place to mention here that there are people who stress that since corruption by lower staff in all government offices effects the common man most, these people too should be covered under Lokpal because without penalising the guilty staff at the lower levels the corruption in the country cannot be controlled. As against this there are others who assert that persons from peon to the subordinates and middle level officials should be covered by the existing Vigilance and corruption departments.

It is the considered opinion of many jurists that a Lokpal is not supposed to deal with all the cases that are brought before him for there are innumerable law and order cases pending in several law courts for years which have not been decided so far. As a matter of fact the Lokpal should deal with those cases of high corruption which pertain to the misuse of the powers causing huge loss to the national exchequer due to the deliberate mischief on the part of the higher functionaries. Routine omissions and commissions or even losses committed in good faith should not be brought before Lokpal. An honest, trust worthy, transparent, non-party man, non-controversial, just, conscientious and truthful person should be appointed as Lokpal along with eight supporting Lokpal through a proper (Screening and Search Committee) for a period of five years with the condition that they shall not be given the second term and they shall never be engaged in any government or private office in any capacity till death after retirement. They should be provided pension and other facilities after retirement so that they may not be financially constrained. The (Screening and Search Committee) can be constituted by taking suitable persons and reliable and men of integrity from various segments of the country. The Screening and Search committee should submit three names for Lokpal and sixteen names for supporting Lokpals in alphabetical order to the Selecting Committee consisting of the eminent people of the country whose integrities must be above board. The selection committee also has the right to refer back the name or the names forwarded by the screening committee. In that case the screening committee shall submit the panel of new name or names. Most of the eminent citizens feel that The Lokpal should be an investigating agency for the higher up and it should report directly to the Supreme Court. The CBI should be under the direct control of the Lokpal or if it is not under direct control of the Lokpal it should be an autonomous body free from the clutches of the government. The director of the CBI should also be appointed by a reputed collegiums. The Lokpal and the supporting Lokpals should be a Constitutional body with their own powers, rights and duties but they should not be a glamorous or super authority like President of India or Prime Minister of India. The decisions of the Lokpal in matters of investigations should be final. However, if the Lokpal or supporting Lokpals are found involved in any well established and valid corruption cases during their tenures they should be examined by Supreme Court. The matters brought before the Lokpal shall not be lingered but they should be expeditiously decided as early as possible so that confidence about the utility of Jan Lokpal may be created in the minds of the ordinary citizens. The Lokpal would decide his or her own strategy to deal with cases brought to his or her notice. The report about every case decided by the Lokpal along with all the details should be submitted to the Lok Sabha and Rajya Sabha for the information of the MPs and the general public. There is a section of the public which wants that there must be some provision to penalise those who deliberately submit wrong and bogus complaints to malign the image of the innocent persons. Besides, there should be a State Lokayukta along with four associate State Lokayuktas for every state on the pattern of the Lokpal and there should be coordination between the Central Lokpal and State Lokayukta offices but the state Lokayukta should not necessarily be under the Central Lokpal. They should be independent and their decisions too should be final.

It will not be out of place to mention here that the Indian Parliament passed the Lokpal Bill in December 2013 and the salient features are as follows:

1. *Lokayuktas:* The new Bill mandates states to set up Lokayuktas within 365 days. States have the freedom to determine the nature and type of Lokayukta.
2. *Constitution of Lokpal:* The Lokpal will consist of a chairperson and a maximum of eight members, of which 50 per cent shall be judicial members. Fifty per cent members of Lokpal shall be from among SC, ST, OBCs, minorities and women.
3. *Selection of Lokpal:* The selection committee will have

Prime Minister, Lok Sabha Speaker, Leader of the Opposition in Lok Sabha and the Chief Justice of India. A fifth member of the selection committee for selection of Lokpal under the category of "eminent jurist" may be nominated by the President on the basis of recommendation of the first four members of the selection committee.

4. *Religious Bodies and Trust:* The new Bill includes societies and trusts that collect public money, receive funding from foreign sources, and have an income level above a certain threshold, it excludes bodies creating endowments for or performing religious or charitable functions.
5. *Prosecution:* Before taking a decision on filing a charge-sheet in a case upon consideration of the investigation report, the Lokpal may authorise its own prosecution wing or the concerned investigating agency to initiate prosecution in special courts.
6. *Central Bureau of Investigation:* For independence of the CBI, a directorate of prosecution will be formed. Appointment of the director of prosecution will be on the recommendation of the Central Vigilance Commissioner. Transfer of officers of CBI investigating cases referred by Lokpal will be only with the approval of Lokpal, who will also have superintendence over CBI in relation to Lokpal referred cases.
7. *Hearing:* The government servant will get a hearing before a decision is taken by the Lokpal.
8. *Prime Minister:* The Prime Minister will be under the purview of the Lokpal with subject matter exclusions and specific process for handling complaints against the Prime Minister.
9. *Investigation:* Inquiry has to be completed within sixty days and investigation to be completed within six months. Lokpal shall order an investigation only after

hearing the public servant. Inquiry against the Prime Minister has to be held in-camera and approved by two-thirds of the full bench of the Lokpal.

10. *Penalty:* False and frivolous complaints—imprisonment up to one year and a fine of up to Rs 1 lakh. Public servants—imprisonment upto seven years. Criminal misconduct and habitually abetting corruption—jail term up to 10 years.

Many people also strongly feel that the Lokpal Bill has been passed in hurry by the Parliamentarians due to public pressure and the Bill is half-baked. There is general impression in the public that since the CBI has not become completely independent, it will be difficult to punish the higher ups. Besides, people believe that it will be cumbersome for the vigilance department to deal with lakhs of people. However, people by and large have appreciated the Bill as it is a right step in right direction and it would cause some dent to corruption in the country.

**Central Investigating Commissioner**

It is also the general perception of our countrymen that there should be an investigating agency to control corruption and antisocial activity in private sector because without controlling nefarious activities in this sector the corruption in the country cannot be dented. Country is horribly suffering from the adverse activities of musclemen, mafia, creators of black money, participants in foreign exchange bungling, smuggling and other illegal activities. We hear everyday cases of land grabbing, kidnapping, black money in foreign banks, match fixing and Satta business. Likewise several citizens are the victims of big scams by some of the fraudulent builders; many have suffered at the hands of few unscrupulous financial companies as well as the inhuman activities of some of the recruitment agents. Many civilians are exploited by the money lenders, commission agents and the whole society is at the mercy of the hoarders, adulterators and cheaters. Similarly, many people have grievances against the mal practices of some of the pharmaceutical companies, dubious activities of some diagnostic centres, false claims of the fake healers of dreaded diseases and blackmailing by some of the irresponsible persons in media and mass communication. In their opinion the country needs an honest, dedicated, transparent, just and trust worthy Central Investigating Commissioner to control the evil and corrupt activities in above areas. The misadventures at the lower and middle levels should be dealt with by the existing consumer redresser forums and other law enforcing agencies. An honest, competent and man of integrity should be appointed as central Investigating Commissioner along with four assistant Investigating Commissioners by a collegiums consisting of eminent people of the country for a period of five years with the condition that they shall not join any government or private job after retirement till death. They should be provided pension and other facilities after retirement so that they may not face any financial difficulties. It should be the duty of all the investigating agencies to co-operate with the Investigating Commissioner. The decisions of the Central Investigating Commissioner should be reported to the chief justice of the Supreme Court as well as they should be reported to Lok Sabha and Rajya Sabha along with complete details for the consumption of the general public. However, if there are any valid and substantial corruption charges against the Central Investigating Commissioner or associate Investigating Commissioners arising out during their tenures as Investigating Commissioners, they should be dealt with by the Supreme Court.

The Central Investigating Commissioner should be a Constitutional authority and it should be the duty of the Central Investigating Commissioner to decide the cases brought to his or her notice expeditiously, transparently and justly. Similarly, there should also be a Director – Investigations at the state levels along with four assistant Directors on the pattern of Central Investigating Commissioner and they should be independent and their decisions should be final. The Investigating Commissioners would decide their own strategies to tackle cases brought to their notices. Needless to say, that there should be some provision of penalty so that false complaints are not unnecessarily filed. There is no guarantee that the corruption in government offices and in the private sector and in high offices would be completely eradicated by merely appointing Lokpal and Investigating Commissioner and leaving citizens, civil society and political parties free because human ingenuity is much sharper than all the laws of the land. The corruption, malpractices, adulteration and cheating would certainly decrease but the degrees of decline would depend upon the effective execution of the Acts, Statutes and Ordinances.

**Citizens' Charter**

It is an admitted fact that corruption is not committed merely by the higher ups in the government and private sectors but also by various other segments of the society including the citizens of the country. They are also not immune from the lures of corruption. It is the firm faith of meaningful citizens of the country that if we control Government Officials and People on the top in the private sector and leave the citizens untouched; we cannot succeed in improving the deteriorating conditions of the country. We have to make our citizens alert, responsible and conscientious by bringing the Citizens Charter of rights and duties. We have Fundamental Rights guaranteed in the Constitution but we do not have a Citizens Charter covering their fundamental duties and responsibilities.

**Citizens Rights**

My learned countrymen!

*"All men are endowed by their Creator with inalienable rights; among these are life, liberty and the pursuit of happiness" (Jefferson)* However, one should know that *"There is no right without a parallel duty, no liberty without the supremacy of the law, no high destiny without earnest perseverance, no greatness without self-denial."*

*—Lieber*

Human rights are inseparable part of modern civilisation. The Citizens Charter pertaining to their rights must ensure that all persons are equal before law and they are entitled to equal opportunities and protection of law irrespective of the caste, creed, colour, religion, sex and place of birth. It should also be guaranteed that the life, liberty, honour and possession of citizens shall be safe and secure and no person would be exposed to injury or death except under the due process of law and the sanctity of one's dead body too would be inviolable and it shall be handled with solemnity. Besides, the conditions of the Charter are deemed to be amply fulfilled when every individual has a right to protect his secrecy and privacy, honour, reputation and dignity against deliberate attempts at defaming and black-mailing him and leveling groundless charges against him. The citizens rights are also amply guaranteed when everyone is allowed to earn lawfully according to his abilities and he is also permitted to own his individual and collective property as per the rule of law and no property is expropriated in the public interest save by paying fair and reasonable compensation. When everyone has a right to move freely and reside wherever one deems fit within the boundaries of the country and no one shall forcibly evict him from his residence without recourse to due process of law. When every person has a right to marry and to form a family and bring up children in accordance to his religious practices or social conventions and no one is married against his or her will or suffer any diminution on account of marriage. When the members of the family share their responsibilities and obligations according to their sex, natural capabilities, talents and inclinations bearing in mind their common responsibilities towards their families. When parents who have become old, they are entitled to proper care and compassion from their wards and mothers have rights for special care being the foundation of the family.

When, every married woman has a right to receive means necessary for her maintenance suiting to the status of her husband and in the event of divorce a suitable alimony according to the law. When every woman can seek dissolution of marriage in accordance to the terms of the law and inherit her husband's, parents, children and other relative's properties. When all the children have the rights to be brought up properly and other members have the rights to be treated nicely according to family traditions. When every citizen, including those who are handicapped and disabled, have rights to adequate food, shelter, clothing, medical and health care, education, social security and other conveniences and comforts consistent with the means and resources of the country. When every individual has the fundamental right to freedom in all phases of his life and to protect his freedom through peaceful and constitutional means and no attempts are made to usurp his freedom save under authority of law. When all the residents of the country are treated justly, fairly and in accordance to the law and all have liberty to protect their legitimate rights, seek appropriate remedial measures and are not discriminated in protecting their rights, freedoms and liberties before independent judicial bodies. When all persons get equal wages and benefits for equal work and efforts and no one is denied any opportunity in any sphere of life or discriminated against in any manner in any field or exposed to physical and mental risk in any segment merely by reason of belief system, race, religion or language.

When labourers are treated generously and not only paid wages regularly but also provided adequate rest and leisure. When no one is declared guilty and punished in accordance to law for any offence save when he has faced the fair trial, given reasonable opportunity to defend and is declared guilty by independent judicial tribunal. When no act is considered a crime unless it is declared as such by the law of the land and no punishment can be awarded in excess of the seriousness of the offence and without taking into consideration the circumstances under which the crime was committed. When a citizen is not killed in fake encounters for getting prizes, promotions or to satisfy the hunger of revenge and no one is illegally detained or unnecessarily harassed being of a particular caste, religion or creed. When no one is subjected to inhuman tortures relating to his mind, body, soul and he is not insulted, humiliated, degraded or threatened injury to himself, or to anyone held dearest by him or not compelled to confess to the commissioning of a crime or not forced to consent to act which is injurious to his interests.

When a citizen is not dragged in the courts except when the finger of suspicion is raised against him and he has a right to protection against the harassment against official agencies. When religious and ethnic minorities and the downtrodden sections of the society are not discriminated but looked with compassion and care. When they are free to establish their religious institutions, preach and practice their religions and also to establish the educational institutions of their choice, impart instructions in their mother tongue and to promote their culture and maintain their special identities. When every citizen is entitled to assume any public office according to his capacities and capabilities and when no one is debarred from the fullest use of the natural endowments provided by the Lord. When everyone has freedom of speech, expression, thoughts, beliefs and ideas within the limits of the law and there is no restriction on right to freedom of conscience and worship according to ones belief system. When every individual has complete freedom for the development of his personality and to participate individually or collectively in any social, political, cultural or religious function and he is also entitled to establish such institutions for the enjoyment of his social, cultural, political or religious rights. When every person, persecuted or oppressed has a right to seek refuge and asylum in other countries irrespective of his caste, creed, religion, sex and place of birth.

## Citizens Duties and Responsibilities

My well-wishers! In the same way, various provisions in the Directive Principles of State Policy of our Constitution indicate the responsibilities of the state but any document charting the Responsibilities of the Citizens in various aspects of their lives is missing. We need such a document badly. Duties have played an important role in Indian society. We have been hearing it since centuries that

*"Do thy duty; that is best; leave unto the Lord the rest" (Longfellow) "Let us do our duty in our shop or our kitchen; in the market, the street, the office, the school, the home, just as faithfully as if we stood in the front rank of some battle, and knew that victory for mankind depended on our bravery, strength, and skill. When we do that, the humblest of us will be serving in that great army which achieves the welfare of the world."*

—*Theodore Parker*

The importance of the duty would be highlighted by the story telling that;

*"a mighty king wanted to go on a pleasure trip along with his queens, servants, bodyguards and paraphernalia to nearby picnic point at twelve o' clock in the night. The moment he came out of the fort, his night watchman came and spoke with folded hands that they should postpone the journey as it was not a good omen. The king kicked him aside and started proceeding towards his chariot. The watchman lied down in front of the chariot and told the king that he could go only after moving the chariot on his body. Having seen the watchman so adamant, the senior queen persuaded the king to postpone the trip. The king postponed his journey but side by side sent another delegation in the guise of the king and his courtiers. The king was highly surprised when he came to know that all whom he had sent in the disguised forms of king and his courtiers were killed in the way by the enemies of the king in surprise attack. The king called the night watchman and asked him the reason of stopping him from going on to the trip; The watchman said that at about half an hour before the king was to go on his pleasure trip, he saw a dream that the king was going along with his darbaris on a journey, suddenly he was attacked and all who were with the king were killed. King became very happy. He called the special Darbar to honour the watchman and gave him titles, land and costly gifts but side by side terminated his services with immediate effect. On asking by his closest associates*

*the reason for terminating the services of the watchman, the king replied that he gave him honour and gifts because he had saved the lives of the king, queens and others but terminated his services because he was negligent in his duties. When he saw the dream at about half an hour before his departure meant that instead of keeping watch he was sleeping which clearly showed that he was not performing his duties properly, hence he punished him for the violation of his duties."*

Despite the fact that the night watchman had saved the life of the king, the king did not condone him for violating his duties. This shows that people in olden days made no compromises in matters of duties since duties were considered as an integral part of a civilised society and it was expected from the people that they would perform their duties in true spirit.

The duties of the citizens should be clearly defined and identified. From our point of view the citizens are supposed to have fulfilled their duties and responsibilities. If they perform their duties religiously with utmost responsibility such as they are loyal and sincere to their country and love their country with the core of their hearts and are always ready and willing to sacrifice their lives, honour, liberty and property for the sake of the nation. They do not perform, assist or abet any activity prejudicial to the interest of the country. They are the protectors of national property, guardians of national resources and never indulge in deforestation, pollution and dumping of waste material in rivers and seas. They pay their taxes regularly; abhor tax evasion, black money and theft of foreign exchange. They promote national products, help in generating income and employment. They help in arresting terrorists, fifth columnists, anti-social and anti-national elements and those who sabotage. They are law abiding, truthful, trust worthy, faithful and peace loving. They fulfill their promises and contractual obligations when they make any and do not take part in cheating, theft, misrepresentation, coercion and fraud. They do not adulterate, never give or take bribe, avoid all types of corrupt practices and are honest to the core. They weigh properly, deal ethically and are fair in their trade practices. They hate begging, superstition, games of chance and intoxicants. They are pragmatic, progressive, dynamic, God-fearing and morally sound. They are sympathetic to their nationals, kind to the poor, helping to the destitute and considerate to their colleagues. They lavishly spend on charity, feed the hungry, clothe the paupers and provide shelter to the downtrodden. They avoid falsehood, violence, pride and anger. They control their passions, greed and selfishness and tell what is true and do what is just and speak what is worthy and hear what is commendable. They are just, impartial, transparent and never discriminate on the basis of religion, belief system, caste, creed, sex or place of birth.

They obey and look after their parents, love and train properly their children, behave nicely with their spouses and are helping to their kith and kin. They keep all types of information confidential about each other after divorce which they had obtained about their spouses during the period of their marriage and the disclosure of which could prove detrimental to their interests. They avoid niggardliness and extravagance and wasteful expenditure. They dress properly and avoid indecencies of all types. They take nutritious meal and discard the junk foods. They protect their culture, dynamic customs, healthy traditions and precious national heritage. They promote art, architecture, crafts and literary and cultural activities and games and sports. They perform yoga, promote cleanliness and are early risers and early sleepers. They protect the rights of all citizens including the rights to life, honour, liberty, property and possessions and come to the rescue of those who are struggling to protect their legitimate freedoms. They rise against injustice, infringements of human rights, exploitation and struggle for seeking remedial measures provided by law and to get adjudication before an independent authority. They do not obey any command which is contrary to law of the land no matter by whom it may be given. They own their own legitimate crimes and do not involve family members, friend and relatives or pass them upon those who had nothing to do with them. They do not disseminate falsehood, propaganda material and matter prejudicial to the interest of the society or circulate reports, articles, matter which may outrage public decency or do not indulge in backbiting, slander, and spying, nicknaming, anti-social activities or cast defamatory aspersions on others. They go in search of knowledge and also in pursuit of truth wherever it is available. The list of duties and responsibilities is big but if the above duties are faithfully performed by the citizens much improvement can be brought in the effective functioning of the society.

**Code of Conducts for Government and Private Employees**

Just as the Citizens Charter underlying the rights and duties for the citizens is necessary similarly the Code of Conduct reflecting the good moral character for government and private employees is also essential.

> *"The noblest contribution which any man can make for the benefit of posterity, is that of a good character. The richest bequest which any man can leave to the youth of his native land is that of a shining, spotless example."*
>
> —*R.C. Winthrop*

> *"A good heart, benevolent feelings, and a balanced mind, lie at the foundation of character. Other things may be deemed fortuitous; they may come and go; but character is that which lives and abides, and is admired long after its possessor has left the earth."*
>
> —*John Todd*

True character is generally reflected at the work place or while dealing with people.

The admirable principles of the character such as discipline, self esteem, commitment, conviction, courtesy, courage, hard work and sense of responsibility should find their place in the code of conduct for government officials and private sector employees. Employees should be made accountable and there must be a deadline to complete the task brought before the authorities. It should be ensured that matters are not lingered but decided within a reasonable period of time. Positive thinking, power of perseverance, spirit of giving more than taking, pride of performance, learning by mistakes and power of rationalising should be prominently projected in the conduct rules. Trust, credibility, obedience, integrity, motivation, ethics and morality should form the basis of guidelines for the employees. The conditions of the code of conduct for the employees are largely satisfied, if it is made incumbent upon every employee whether he gets the higher pay or lower pay or whether he is the supervisor, manager or subordinate that he or she would come to office neat, clean, well dressed, fresh, cheerful and in time. He would report for duty within a reasonable time after getting his attendance recorded. He would not waste time in gossiping, leisure, idle talks or in meeting formalities but report for duty within reasonable time after changing clothes if any, collect the necessary instruments or files, equipments or material and start his work as stipulated with enthusiasm. During the duty period he would co-operate with other colleagues, help them wherever needed and keep patience, perseverance and calm. He would obey his bosses, respect the colleagues and be kind to his subordinates and avoid unnecessary arguments, backbiting of the superiors, criticism of the compatriots and blaming the subordinates. He would avoid doubting, suspicion, acquisitiveness and spying. He would be loyal to his institution and sincere to the organisation and would not take part in any activity prejudicial to the interest of the organisation. He would not hesitate to fight through peaceful and legal means for his genuine rights but would not incite or instigate people to go on strike, cause violence and shut downs. He would protect the property and the interest of his organisation and come to the rescue of the same when situation so demands. He would be co-operative, trust worthy and reliable. He would not express his grievances in vulgar manner but report them to appropriate authority for redresser. He would never sabotage, never act as a fifth columnist and never indulge in commissions and cuts for doing his legal duty. If he is in commanding position it is his duty to provide congenial atmosphere at the work place for every individual such as clean and lighted rooms, smoke free atmosphere, continuous electricity supply, pure drinking water and pollution free surrounding. He should see to it that no employee is over burdened, over worked, exploited or asked to do work and duty beyond his powers .He should ensure that the employees are paid reasonable wages and salaries in time as well as other contingency benefits such as leave salary, city compensatory, educational and medical allowances and the organisation also makes it sure that their retirement benefits are ensured. In the event of injury or loss of life during service period, the organisation should stand firm and help the dependents of the employees as per rules. No one should be hurt by words of mouth, conducts, gestures, postures and deeds and no compromise should be made with the respect, dignity, honour and ego of any employee. Everyone should be treated with utmost respect due to him or her and he should not be humiliated, tortured or exploited in any manner. He should have freedom to express his genuine ideas and grievances as per the rules of organisation and be free to leave the organisation if he deems fit as per his contractual obligations. Needles to say that all civilized societies value the dignity, honour and safety of their employers and employees since without showing mutual respects no society can function properly.

**Code of Conduct for Political Parties**

The peaceful climate in the country in any democracy is generally vitiated by the defective policies of the political parties. Some of these parties indulge in nefarious activities to promote their personal interests and hence they should be brought within the frame work of a sound code of conduct.

> *"Two kinds of men generally best succeed in political life: men of no principle, but of great talent: and men of no talent, but of one principle- that of obedience to their superiors."*
>
> *—Wendell Phillips*

*"To be a chemist you must study chemistry; to be a lawyer or a physician you must study law or medicine; but to be a politician you need only to study your own interests."*

*—Max O'Rell*

*"The political parties that I would call great, are those which cling more to principles than to consequence; to general, and not to special cases; to ideas, and not to men. Such parties are usually distinguished by a nobler character, more generous passions, more genuine convictions, and a more bold and open conduct than others"*

*—Fe Tocqueville*

The leadership of every political party should, therefore, be in the hands of those people who are visionary, inspirational, generous, dependable, reliable, consistent, caring, just, transparent, humble and empathetic. They should be committed to values, socially responsible, gracious, good listeners, open minded, sensitive to public issues, good role models and leave healthy legacy behind. They should never attack below the belt, never indulge in petty politics, trivial issues and in activities prejudicial to the interest of the country and the people.

While designing a code of conduct for such parties it should be made incumbent upon them that they would be duty bound not to do anything which is contrary to the safety, security, progress, harmony, dignity, grace and the interest of the country. They would not encourage, help and abet sedition, revolt, division and disintegration of the country. They would emphasise on the principles of give and take, live and let others live and do to others what we expect others to do to us. They would not try to divide people in castes, classes, religions and other subsections with a view to create in them hatred against each other. In order to seek the votes of the people they would not take the advantage of their sensitivities, emotions and weaknesses. They would constantly keep in mind India's composite culture, unity in diversity and diversity in unity. The political parties would not work as hostile or contrasting groups but as colleagues and compatriots. They would be slow to suspect but quick to trust, slow to expose but quick to shield, slow to downgrade but quick to appreciate and slow to provoke but quick to conciliate. The manifestos of the political parties would not reflect any evil designs or tendencies detrimental to the larger interest of the people as well as the country. They would highlight the healthy, constructive, sane, progressive and dynamic issues and discuss them in the climate of calm, compassion and seriousness. They would not indulge in opposition for the sake of opposition and would not resort to leg pulling and slandering. They would resist raising funds by going to the vested interests who demand quid *pro quo* or to anti-national elements who are the enemies of the country. They would not compel government officials to raise money for them by misusing government machineries and resources and over burdening general public. They would not violate election rules and rules of conducts devised by Election Commissions and perform their duties justly, honestly, transparently and equitably irrespective of the fact whether they are ruling the country or are in the opposition. Their members would obey the Party Manifestos, Whip of the party, directions of the Chairman, Lok Sabha, Rajya Sabha and the Chairmen of State Assemblies and their leaders and would not cross the floors. They would not try to raise their salaries, allowances, conveniences and benefits beyond proportions and would not waste the funds of national exchequer by visiting unnecessarily to foreign lands. They would not create hurdles in the proper functioning of the Parliament and Assemblies by unnecessary creating chaos, going to the well, shouting slogans, disturbing speakers and creating violence in the houses. They would not misuse their powers and funds whether they are ministers or merely the members. The political parties would not develop in them the extra territorial loyalties with political parties of other nations based on ideological, regional or parochial considerations that are harmful for the country. They would always fight for the betterment of mankind both at national as well as international levels and would not do anything that may lower down the dignity of the country as well as the grace of mankind.

### A Monitoring, Assessing and Controlling Authority

Democracy is supposed to be the government of people, by the people, for the people but mostly it is run by government officials and a few elected representatives of the public. The sixty years experience of Indian democracy reveals that whatever money is sanctioned for the government projects or for the benefit of the marginalised sections of the society, nearly one tenth reaches up to the ground level and most of the funds are usurped by the officials and the men in power. The funds are certainly audited but the audit reports find few takers. Besides, there is no check on the quality of work by any independent agencies with the result that the sub standard material is used which withers away with the vagaries of nature. Moreover, it is also alleged that certain funds marked for weaker sections never reach them. They either remain unspent or are diverted to other segments. As a consequence of which the very purpose of government spending becomes redundant.

> *"If the master takes no account of his servants, they will make small account of him, and care not what they spend, who are never brought to an audit."*
>
> —*Fuller*

There is an urgent need to institutionalise the mechanism for monitoring, assessing and controlling of various funds with a view to suggest policy measures on timely basis. An autonomous Monitoring, Assessing and Controlling Authority on the pattern of Auditor and Accountant General of India can serve the purpose. This body should see to it that not only the funds are properly utilised for the purpose for which they were ear marked but the quality of material should also be ensured. This cannot be done unless and until the government associates the trusted academicians, reliable professionals and honest members from civil society with this authority who should closely monitor and watch the activities of the government officials and the elected representatives as watch dogs. This authority should assess and evaluate the extent of development benefits that accrued to various segments of the economy as well as the misuse of funds by various persons and agencies. Over and above this, the MP's, MLA's, members of Municipal Corporations and Panchayats and as well as functionaries of *Zila Parishads* too should be given more powers within their constituencies so that they may ensure that the various schemes designed for their sectors may be fruitfully executed.

**Overhauling of Archaic Social, Cultural and Religious Practices**

If we bring changes in the mindsets of the individuals and the groups and do not change our social, cultural and religious institutions wherever they need improvement, we cannot succeed in achieving our objectives. The experience teaches us that many European countries succeeded in accelerating growth by reorienting their obsolete customs and practices. Change is the law of nature. Everything is changing with the changes in time, space and consciousness. The society too cannot remain static.

> *"In this world of change naught which comes stays, and naught which goes is lost."*
>
> —*Mad Swetchine*

> *"He that will not apply new remedies must expect new evils."*
>
> —*Bacon*

In the dynamic world those survive with dignity who adjust with the changing times with balanced attitude and sense of proportion. *"Society undergoes continual changes; it is barbarous, it is civilised, it is Christianised, it is rich, it is scientific; but this change is not amelioration. For everything that is given something is taken. Society acquires new arts and loses old instincts. The civilised man has built a coach, but has lost the use of his feet; he has a fine Geneva watch, but cannot tell the hour by the sun."*

*—Emerson*

Indian society too is changing very fast. It is gaining in one field and losing in many. Everyday we hear of the murders of lovers for marrying outside their castes or within the prohibited degrees. Many bridegrooms are forcibly married to girls not approved by them merely because the parents and relatives of the unfortunate girls cannot find the bridegrooms or are unable to pay the required dowries. Likewise, there is cultural suffocation. New cultures and new ways of living are flattening Indian culture and new moralities and diverse values are denting the age old moral system of the country. We need corrective measures in such a way that the spirit of our dynamic systems is not violated and side by side the healthy changes may be adapted in our social, cultural and moral milieus.

My Countrymen! Is it possible to correct all the above maladies and deficiencies merely by framing legislations? Our experience of setting things right through legislations is not encouraging. We have Indian Penal Code, Criminal Procedure Code, Civil Procedure Code and Indian Evidence Act to control crimes but the magnitude of crimes is increasing day by day. We have officials to look after adulterated products, examine weights and measures and control hoarding but ground situation is that hardly any food item is immune from adulteration and the situation is worsening day by day. The Income Tax Department, the Vigilance Section, the Foreign Exchange Regulation Act are there but the black money is mounting in foreign banks. We have seen the fate of the Right to Education Bill and other Bills pertaining to torture of bonded labourers and the children. We are also aware of the pathetic conditions of many laws framed by government to reform economic, social, moral and religious systems. The government of India has introduced reservation in government jobs and educational institutions for the Scheduled Castes and

Scheduled Tribes and the Backward Classes and has passed many laws to protect the atrocities upon *Harijans* and *Dalits*. It has framed laws to ensure help and assistance to parents, to give half of the property to divorced woman and to give equal share to females compared to males in the ancestral property. It has also endeavoured to provide work for a certain days to the poor and to create infrastructural facilities in slums and *ghettos*. However, the result is not to our satisfaction.

**Laws have Their Own Limitations**

The basic question arises as to how far can we achieve our objectives by merely framing laws when the general impression is that the laws are meant to flout them and to find out holes in them?

*"Laws grind the poor, and rich men rule the law."*

*—Goldsmith*

"They help the mighty and crush the weak." *These written laws are just like the spider's webs; the small and feeble may be caught and entangled in them, but the rich and mighty force through and despise them." (Anacharsis)* "The laws benefit the big ones and harm the small entities". *Laws are generally found to be nets of such a texture, as the little creep through, the great break, and the middle size are alone entangled in."*

*—Shenstone*

*"Laws are like cobwebs which may catch small flies, but let wasps and hornets break through"*

*—Swift*

The framing of the wonderful laws is no problem, the difficulty arises when we try to implement them in their letter and spirit. In addition to it, the multiplicity of laws shows the weakness of a state.

*"A multitude of laws in a country is like a great number of physicians, a sign of weakness and malady."*

*—Voltaire*

*"When the State is most corrupt, then the laws are most multiplied"*

*—Tacitus*

Besides, there is limitation to the application of laws. All social and cultural maladies cannot be cured through the promulgation of laws.

*"To seek the redress of grievances by going to law, is like sheep running for shelter to a bramble bush."*

*—Dilwyn*

*"Economic depression cannot be cured by legislative action or executive pronouncement. Economic wounds must be healed by the action of the cells of the economic body, the producers and consumers themselves."*

*—Herbert Hoover*

*"There is no country in the world in which everything can be provided for by the laws, or in which political institutions can prove a substitute for common sense and public morality."*

*—De Tocqueville*

Those countries which tried to correct their social, cultural and moral systems through the enactment of laws failed miserably.

*"Let but the public mind once become thoroughly corrupt, and all attempts to secure property, liberty, or life, by mere force of laws written on parchment, will be as vain as to put up printed notices in an orchard to keep off canker-worms."*

*—Horace Mann*

"Moreover, can we revive the spirit of selflessness, sacrifice and service to mankind by legislative measures in those that are greedy, acquisitive and selfish? Can we change the mindset of arrogant, hot-headed and nasty people by imbibing in them the passion for needy, downtrodden and helpless with the help of rules and regulations? Can we develop the love for animals, affection for kith and kin and respect for humanity by changing Statutes? Can we create in the sordid, dead and morbid souls the attraction towards peace, piety and righteousness just by bringing Ordinances? Can we bring any change in the consciences of the conscienceless, wicked and lewd people for truth, justice, equity and good conscience by introducing Acts? The answer perhaps is no.

> *"We should never create by laws which can be accomplished by morality."*
>
> —*Montesquieu*

Many countries have corrected their derailed system by adopting a basket of policies. For instance, they made general public conscientious, honest, dedicated and transparent by bringing revolutionary changes in the mindsets of the people. Besides, they developed the spirit of dedication, honesty, transparency and commitment among the people manning various affairs of the government and created in the governing machinery the will and power to detect and punish the culprits without any fear or favour. Likewise, they created the fear of the state among people for fear of the government plays a dominant role in maintaining law and order. For instance, it is claimed that in South Korea if anyone participates in eve teasing or looks at any girl with malicious intensions or molests a girl or commits a minor crime, he is sent behind the bars for five to ten years. However, if he goes to brothels or to call girl centers which are legal or maintains a live-in-relationship with any partner with her consent it is not considered crime. Thus, in South Korea crimes are very few though routes are opened for leading a perverted life in permissible areas. Similarly, in Saudi Arabia one is beheaded for committing adultery and one's hand is cut off if he commits theft and hence, people resist committing any crime.

The ideal solution for a democratic country like India is that we should transform people by changing their mind-sets, arousing their consciences and bringing revolutionary changes in their perceptions, conceptions, ideas and belief systems so that heart to heart they become progressive, dynamic and enlightened. It has been rightly said that:

> if there is uprising among civilians we can call the police and if the policemen rebel we may invite the military but when military revolts our system breaks down.

Thus, if we want to control the people the best course of action is that we should control them by themselves. We should sharpen their inner instinct, their conscience and their good sense which always guide them to follow civilised ways to solve their problems peacefully, constitutionally and democratically. Save this there is no method to control people in any form of government.

**Our Main Problem**

My brothers! Our main problem is that most of our politicians have lost their luster, the government has generally become indecisive and its fear has vanished to a large extent from the minds of the people and the general public too is not hearing the voice of its conscience. As a matter of fact the condition of the country is such that it can be depicted only by the story of an Emperor *who saw a dream in which he found that there would rain heavily in his capital after seven days and whoever would drink the rain water would become mad. He consulted the astrologers and all of them agreed that the dream was true and there would rain after seven days and he who would drink that water would lose his senses. The Emperor called the meeting of his top most advisers and informed them about his dream and the opinion of the astrologers. They assured him to find out the suitable solution before the onslaught of the rain. The rain actually came as predicted and he who drank the rain water became mad. However, the Emperor and his family members, advisors and the coterie remained safe from the danger as they had collected the pre-rain water in the reservoirs and were drinking out of that. The impact of the rain water was so severe that those who drank that water became insane. They levelled baseless and foolish charges against one another and the law and order cases mounted astronomically because they pertained to the lunatics. The Emperor's Court failed completely to deal with the nonsensical issues of the mad people. There was all round resentment in the state and people started saying openly that the Emperor and his advisors had become lunatics since the day it rained a few days ago. When the Emperor heard it, he was dumb founded and again called the meeting of his advisors and told them the reaction of the people. One of the advisors who possessed wisdom spoke that what the Emperor saw in the dream was absolutely correct and what the general public was saying was also not false. He stressed that instead of wasting time in discussion it would be in the interest of the Emperor and the state to find out the solution to the vex problem which he knew. All agreed and asked him to present his proposal before the meeting. The genius went outside and brought few glasses of the rain water and asked them to drink. Everybody drank the rain water and nonsense prevailed upon them and being themselves lunatics decided the cases of the mad people to their entire satisfaction which compelled the general public to proclaim that thank God that the Emperor and his advisors had come to their senses.*

Thus, in a situation where majority is yielding to perverted forces and making compromises, a few sane voices cannot bring any material improvement. When most of the state machinery and the civil society has drunk the "polluted rain water" the easiest solution is to drink the same and become as they are for it is worthless to sell mirrors in the lands of the blinds. However, this is not the permanent solution for a big, mighty and great country like India. It would destroy all our systems, values, heritage and golden past. If we have to survive as a vibrant nation with our distinct identities, values, culture and traditions, we would have not only to correct ourselves but also bring those to the straight path who have gone astray. The task is certainly difficult but not impossible.

History is witnessed to the fact that no country could survive with dignity without ambitions, visions, missions and viable strategies; no nation acquired a place of honour without elegance, majesty, grace and magnificence; no territory marked its place on the annals of history without dedicated hard work, exemplary conducts, admirable values and innovative thoughts and no state boasted of its grandeur without its history, past glory, golden heritage and bright future. Likewise, no system can work efficiently without the backing of truth, justice, equity and good conscience; no organisation can function effectively without the support of sincerity, devotion, dedication and honesty and transparency; no structure can operate optimally without character, commitment, courtesy and courage and no establishment can move scientifically without the help of experience, expertise, values and sound judgment. Suitable changes in the laws of the land and the necessary amendments in the rules and regulations and the overhauling of various systems of the country would certainly go a long way in shaping the destiny of the country but side by side we will have to develop in us our sterling qualities which we possessed but have lost over time failing which the entire system would fall flat.

# 3 We have Lost Our Sterling Qualities

My wise countrymen! When we impacted the world we possessed sterling qualities and we were known for our generosity in the designs, humility in the execution and moderation in success. We were not only conscientious but also cultured and refined beings. We had an appreciation for the arts, literature, painting, sculpture, music, religion, technology, sciences, and politics as well as to the process of starting and promoting development and to the totality of society's achievements. Our culture was rich, progressive, dynamic, growth-oriented, and purposeful and rooted in our value system which our elders had preserved since time immemorial in the shape of epics, legends, fairy tales, folklores, customs, habits, life-styles and ways of living. The whole social, economic, political and worldly order of ours was based on the comprehensive and all-pervading material, moral and spiritual premises which sustained us for centuries as dynamic, progressive and pious people.

## Our Qualities

My countrymen! We were result-oriented people. We were aware of our constraints but focussed on our strengths. We did not do different things but did things differently. We did not do extraordinary things but did ordinary things extraordinary well. Experience taught us that most people faltered in life not because of lack of ability or intelligence or resources but because of lack of direction, character, desire, dedication and discipline. The geniuses have said that there is nothing in the world which human beings cannot achieve through honesty, courage, compassion, persistence and commitment and discipline as well as by altering the mind-sets. To get the winning edge we have to strive constantly for excellence and not perfection as there is nothing like perfection because even the best can be improved. We should set our goals clearly specifying what do we want and why and how would we achieve that and what would be the time limit? The dynamic social norms, vibrant cultural notions, exemplary moral practices, pious religious values which sustained us for so long have gone too far from us. The positive attitude, holistic approach, wonderful self-esteem, power of persistence and spirit of giving more than what we get and the pride of performance which were our hall marks have left us alone. The passion for truth, the fancy for justice and the craze for equity are no more in our veins. Our lack of priority, fatalistic attitude and not learning from past have brought us in wilderness. It is because of losing these admirable qualities that we have become selfish, self-centered and individualistic. The voice of conscience which used to control us from doing wrong things has vanished from our minds, hearts and souls. Our abilities to use talents, our capacities to recognise opportunities, our intellect to motivate people and our decent upbringing which were differentiating us from others have dented us. Since we have divorced our value system, we do not mind taking bribes, fear least in cheating people, and fearlessly indulge in sins, criminal and lewd activities. As most of us are not conscientious we believe in pushing aside whoever comes in our ways. Being not true to our self we have abandoned all that we had inherited from our elders, teachers and well–wishers. The notions like piety, righteousness and good moral conducts are merely hollow words for us so also are the healthy traditions, resounding conventions and vital ethos of our classical culture. For us, ends justify means and being materialistic we relish most in material prosperity rather than the synthesis of material, moral and spiritual endeavours.

Lord has given us physical body and it needs food, clothing and shelter. He has bestowed us brain which demands sense, wit, aptitude, perception, wisdom and genius. He has given us heart which requires feelings, emotions, love and affection. He has provided conscience which is guided by right and wrong, good and bad, sin and piety and moral values. He has gifted us the soul which thrives upon piety, righteousness, prayer, worship and faith. Think for a moment do we need merely the bread to satisfy our physical body or we also need aesthetic basket, emotional quotients, cultural and moral doses and spiritual connotations to satisfy our social, cultural, moral and spiritual needs? Can we survive as a viable and progressive nation without the support of our valued ideals when the facts testify that all debacles in history have been due to moral failures? Can we buy happiness from money when sages say that you can buy pleasure but not happiness, cot but not sleep, drug but not health, women but not wife, books but not intelligence and food but not appetite? The answer is no because without these comprehensive and holistic ingredients no country can set an example for other countries and function as a trendsetter as well as a vibrant and worthy nation.

**Indians were Virtuous**

My Colleagues! Indians were renowned for their virtues. They believed that it was not money or possessions that made man admirable but his virtue. They held that he who aspired for the good of others had already secured his own since those who scatter with one hand gather with two.

> *"Virtue is certainly the most noble and secure possession a man can have. Beauty is worn out by time or impaired by sickness—riches lead youth rather to destruction than welfare, and without prudence are soon lavished away; while virtue alone, the only good that is ever durable, always remain with the person that has once entertained her. She is preferable both to wealth and a noble extraction."*
>
> —*Savage*

They practiced in giving rather than taking and they felt much for others and little for themselves and used their wealth, thoughts and deeds for the advancement of the good of others. They always forgot what they gave and never forgot what they received.

They held that;

*"To the generous mind the heaviest debt is the debt of gratitude, when it is not in our power to repay it."*

*—Franklin*

They firmly believed that;

*"He who receives a benefit should never forget it; he who bestows should never remember it."*

*—Charron*

Our elders never forgot their benefactors but it is a tragedy that our modern generation has become mostly ungrateful. What to talk of repaying debts or appreciating their kind acts, they criticise them and talk ill of them and never greet them and turn aside if they happen to confront them. As a consequence of which many people have abandoned helping others and doing good deeds.

The story goes like this;

*"A saint was delivering the sermon and a stranger entered. The disciple told the saint that such and such person had come who often talked ill of him. The saint ignored it. He again repeated the same, the saint again did not reply. When he told him the third time, the saint angrily retorted that the person in question could not abuse him because the saint had never obliged him."*

Another story states that;

*"A king went in the jungle along with his courtiers on hunting. Unfortunately, he lost the way and fell in the blind well. Hearing his cries the peasant who was returning home went near the well and rescued the king. The king thanked the peasant, offered him his ring and told him to come to him when in trouble along with the ring as he was his king. The peasant never felt the necessity to go to the king but when he wanted to marry*

*his daughter his wife persuaded him to go to the king along with the ring with a view to seek his help. When the farmer entered the Darbar of the king and showed the ring to the king, the king stood up and showered immense respect and wealth upon him. However, the moment the peasant came out of the fort, he was killed. The one who was asked to kill the peasant was extremely puzzled. He asked the king with folded hands whether he did the right thing since he had killed the saviour of the king. The king replied that he did the most right thing because when the peasant came before the king, the king felt low before the peasant and found it difficult to face him due to the obligation that he had made. He ordered his death because he never wanted to face the similar situation again."*

It is said that in good olden days it was written on the doors of the Egyptians that beware of those whom you have obliged. It has been generally observed that many retired people complain that their junior colleagues whom they had obliged by going out of the ways do not recognise them and never come to them even on important occasions. Many former dignitaries of the highest ranks are found roaming in Delhi and State capitals and people seldom greet them with love and admiration. Many of these eminent persons cannot dare to go to their respective departments and offices perhaps because of the fear that many whom they had obliged might be standing with sword in their hands. It was perhaps because of this reason that our elders always told us not to expect any reward from those whom we have obliged and asked us to continue obliging people forgetting the obligations forever and throw the obligation in the wells.

My Dearest Companions! Our present situation is that we very often complain that we are alone in the crowd of people. Our neighbours have deserted us, our colleagues are after us, our relatives have become aliens and our servants have become ungrateful. We have forgotten that this was not our position in good olden days. We were an entirely different people because of our multi-dimensional development, holistic transformation, exceptional behaviour patterns and wonderful images. Being peace-loving, we seldom quarreled on road sides in loud and abusive tones but addressed even our adversaries with respects. We made it a point to disengage the two warring groups wherever we confronted them and made peace between them. What to talk of human beings we disengaged even fighting animals on the road sides due to our love and compassion for living beings. We never allowed our differences to come in open and never permitted the matters of our families to go outside our doors. We kept our public and private lives separate and never encouraged Sohan and Mohan to peep into them. Whomever, we met we greeted them with good greetings and whomever we addressed we addressed by using Shri, Mr, Sahib, Ji and never addressed people as they are being addressed today despite being most respected and dignified. We never threw dirty looks with bad intentions towards the nearby passing females but kept our eyes low.

We were recognised by the hallow of good conducts on our faces, spirit of piety in our consciences, intellect in our minds, courage in our hearts and truth on our tongues. It were we who never bowed before falsehood; it were we who never compromised with evil forces; it were we who raised the flag of truth, justice and piety in the world and it were we who showed the path of peace, progress and harmonious living to humanity. We were known for our free inquiry, large-hearted tolerance and non-violence. We invented *zero*, we discovered the secrets of infinity and we dwelt upon indeterminateness. When we mediated, we were so lost in our meditation that even the birds laid nests in our hair. Our prayers could cause rains, our blessings could produce wonders and our devoted ladies could revive the dead. Whatever, our gifted saints uttered was accomplished and our worship, adoration and prayers provided contentment, consolation and salvation. When we came to charity, we sacrificed whatever we had with us. We avoided alcohol, never touched the prohibited diets, abhorred gambling, games of chance and bad company. We never killed even the insects unnecessarily and practiced what we preached.

We had greatest respect for human life. What to talk of throwing human beings out of the running trains or killing people in road rages on slightest provocation or kidnapping and murdering people for ransom or revenge, we even hesitated to cause any harm to the trees. For us abusing, taunting or showing any disrespect to any human being was a greatest sin. We believed in the philosophy of *Karma* and abhorred committing of suicide or having any jealousy with anybody due to his riches, power or influence. We never mutilated, disfigured or showed any disrespect even to enemy soldiers who were killed during combat operations and never raised swords during war against women, children, old, sick, religious heads and those who were unarmed. We never destroyed the enemy property and their crops, never violated the chastity of their women folk and never humiliated their prisoners of wars after conquering them but treated them nicely. We showed equal respects for all religions, cultures and ways of living and never discriminated people on the basis of their social, cultural and religious differences. We hated flattery, back-biting, skimming and black mailing and never stabbed people at their backs. We never left the injured on the road side unattended due the fear of litigation but helped the patients risking our lives. We could never think even in dream to violate the personal secrecies of young couple by hiding cameras in hotel rooms or ditching people by making false promises or throwing the innocent girls in brothels by promising to marry them.

We were optimists, proactive and hard working. We were never defeated by failures since we always thought that there must be a better way of doing things. We seldom considered problems as obstacles but treated them as solutions in disguised. We were aware that despite continuous failures since the age of 21, Abraham Lincoln succeeded in becoming the President of the United States of America at the age of 52. We had read that Thomas Edison failed several hundred times but ultimately lighted his bulb. Henry Ford II was not always lucky, he had been miserably broken in his youth days. Beethoven had been shown the doors before he became the world fame musician. It took nearly forty years to Noah

Webster to compile Webster's dictionary and Milton rose several thousand mornings at four a.m. to write his Paradise Lost. Andrew Carnegie was just an ordinary man but due to his focussed attention he became one of the largest steel manufacturers of the United States of America. The world history shows that many shepherds and peasants were crowned as the Emperors and the conquerors of world fame merely by their capacities to re bounce after continuous failures. The Guinnes Book of world records testify that miracles were committed by the handicapped in the fields of sports and the day to day matters. The contemporary examples from modern India also reveal that many eminent personalities like Lal Bhadur Shastri, Dr Abdul Kalam, Dehrubhai Ambani and others became great despite their meager backgrounds merely due to their dedication and consistent hard works. We not only knew how to ride but also knew how to fall. If we did not find the way we made one for us. We always believed that there was plenty of room at the top but there was hardly any room to sit therein. We knew that even if we were on the right track we could be run over if we sat there. We always rose against the winds and if we had eight hours to cut the trees we took two hours in sharpening our axes. We took pleasure in doing what the people said we can't do. Others worked from eight to five and we worked from five to eight. We were really gentlemen. We disagreed without being disagreeable. Not only our elites were conscientious but the baser elements of our society too possessed admirable conscience. The following story could reveal that our most conscienceless people too had some conscience.

> *"There is a story about a horse of a beggar which was most elegant and it had hypnotised the Sardar of the dacoits and he wanted to buy it at any cost but the beggar was not willing to sell the horse at any price since he loved it more than his life. The beggar had no family, no relatives and no charm in his life except that he used to ride every evening on the horse and take the round of the jungle. One day while the beggar was returning from the jungle he heard the cries of "save", "save" from nearby*

*area. When the beggar reached the spot, he found that a handicapped wanted to be taken out of the jungle to save his life. The beggar readily agreed and put him on the saddle of the horse. The moment the handicapped rode on the horse back he took the reins in his hands and ran away saying that he was the Sardar and had succeeded in getting the horse of his choice. He told the beggar that he wanted to buy the horse but could not get it. He then tried to steal it but there also he failed. He, therefore, had no alternative but to get the horse in the garb of an handicapped. Thereupon the beggar told him that he could say to the people that he bought the horse at an exorbitant price or stole it cunningly or got it by force but should never say that he got it in the guise of an handicapped for in future not one would trust the handicapped. The beggar returned to his abode disgusted and disheartened but to his great surprise when he got up early morning he found the horse tied to the nearby tree with the words 'Sorry Baba'."*

**Our Measuring Rod in the Past**

We find that our measuring rods too have changed. In the past we paid respect to our elderly people and the elders were so dearest to us that we could do anything for them. We showered our respect for every old man irrespective of the fact whether he was high caste or *Dalit,* rich or poor or otherwise. We addressed them with greatest respects and regards and never pointed their mistakes and never laughed at their follies and obeyed even if they were sometimes not right. We called them with great admiration and we did not dare to show any disrespect towards them when we felt annoyed or disgusted by their unreasonable behaviour. We helped them when we found them on road side crossing the busy traffic. We came to their rescue when they sought our help in finding some place, person or direction. We fed them when they were hungry, provided them decent dressing material and looked after their interests with intense love, caution and care. To our own elders, we did not utter even *"uf"* when we felt some inconveniences. We made it sure to provide them all comforts and luxuries that we could afford, heeded to their advices, consulted them on important matters, offered worthy hospitality to their friends when they visited our homes. When our aged ones died, we gave them decent farewell worthy of their status. After their demises we spared charity, fed the hungry, clothed the pauper so that their souls could rest in peace and tranquility and remembered them with exaltation and admiration till we breathed our last breaths.

My Fellow brothers! During our days we had the fortune of having seen saints who abhorred worldly charms and who were mostly involved in the love of their creator. Generally, they lived away from cities in jungles or far-flung areas and avoided the companies of city dwellers. They never expected any material help from the general public and if anything was presented to them it was distributed among the poor. Nobody could expect any untoward thing from their sides. We feared to face them due to their grace and glory. We showered our respects in abundance upon such saints and men of piety because we considered them God's men being in the service of the Lord. We revered them, adored them and respected them not for worldly charms but for getting consolation and obtaining their blessings. We always demanded guidance from our saints for living a purposeful life and getting peace of mind. We visited them very often when they were alive and did not forget to visit their tombs and places of final abodes even after their deaths. We also sought worldly helps from them when any eventualities occurred in our homes. It is most unfortunate that those saints who helped us to make our worldly life safe, secure and beneficial are conspicuous by absence. Indian society has been always considerate towards its *gurus* and religious heads since unknown times, we respected our *pujaris* and clergies of religious places, our *dharma gurus, Acharyas,* Preachers and others.

My dear and near! We also judged the status and dignity of the individuals from their intelligence, brilliance and wisdom. The geniuses from every field were accorded greatest respect in the courts of the kings, emperors and the rulers. The wise ones especially our teachers and guides were adored and revered by high ups and the commoners alike and they were mostly the centre of attraction for all beings. *Gurus* and teachers and men of learning from every caste, class and background were showered highest respect in Indian society. We touched the feet of our teachers and the mentors; we learnt from them the niceties of our religion, secrets of philosophy and charms of astrology and efficient skills for livelihood. Our relationship was based purely on love, sincerity and admiration rather than any other consideration. We helped them when they were in dire needs, we showed our respects whenever we happened to meet them and we never remained ungrateful to them in our lives. We read their books and articles with great admiration and heard their lectures with rapt attention. We invited them on important occasions and honoured them by giving them respectable seats and introducing them to other important dignitaries.

We had a special place for men of decent background. The respectable people from higher and dignified families who had done something good for society were given honour, ovation and respect. They were received with greatest esteem by government officials and civil society and they were consulted on important matters. During their lifetimes they were considered as the symbols of the society and after their demises roads, localities and parks were named after them. At many important places such as Railway Stations, Crossings and Parks their statues were planted along with brief inscriptions written on the tablets. For many years, their children, grand children and great grand children were addressed by associating them with their names such as the son of Lala Shive Prashad, the grandson of Deputy Amar Singh, the great grandson of Sardar Ummed Singh, the nephew of freedom fighter Krishna Kumar Yadave and the daughter of architect Hidayat Husain.

The retired persons from every department were looked with great admiration and respect. The society recognised their past services and gave them a place of honour. They were very often consulted by their juniors on important occasions. When they visited their old departments they were paid respect and their problems were solved on priority basis. If they were in trouble and approached their colleagues for help and assistance, they were not disheartened. The Army, Police and Security Forces were renowned for giving special respect to their retired personnel. Likewise, the Education Department, Income Tax, Sales Tax and other government Departments too were not lacking in their duties towards their old colleagues. The former Presidents, Prime Ministers, Chief Justices of India, Chief Ministers, Ministers, High Court and District Judges, MPs, MLAs, IAS, IPS and other Central and Provincial level officials too were received with grace and dignity. In the same way, the specialists, competent people and experts in every business, profession, vocation and trade were respected and addressed with great esteem. Many wrestlers, players, musicians, tailors, carpenters, masons, restaurant owners and others were given due regards in the society due to their expertise. The localities and products were recognised by their names such as so and so lives near the house of Ram Singh Phelwan, such and such material is available near the shop of Vaid Anand Ram and the *kebabs* of Kallu, *Lassi* of Hira Lal and *chat* of Gopi Chand are famous and delicious. The younger people considered it a pride to be associated with the names of their elders such as the son of tailor master Akbar Ali, the grandson of Ganesh Prashad *mithaiwale* and the neighbour of mason Hari Ram.

Likewise, there was immense respect for women in the society. Women were addressed with great respect and admiration such as *Amma,* Aunty and Sister. Every women irrespective of the fact whether she belonged to higher caste or lower caste or she was the mother, sister, wife or daughter of any rich or poor person, she was adored with great respect. People used to give seats to women in trains, buses and helped them whenever they were in trouble. They were given priority wherever queues were formed and they got special treatment in getting tickets, ration, water and everything of their use. Nobody could dare to touch any lone woman on the road or in any public place. Women were safe and secure from eve-teasers and molesters and they could freely move laden with their ornaments in odd hours. The miscreants and the vagabonds were given such a lesson by the on—lookers that others could never dare to do heinous acts in future. There were many cases when several youths sacrificed their lives in saving the women from the clutches of the criminals even though they were neither related to them nor knew anything about them.

We were also hospitable and our hospitality was worth seeing. We welcomed our relatives, friends and acquaintances who visited us as our guests and behaved with them cordially and kept them in our houses for months without giving them the impression that they were burden to us. We served them the best and cared for them more than our own kith and kin despite our meager resources. Likewise, when any stranger came to our house for some purpose we welcomed him with open heart and obliged him by doing his work. We never allowed the beggars, way farers and the needy to go empty handed from our houses. Our houses were seldom left without guests and we considered ourselves unlucky the day any guest did not visit our houses. Similarly, we helped our friends, neighbours and well-wishers when they were in dire needs. We cooperated with them at the time of the marriages of their wards, helped them while they were constructing their houses and came to their rescue when they were trapped in litigations, law and order problems, sickness, debts and other eventualities.

The basic purpose to write these matters was to show to our younger generation that Indian society of yester years was not a celebrities-oriented society but an all-pervading and all-embracing one. Every individual young and old, rich and poor, man and woman, learned and commoner, labourer and professional and government active servant and the retired one all had some place in the society. No one felt outcast or redundant. People were personally known to one another, they were dependent upon their counterparts and they felt that they were an integral part of the society. It was because of the close-knit relationship between various segments of the society that suicide cases were few, crime rates were the lowest and psychiatric and mental patients were practically absent. If we now look at our present society, we find that in this glamorous society only those are significant who can find any place in the news channels or on television screens or who are rich and famous. The rests are merely the residuals. Most of the people are aliens and strangers to each other. Despite living in the same complex they are not known to one another. Such a society is not conducive to healthy and balanced development of the country.

What has happened to us that despite being materially rich and intellectually sound we appear socially shaky and culturally hollow? We have an army of intellectuals, geniuses and experts in the field of science, technology, management, medicine, health care, infrastructure, education, industry, trade, commerce, legal profession, sports, cinema, music and architecture yet by any standard India is not nearer to the top. We have wonderful educationists and academicians whose role in transforming the educational systems of African, Middle East, Central Asian and Far East countries; is tremendous. They have established knowledge parks, colleges and universities as well as many hubs of educational institutions in every corner of the country. Innumerable people are getting higher degrees and a multitude is benefitting from their services but we find that hardly a few institutes of ours are of world standard. We have management and computer centers that are producing every year many management graduates and computer experts. They are not only absorbed in our big business concerns but also get appointed in running several multi-national companies. However, our tragedy is that we have not been able to produce Indian multi-national companies in large number that could impact the world. Our legal experts and economists are working in international institutions as well as they are guiding several world class concerns in their ventures as experts, advisors and consultants but the impact of their geniuses is not visible at the level of the country. We have excellent physicians and surgeons whose fame has reached far and wide. People come from neighbouring countries for treatment and consultations. The treatment provided by them is not only affective but also cheap. Our few hospitals and diagnostic centres are of world fame and Indian origin medical practitioners can be seen in every part of the world but despite this India is lagging behind in the field of health care. We have also marvelous scientists, researchers and consultants who are manning several scientific academies and laboratories and publishing research papers in referred journals of world fame. Likewise, our engineers are not behind anyone in the globe. They have laid a chain of high ways, fly ways, malls, bridges, splendid buildings and produced "A" class products but still our country has not left any imprint in the field of science and technology. People have seen our contribution in the field of games and sports especially cricket, hockey, archery, tennis, badminton, chess, but save a few games we have not shown miracles in other fields. In the same way, our actors, actresses, musicians and dancers are glamorous but they too have not earned many Grammy Awards. It appears that there is some lacuna somewhere which is not allowing us to win friends and influence people. We are perhaps developing unidirectional and have neglected the multi-dimensional aspects of our personalities as a consequence of which we have lost our magnificent abilities and capacities.

**Distorted Vision**

It appears that we have perhaps adopted a distorted and narrow vision of life. We probably believe that happiness can be achieved through economic prosperity, political acumen and strategic changes. Many meaningful personalities of the country emphasise that happiness can come if the country accumulates pounds, dollars, euros and other foreign currencies in abundance. Certainly economic prosperity would come in India and poverty would be dented to a large extent but the dollars and pounds would hardly provide lasting peace of mind to our people. They are forgetting the vital fact that when heaps of dollars and pounds could not give peace, contentment and happiness to United States of America, UK and Switzerland, how the few digits of dollars and pounds would bestow happiness upon Indians. These countries are certainly prosperous materially but not necessarily happy. Besides, it is worth noting that in the quest of becoming rich they have not only lost their sweet homes, kith and kin, friends and acquaintances but most of their significant social, cultural and religious institutions. Not only they have failed to make their countries rich and prosperous, there are millions of people in their countries who are languishing in poverty, hunger and diseases. These countries are not only losing the grip on the world politics but are also the victims of economic depression and monetary crisis.

One should know that happiness is essentially a state of mind or a subjective term. It is,

> *"Like the statue of Isis, whose veil no mortal ever raised."*
>
> *—L.E. Landon*

It consists in being satisfied from what we have got as well as what we haven't got. It is not how much we have, but how much we enjoy from what we have.

> *"If one only wished to be happy, this could be easily accomplished; but we wish to be happier than other people, and this is always difficult, for we believe others to be happier than they are."*
>
> *—Montesququieu*

The foolish people generally seek happiness in the distance where the grass looks green but the wise men find it under their feet. Being the state of mind it means different things to different people. To some it is health, to others it may mean wealth, to many the love of the kith and kin and to several the achievements of goals but certainly it cannot be achieved merely by piling the heaps of gold, silver and costly resources. Experience reveals that those who seek happiness in money are really in a miserable state of mind.

*"Money is a bottomless sea, in which, honour, conscience, and truth may be drowned."*

*—Kozlay*

*"Money is a good servant, but a poor master."*

*—D. Bouhours*

*"Money is like manure, of very little use except it to be spread."*

*—Bacon*

*" Money is not required to buy one necessity of the soul."*

*—Thoreau*

*"A wise man should have money in his head, and not in his heart."*

*—Swift*

*"It has been said aptly that "Put not your trust in money, but put your money in trust."*

*—O.W. Holmes*

Money never made a man happy yet, nor will it. There is nothing in its nature to produce happiness. The more a man has, the more he wants. Instead of its filling a vacuum, it makes one. If it satisfies one want, it doubles and trebles that want another way. Actual happiness lies in virtues, in service to mankind, in dedication and in achieving the noble objectives.

*"Happiness is like manna; it is to be gathered in grains, and enjoyed every day. It will not keep; it cannot be accumulated; nor have we got to go out of ourselves or into remote places to gather it, since it has rained down from Heaven, at our very doors. Seek happiness for its own sake, and you will not find it; seek for duty, and happiness will follow as the shadow comes with the sunshine."*

*—Tryon Edwards*

My Learned Ones! It is certain that he who runs after material prosperity to get happiness ends up in frustration because need can be satisfied but the greed always remains unsatisfied.

*"It is said that one day Lord appeared before one of his devoted disciple who had a grievance that despite his sincere devotion the Lord was not happy with him as he was starving and the God had closed his eyes. The Lord showed him His 'Treasure House' which was full of infinite varieties of gems, jewels, pearls, coins, ornaments and valuables and told him that He was giving him the time till sun set to come out of it with as much treasure as possible failing which the door would be closed and he would be thrown out. The moment he saw the Treasure House, he was dumb founded. He started collecting the best but the tragedy with him was that the moment he opted for the best, his eyes felt upon better than the best and he ran after that. In this process he went too far and the sun set and he could not decide and was thrown out of it empty-handed.*

It is said that;

*"When Alexander the Great was on his death bed, he called his courtiers and advised them to keep his hands open and outside the coffin so that the general public might see what he carried with him after his death."*

Similarly, it is stressed that many wise kings and emperors left the messages behind them written in golden letters that they were deceived by the illusory world.

**We have Become Directionless**

Is it not true that many of our people have become directionless? What our elders did in the past purely out of the love for humanity have become a lucrative profession? Is it not a fact that the schools, colleges, universities and scientific and technical institutions which were meant to educate people and remove ignorance from their hearts have become profitable propositions? Is it not a reality that the hospitals, nursing homes, diagnostic points and super-specialty centres which were designed to remove sickness from the society have been generating exorbitant profits? Is it not an actuality that hotels, shelter homes, lunatic asylums, orphanages, destitute homes and dormitories which were meant for the downtrodden, less-privileged and have-nots have entered in the category of money earners? Is it not apparent that the temples, churches, synagogues, mosques monasteries and Gurdwaras, where people went for seeking Lord's blessing are not immune from the impact of money? Do we not see that advising, counselling, consultation, sermons and lectures which were for the guidance and benefit of the ignorant, illiterate, unaware and uninformed have been listed under the category of useful trades? Is it not a reality that if we take any help from our fellow friends be it the purchase or sale of property, buying any product, purchase of tickets, acquiring any service or doing anything through someone, commission is paid lavishly? Do we not observe that many unscrupulous NGO's who are serving the society in one way or the other are being guided by monetary considerations? Thus, we find that the concept of friends, neighbours, colleagues, helpers, social reformers, elders and advisers has disappeared in the materialist age. We are living in a market where we have to pay for everything. If we want education we have to offer fee, if we want help from the physicians or surgeons we have to deposit consultation fee, if we want water we have to pay a price, if we want shelter we have to remit hotel charges, if we want sermons we have to give donation and if we want to buy or sell anything we have to disburse commission irrespective of the fact whether we are capable or not.

Thanks to the power of money, charms of the governing structure and quest for name and fame that all standards of greatness, wisdom, grace, dignity, respect, piety and magnificence have changed. The material prosperity and the worldly lures have hypnotised people. Sons and daughters have been separated from their old and infirm parents in search of money and comforts, brother is after brother, sisters are bitter, relatives are jealous, neighbours are averse and friends and acquaintances have become aliens. The significance of age, the respect for intellectuals, the dignity of respectable people, the regard for women, the affinity for values, the love for friends and colleagues, the fascination for moral and cultural notions and the charm for charity, spiritual perceptions and human dignity have fallen flat. Power centres have been created around those who are in the governing structure or who possess abundance of money and wealth or who command muscle and nuisance power. Even the most respected and dignified parts of society and the district officials consider it their pleasure and privilege to have contacts and connections with such people. The governing principle in the present day society is that more the money, more the respect and *vice versa.* In the quest for money innumerable families have been ruined and several influential and meaningful people have gone astray. Many talented girls even from good family background have resorted to unconventional activities merely to earn money. Markets are full of fashion goods, branded items, delicious food joints and glamorous beauty parleys. Late night parties, cheap and murky entertainments, speedy driving and gossiping in the bars have become fashions. Attractive advertising campaigns undertaken by the celebrities with a view to promote the sale of ordinary products at extra-ordinary prices in lieu of their exorbitant service charges have become part and parcel of modern households.

The television serials are full of talent search shows which are diverting the attentions of the youths from studies towards dance, drama and cinema. The multi-national companies have introduced innovative methods in the field of cricket as a consequence of which general public is mesmerised. The money which is given to players in cricket, tennis, and boxing and in quiz shows as well as to the winners of medals in international meets has changed the perceptions of parents towards games, sports and entertainment shows. The astronomical salaries provided by the multi-national companies to Indian kids have made them the centre of attraction irrespective of the fact whether such units are in the interest of the country or not. The mind-set of the whole young and the new generation has changed. Our youths know the names of the important actors, actresses, dancers, directors, players and the celebrities but they are not aware of country's scientists, innovators, intellectuals, leaders, reformers and statesmen. The need of the hour is that our children should be given *sanskars* or family traits about good qualities concerning dress code, dietary habits, manners and etiquettes by parents and the members of the family. Besides the lessons on morality, culture, ethics and good moral conducts in the light of the lives of great men should be provided at the levels of the schools, colleges and universities, so that the portals of learning may become temples of learning rather than the places of entertainment and enjoyment.

**The Fragmentation of Indian Society**

Indian society was an amalgamation of well-established and well-tested social customs, vibrant and vital cultural practices, sound and viable moral norms and pious and spiritual principles based on wisdom, experience and good moral conducts. The society was a dynamic unit which combined all the segments of the society into a composite whole. There were no hostile divisions, no antagonistic water-tight compartments and no clashes of interests. It was like a healthy body where all parts functioned harmoniously enriching each other. The young, old, rich, poor, educated, uneducated, dignified and the commoners lived within the same locality, same area and same neighbourhood. There was lively relationship between various sections of the society. The haves used to care for the have-nots and the have-nots too were always willing to sacrifice everything possible for the benefit of their well wishers. Unfortunately, during the seventies when the doors for employment were opened in Afro-Asian countries, the sudden emergence of the neo-rich changed the whole colour and complex of Indian society. The use of high mass consumption as well as the demonstration effect and the rat race between people accompanied by the impact of cultural invasion from the Western civilisation exercised such a damaging effect upon the minds of our people that most of the good qualities which they possessed withered away one by one like the packs of cards. Indian society which was based on solid foundations became ritualistic and showy. People performed their social, cultural and religious ceremonies as usual, communicated with their colleagues normally and behaved in their habitat customarily but the usual warmth which was in their dealings vanished away and it was replaced by pomp and show and formalities. Thus, whatever sterling qualities we had we lost them badly and the bond between various parts of the country loosened and the Indian society got fragmented into water-tight compartments according to the socio-economic conditions of the people. Broadly speaking, there emerged three broad divisions—namely, the poor and the downtrodden, the rich and famous and the mediocre and the middle class. Besides, there is a sea change in their behaviour pattern compared to the past.

**The Poor and the Downtrodden**

Many of the extreme poor who were generally God-fearing, simple minded, honest and straight forward have become altogether a different product. Several of them have television sets, fans and coolers and mobile phones. Many wear second-hand jeans, bright clothes and fashionable shoes. They are tolerant in their attitudes and follow liberal ways of living. Divorces, family disputes and quarrels are very common in this segment of the society. Having seen the glamorous food joints, branded clothes, glittering sign boards, mighty malls, splendid cars, majestic mansions and glaring prosperity around them they too have become money-minded. They too want comforts and luxuries of life but fail due to the constraints of resources. Due to extreme frustration for not getting suitable jobs and employment the frustrated ones usually indulge in drugs such as hashish, opium and drink cheap alcohol in plenty. To become quick rich, a few spend their hard earned money on lotteries and batting and incur huge losses in the process. They toil as workers, landless labourers and rickshaw pullers. They spend beyond their means at the time of marriages, sickness and festivals and indulge in borrowing money from crooked money lenders at exorbitant rates. Many of them return home drunk and beat wives and children. The addicts starve their children and compel their wives and children to work as domestic servants. They attend religious gatherings; participate in religious processions and festivities but for the sake of psychic satisfaction because they are completely ignorant about the true spirit of religion. A tiny section among them is so ruthless that one cannot depend upon their promises, commitments and utterances. Those poor people who have migrated from villages to the cities mostly live in slums, out-houses and the *ghettos.* The private lives of those who live in congested areas and depleted surroundings is not up to the mark and they can be easily marked by their shabby dresses, depressed faces and frustration engraved on their foreheads. Most of them suffer from dreaded diseases, ignorance and superstition. A major part of their income is spent in buying medicines and paying consultation fees to the quacks. Constrained by financial circumstances a few of the dishonest poor people do not hesitate in taking part in thefts, cheating, smuggling and unsocial activities. The old, sick, handicapped and helpless people from among the poor suffer most and some of them resort to begging. Most of the children of these unfortunate people work in the factories and private homes as domestic servants and never see the face of schools and colleges. They pass their leisure time in cinema halls, gossiping, cheap entertainment and idle talks.

**The Rich and Famous**

As against this, the rich, famous and haves are on the other extreme. They are from among the privileged political families, the glamorous business houses, the successful exporters, importers, builders and highly paid bureaucrats, technocrats, legal luminaries, professionals, artists, actors and producers and literary figures. Several of them have a liking for western ways, European styles and American patterns. They relish imported brands of clothes and consumer durables and have a fancy for fashionable goods.

Foreign branded liquor is part and parcel of many of these people. Their children, wives and friends lead a luxurious life full of gay and gaiety. Costly and branded foreign liquor is generally served in every party, on every occasion and at the time of every important ceremony of these dignitaries since it is considered as the sign of forwardness, enlightenment and advancement. Those who abhor it are considered as backward, orthodox and conservatives. Many important works are being taken by serving foreign liquor and other means of entertainments. Likewise, many of them have no hesitation in consuming any type of food items such as vegetarian, non-vegetarian, Chinese, Korean, Persian, Continental, Occidental and Oriental without any reservation. They care least which diet has been prohibited by their holy books and their religious dictates.

They feel proud and honoured in communicating in English since English is widely used in their houses and elsewhere as medium of communication. Almost all the behaviour patterns of a significant number of these elites are Western in nature. They move within their equals such as big businessmen, high government officials, renowned physicians and surgeons, rich engineers and important professors and famous lawyers. They own mighty and magnificent mansions, latest models of costly cars, an army of servants and rich bank balances. They represent the country in foreign countries in various capacities. They are mostly found at food joints, fashion houses, health-care centres and kitty parties. They enjoy their leisure time in picnic parties, music, entertainment and merry-making. Some of them use ultra modern clothes and their dress codes reflect the Western tone and style. From their dresses, addresses, gestures, postures, body languages they resemble with Americans and Europeans as gold resembles with gold. The foreign influence and the Western culture impact are amply reflected in their reading habits, living styles and behaviour patterns. Many of them believe in material prosperity and use their powers and resources to acquire it. Generally, the most advanced among them are highly liberal in their views. They do not mind free-mixing, alien ways of living and foreign customs. Divorces, separations, living in relationships are very common among many of them. Some of them are certainly least religious though by name sake they call themselves as Hindus, Muslims, Christians, Parsis or Sikhs.

**The Mediocre and the Middle Class**

In contrast to it, most of the commoners fall within the above two extremes. They are mostly artisans, farmers, petty shop-keepers, teachers, lower government officials, professionals, mechanics and technicians and ordinary people. They are simple ones and believe in family values, traditions, ethos, customs and rituals. They go to temples, mosques, churches, gurdwaras, offer prayers and pay their tributes. They attend the sermons of the saints, participate in religious processions, travel to religious places, perform Hajj and havans and celebrate religious festivals with pleasure and happiness. They are mostly religious and conservative. They usually belong to the middle class and are considered as the backbone of the nation. In real sense, they are the custodians of the heritage, value system and moral and religious norms of the country. One can rely upon their promises, commitments and assurances for by and large they are reliable. Some of them are certainly perverts. These misguided people take bribes, cuts, commissions, liquor, drugs, and hashish and participate in gambling and betting. They too cross the limits of their religious dictates in matters of dress, eating habits and behaviour pattern. Fortunately, their number is not overwhelming.

It is the irony of fate that a large chunk of this segment of the society which gives shape, colour and form to the tone and tanner of the society is after money. Due to inflation, rising cost of living, high cost of accommodation and abnormal school fees a minor section of this segment too has started indulging in unfair means to meet domestic needs. The passion for family values, attraction towards customs and conventions, regard for moral dictates and ethical norms and love for spiritualism is fading fast in this section. Most of the middle class, especially, the educated ones are becoming the victim of fashion, branded clothes, fast food and western ways of living. It is feared by looking at the current trend that in near future India's rich heritage, classical touch and religious and traditional flavour would undergo a sea change.

Indian society is not a homogeneous unit. There are diverse politico-economic groups, social contradictions and cultural dichotomies in the country. Some segments of the country are more active and awakened in contrast to many others which are submissive and sleeping. Besides, the cultures, ways of living and perceptions about life and death of all Indians too are not identical, so also their interests. In such a society one cannot think of similarity of mind-sets and identical patterns of living. The tragedy with the country is that the strong , dynamic and the progressive institutional framework which bound the various individuals, socio-economic groups and politico-cultural sections of the society into a composite whole is in shambles. Consequently, all segments of Indian society have become rootless. In order to come out of the present malice in which the country is trapped every section of Indian society irrespective of its background shall have to work hard to revitalise its institutional framework which the various segments have lost over time.

# 4 We have Shattered Our Institutional Framework

My Countrymen! Our strength in bygone days lied in our vital, agile and classical institutional framework which was firmly rooted on strong foundations erected by our forefathers. Our elders had left for us their admirable ideas and sound institutional structures such as simple living and high-thinking, equitability of genders, decent rearing scheme for children, affectionate security structure for parents, sound joint-family system, viable neighbourhood, vibrant education arrangement and the affective governing mechanism. But with the passage of time, we have uprooted the whole structure one by one, and now we are rootless. We had the fundamental dress code, dietary rules, marriage customs, inheritance and succession laws, etiquettes for good conducts, procedure for prayer and worship and well-marked behaviour patterns for males and females. We also had well-demarcated categories of acts to be done and not to be done and we had ideal perceptions about life, death and after death. Whatever system our elders had developed over centuries was enough to sustain us as civilised, enlightened and dignified human beings but it is most regrettable that we have been laid astray by alien ideas, materialistic notions and strange perceptions.

**Simple Living and High Thinking**

Once upon a time, India was a treasure house of wealth and prosperity. People from far off places like Babylonia, Scandinavia, Africa, China and Indonesia visited this country for carrying out trade, acquiring education and developing political and cultural relations. Our forts were strongly fortified, our roads were well-protected and our trade routes were extraordinary. Foreigners were impressed by our cities, *hats, ghats* and money exchanging points. They were dumbfounded having seen our prosperity and acumen. They praised the simplicity and dexterity of our forefathers, they talked very high of our law and order and they glorified our commitment and the sense of proportion. The supreme simplicity of our culture was visible from the character, manners and style of our elders. They were simple in intentions, pure in actions, frank and straightforward in dealings. They believed that these pomp and show were trivial and the materialistic charms were mere illusions. The purpose of life in their opinion consisted in balanced development of human personality as well as the service to mankind. Our ancestors did not give much importance to the achievements of physical gratifications. They held that each individual needed merely some breads of corn and a simple curry to eat, a few glasses of water to drink, a *dhoti* or pair of shirt and trousers to wear, one pair of shoes to cover the feet and a cot of six by three feet to sleep and four to five square meters of land for burial or cremation which could easily be got by normal efforts. They knew that after death nothing would go with them except their *karmas.* These mighty forts and fortresses, glittering coins of gold and silver, herds of elephants and horses, stores of grains and commodities would be left behind and the army of servants and attendants as well as the kith and kin will accompany them till cremation or burial grounds and shall return soon after consigning them to their fates. The wealth and resources which they collected with hard work and toil would be enjoyed by others as the honey of the bees is usurped by the strangers. They believed that those who lived only for themselves and their children were not better than animals for the birds, cows, crocodiles and ants and insects too live for themselves and bring up their progenies.

Similarly, they also held that those who passed their youth acquiring and enjoying worldly charms were not sensible persons for they ran after mirages and wasted their time in doing nothing. In their opinion, wise were those who devoted their lives in acquiring knowledge and wisdom, in making others happier and prosperous, in serving the society and humanity and in remembering their Creator and the Benefactor. They spread the knowledge of mathematics, astronomy, astrology and *yoga* among different segments of the world and enlightened the humanity by their intellectual, moral and spiritual powers. They bowed with grace and dignity before every one who approached them and provided protection to every shelterless who came to them for help. They treated the whole humanity as an extended family of brothers and sisters and aimed at benefitting mankind by their wealth, wisdom and deeds irrespective of their backgrounds, castes, creeds, colours, religions, sexes and places of birth. Their main objectives always remained non-violence, benefit to mankind, and peaceful co-existence.

The main difference between them and the present generation was that our concept of life is limited to the tips of our noses and they looked beyond that. We believe in avoiding or minimising our pains and maximising our satisfaction and they preferred optimum satisfaction for the whole humanity. Mostly, we are in the quest of material or psychic satisfactions and they were in search of real and lasting one. We take pride in show off and bragging, they kept low profile. Their abodes were very simple, neat and clean. They spent least amount of money on their dwellings, ceremonies and comforts. Our living style is complex, extravagant and showy and we spend lavishly on our houses, functions and entertainments. They respected each person of every segment irrespective of his financial position, family background and educational qualifications but we respect to those who are rich, famous, meaningful and influential. While deciding the marriages of their sons and daughters they looked into the family backgrounds, reputation and status of the families and suitability of the brides and bridegrooms. But, we take into consideration the grace and grandeur of their villas, number and models of their cars, agility and alertness of their watchful attendants, quality and quantum of diamonds studded in the ornaments of their female members and number of their factories, digits of their bank balances and qualifications of their girls and boys. In short, the perceptions of our ancestors were not confined merely to money but extended to time-tested values, customs, and practices and decent norms of the society. Alas! The simple and purposeful life of our ancestors which distinguished them from the rest of the people is no more. It has become the casualty of time.

My brethren! Our elders gave more importance to health, wealth, wisdom and character-building. They used to say that 'if wealth is lost nothing is lost, if health is lost something is lost' and when character is lost everything is lost. Their living was moderate, their life style was balanced and they adopted golden mean while dealing with issues that affected human lives. They gave equal importance on physical fitness, material considerations, moral and cultural values and spiritual connotations. They got up early morning before sunrise and went on foot to take baths in the nearby rivers or ponds or on wells. They greeted whomever they met in the way and asked them about the welfare of their families and near and dear. They generally washed their own clothes on the *ghats* of the rivers and ponds and prayed till sun rise. After that they started their normal works. They considered work as worship and provided highest sanctity to the venue where they worked. They never betrayed their employers and contributed as much as they could. The employers on their part treated them as the members of their families and cared for their needs and never humiliated them or insulted them despite provocations. They shared their pains and pleasures and had cordial relations with them. They encouraged them, promoted them, paid them in time and never annoyed them and never harmed them knowingly. They were generally true to their promises and commitments and seldom ditched or deceived their employees with the intention of causing any harm.

Misunderstandings, if any, were sorted out amicably. After coming from their places of work they met their relations, friends and neighbours in evenings and shared their pleasures and sorrows. They made it a point to attend social and cultural functions and ceremonies of their comrades and invited them for dinners and parties. They also made it sure to congratulate their friends and well-wishers on the occasions of birth days, child birth, weddings, house warming ceremonies and other important functions. They shared the festivals of different communities as if it were their own. They believed in friendship and their friendship that developed at the places of work, market places and during travels generally lasted till death.

People of those days were very choosy in making friends and made friends not by giving gifts but incurring sacrifices. They knew that friendship with the evil was like the shadows of morning, decreasing every hour but friendship with the good was like evening shadows increasing till life. People believed in their friends more than their kith and kin. They were quick in reaching in adversity than prosperity. Their friends absorbed much of the worries and tensions of their colleagues and hence there were no diseases like diabetes, blood pressure, heart ailments and cancer.

Basically, they were simple-minded people and remained contented in what they had and seldom pined for what was not. They considered yesterday as a cancelled cheque as you could not cash it, tomorrow as a promissory note which was not worth relying but they believed only in today since it was ready cash that was to be spent wisely. They lived care-free life and slept without bothering about future eventualities. They gave more importance on physical fitness and participated in *yoga,* games and sports and took simple meals that could be digested easily and had no adverse affect upon their bodies.

If we now look towards our lives we find that we are the victims of hurry, worry and curry. When we gaze at people around us, we find pedestrians moving fast pushing one another, cyclists taking twists and turns, motor cyclist hitting this or that and car owners roaring their horns as if they are in haste. When the fact is that some are worried due to losing the jobs, a few are perturbed because they have been shunted out from the houses by their landlords, many are in shock as the doctors have diagnosed dreaded diseases, numberless are rushing fast as they have to reach their offices in time, multitude has come out to meet family needs, and there is no shortage of people who are moving aimlessly. Likewise, we take oily and juicy diets full of proteins and fats and do very little to digest them. We take tea or coffee or sweets at the instance of our friends without bothering that our stomachs are full. We consume junk foods and do not think for a moment that they could create acidity and ulcers in our bodies. We have a special liking for particular *dhabas,* restaurants, hotels and food joints but we forget that the food items that are cooked at such places are not hygienic. They are certainly tasty but not rich in nutrition. We silently carry dreaded diseases like gastro-entities, cholera and typhoid with us after taking adulterated Continental, Indian, Chinese and other types of foods. Our sluggish culture has certainly given us comforts and luxuries of life but side by side it has made us lazy, lethargic and inactive. What we eat is not digested properly and hence diseases are multiplying in the society. It is surprising that forty to fifty years ago, there were a few hospitals and chemists' shops and only the elderly and weak people were found loitering around hospitals. Now, we find hundreds of chemist shops everywhere, dozens of nursing homes at every step, many diagnostic centers in each colony and several private hospitals in every market where mostly young people are found consulting their physicians and surgeons.

Besides, the television sets, mobile phones, internet connections, i-pads and other electronic objects have made our life hell. The markets are full of such items and every day new products are emerging in the markets with slightest modifications making the old products old-fashioned. Every person, whether he a rickshaw-puller or a student or a worker or a boy or a girl or an ordinary man or an important dignitary is found talking with mobile phone stuck to his ear. The young boys and girls are found talking to their friends during late nights. Similarly, the elderly people are found entangled with their internets and the children with i-pads, as if they are extremely busy in doing some very important work.

It's a matter of surprise that their talks mostly pertain either to chatting or gossiping or fixing some dates or wasting time in doing nothing. It would not be out of place to mention here that the televisions have changed the whole life structure of the Indian society. They have made them easy going, lethargic and obese. People do not want to participate in physical exercises, play games and meet their friends, relations and acquaintances during their spare times as they used to do in the past because they do not want to miss their serials and other programmes. The various channels suiting to the tastes of different segments of people have not only changed the mind sets of our children, youths, elderly people as well as ladies and gentlemen but have also made them addicts to the television shows. The constant and hateful advertising campaigns showing celebrities and charming girls in odd modes not only compel them to buy ordinary products at exhorbitant prices but also develop in them the fancy for actors, actresses, cricketers, dancers and singers. The entertaining programmes and the serials affecting the ideologies of our youths have caused immense harm to our cultural milieus. Mostly, the younger people relish the Western music and dances and they have developed a keen liking for acting, dancing, drama, singing and playing games and sports in preference to obtaining knowledge, sharpening the intellect, acquiring skill and wisdom which do not auger well for the country like India. In essence, it is the electronic revolution which has struck the last nail in the social and cultural coffin of Indian society.

**Equitability of Genders**

It's true that our elders also had a unique view about the rights and duties of the males and females. They held that males and females were entitled to equitable rights that is, they deserve rights which were due to them. Most of them believed that males and females were not perfectly identical in all respects. They were different segments called fair sex and strong sex. It was foolish to compare them for they had been created for different purposes. The nature had provided them with different physical, mental and emotional qualities. Male was superior in some fields and the female was better in other areas. Father is respected being the bread earner and the guardian of the family and mother is crowned as the nurturer of the children and the manager of the family. The respect which the mother commands is unparallel.

It is said that if there is heaven on earth, it is under the feet of the mother. The sages say,

> "a father may turn his back on his child, brothers and sisters may become fierce enemies, husbands may desert their wives and wives their husbands but a mother's love lasts till the end."

In good days, in bad times and in the face of the world's condemnation, a mother still loves, and still hopes that her child may turn from his evil ways, and repent. She remembers the smiles, the laughs and the joyful shouts and the promises of her infant and she can never think him unworthy. In our day to day dealings also we are very considerate between males and females. The respect and regards that we give to mothers, sisters, daughters and wives are in no way less than the affection and love that we bestow upon fathers, brothers, sons and husbands. In Indian society there exist personal relationship between males and females. We address our elderly ladies as mothers and aunts, younger ones as sisters and daughters and elderly males as fathers and uncles and the younger ones as brothers and sons. We cannot conceive a female as an object of entertainment because she belongs to us and she is part and parcel of our body, mind and soul. In our family structure males are the masters in the sense that they work day and night to earn livelihood, protect the family, raise its standard and face all types of eventualities for the betterment and welfare of the family.

As against this, the females are home-centric. They are the queens of the families and the supervisors of the households, planners of the domestic budgets, keepers of the accounts of home expenditures and shapers of the destinies of the children though they also work on the fields along with their kith and kin, toil in the factories and business houses during emergencies and struggle as labourers to meet the two ends. Thus, the Indian society has beautifully blended the rights and duties of males and females in a harmonious manner without declaring any one of them superior or inferior but the two wheels of the cart to carry on the affairs of the family smoothly and effectively.

It is alleged by conventional segment in the country that behind the gender equality there was a deep-rooted conspiracy of the vested interests. They held that so long as our ladies remained confined within their cultural surroundings, they enjoyed their domestic life very gracefully and elegantly enjoying all the privileges of life. They adored costly ornaments, beautified them using several devices and made them as charming as possible but all their efforts were generally home, women and relative centric. They did not have any lust for modern types of clothes, fashionable items and luxurious goods but through media, celebrities, television serials, cinemas and games and sports as well as mobiles, internets and other electronic medium the vested business segments created a plethora of institutions like boutique centers, massage units, health-care clinics, beauty parlours, designing complexes and beach shows which proved not only boon to their business enterprises but also brought about tremendous changes in the mind-set of the Indian women.

After the recent heinous rape of *Nirbhaya* in the national Capital the whole country has reached the boiling point which shows that our countrymen highly respect their womenfolk and they cannot tolerate any insult, injury, disrespect or harm to their mothers, sisters, wives and daughters. They want to make them safe from all kinds of hazards and they have zero tolerance for crime against women. It is irony of fate that different people having different backgrounds are giving different explanations about the crimes against women which have raised several controversies. A large section of Indian society believes that we cannot keep our females within the four walls of our homes for ever. We have to provide them education, job opportunities and means to enjoy material benefits but within our social, moral, cultural and spiritual constraints. In our society, males and females are not mere individuals but they are role models and hence the western types of roles for them are detrimental to the health of the country.

**Equality of Genders did not Give Much to Women Folk**

Many Indian critics say that it is a cruel joke that those societies are blaming Indian society for not providing adequate rights to Indian women who have actually not done justice to their females in the name of gender parity, individual's rights and the equality of sexes. They used to say that since time immemorial the Indian women had commanded unprecedented respect in the society. History is witness to the fact that when they passed nearby every eye bowed down, when they intended to purchase anything people gave them way and when they called someone for help they were gladly obliged. Nobody could dare to gaze at them with dirty looks, no one could think of eve-teasing, none could muster courage to molest them and committing rape upon them was unthinkable. As against this, those who claim to have raised the status of woman in the society have perhaps made their lives hell due to scanty dresses, free mixing, permissive ways and modern life-style. Whenever they go out of their homes they are generally gazed with dirty looks, they have mostly to bear the cat calls of the eve-teasers, face sometimes molestations by urchins in trains and buses and rarely confront horrible rape like situations in lonely areas and many a time they face dangers to their lives. In their opinion the modern society in the name of equitability of sexes has given them nothing but non-conventional ways of living, care-free life style, fashionable items and physical comforts.

According to the National Victim Centre/Crime Victims Research and Treatment Centre, 1992, a woman is raped in the United States of America every 46 seconds. More or less the same is the condition in many foreign countries. Even in India it is alleged that several girls are raped every day. Many enlightened human beings feel that modern society has provided the education facilities to the women at par with men but it has not done justice to them in other fields. They have been engaged generally at lower or lower middle levels. Market has absorbed many of them as sales girls, stenos, private secretaries, receptionists, air hostesses and show pieces. Some vested interests use them as restaurant waitresses, bar and casino girls and dancers and promote the sales of their products by putting their objectionable photographs on calendars. There is no shortage of people who exploit them and their talents for their profit motives and promotional purposes by organising circus shows, beauty contests, music nights, quiz competitions and projecting them in odd positions in objectionable poses on television screens. This type of freedom or equitability of rights in the name of gender equitability and freedom for women is hardly acceptable to many Indian parents. They want to see their daughters on dignified and admirable positions. It is claimed that western culture apparently appears favourable to women but in real practice it is harsh towards them.

This point should not be undermined that women in the world are nearly fifty per cent of the total population of the globe and they are equally educated compared to their counterparts in those countries that claim to have empowered them but we never observe fifty per cent women prime ministers, heads of states, ambassadors, governors, judges, military commanders, consultants, lawyers, physicians, surgeons, engineers and others. Even in the so-called developed countries they are mostly house wives and those that are in jobs are found in health segment, education section, government and private sectors and that too not as officers and Chief Executives but generally as subordinate and lower staff.

Conservative Indian parents put checks upon objectionable and unwanted behaviour patterns of their males and females and believe that it is foolish to assume that the freedom of a man or a woman is violated if he or she is asked to protect his or her modesty and provocative parts or he or she is checked from vulgar shows or stopped from dancing indecently before audiences. Similarly, in their opinion their rights are not violated if they are checked from participating in activities contrary to Indian culture, customs and ethos. They stress that Human rights are certainly violated when the dignity of man and woman is violated, time-tested value system is shattered and the civilised norms of the society are abrogated, established dress code, food habits, etiquettes and conventions of the society are abandoned, well-tested cultural practices are discarded, time honoured moral principles are thrown aside and moral and ethical values are shattered. They claim that men and women are supposed to live decently within social, cultural and ethical constraints and not expected to behave indiscreetly. They further stress that the state as well as the society can certainly put checks upon the freedom of the individuals when it clashes with the age-old practices of the society and the time-tested conventions of the nation.

William P. Faunce says,

> *"We have in America the largest public school system on earth, the most expensive college buildings, the most extensive curriculum, but nowhere else is education so blind to its objectives, so indifferent to any specific outcome as in America. Our trouble has been its negative character. It has aimed at the repression of faults rather than the creation of virtues."*

It is confessed by many Americans and Europeans that most of the college and university going boys and girls are not immune from pre-marital intercourse. Only recently the girls in many American schools were asked to take pills during school hours to avoid pregnancy. It is because of meeting different partners during the student days that most of the marriages in such countries do not last beyond few years and divorces and separations take place soon thereafter. Besides, maintenance laws in these countries work as the deterrents for marriages and rearing of children.

Consequently, there is a scarcity of infants and children in such countries. These countries are left with old people and are facing the shortage of labour which is being met by inviting immigrants from neighbouring countries at terrible economic and social costs. It is the considered opinion of many experts on human relations that mingling of males and females continuously for a longer period of time without any inhibition is bound to result in sexual misadventures. Wherever the boys and girls were given freedom be it United States of America, Europe, Asia, Africa, Australia, Latin America or any part of the world nobody could check them from entering into sexual relationships. Instead of stopping or checking them or declaring such acts as sin or taboos, the society in such areas was compelled to provide them social, cultural and moral sanctions. Many sane voices warn Indian parents by saying that those whose children are mixing freely with their counterparts in colleges, universities, restaurants, bear parties, dancing halls, and outings too should bear in mind that they too would not be able to check them except providing them the needed sanctions.

Many meaningful people tell us that we should wake up and remind our youths about our customs, values, moral practices and national conventions. Provide them higher education, let them enjoy the benefits of excellent job opportunities, allow them to play games, sports and conduct other activities preferably within healthy environment not prejudicial to the interest of the society. They further stress that we should make it sure that wherever there is co-education, sanctity of the boys and girls is ensured and they are not allowed to indulge in activities repugnant to their consciences. Likewise, we should also ensure that the work places where our young boys and girls work are completely safe for our children and they are not exploited by the vested interests by offering them different temptations.

## The Clash of Gender Theory

There are intellectuals, who fear that the mankind would face a clash of genders by the mid of 21st century. As time is passing by human right activists are fighting for gender equality and rights of women in every sphere. Women are getting modern education along with men, they are being given representation in governing structure, they have got property rights and they are free to choose any profession, vocation and trade and it is also left to them to select their own life partners. In their opinion, the modern society has created such a life structure in which the role of women has become dominant. Since most of the time and energy of the boys and girls are passed in the colleges and universities, they tend to date with different partners which is most likely to create in them the quest for new partners which has enough potentials to end in divorces and family discords. They further stress that the permissiveness and liberalism in the surcharged atmosphere cause a sudden decline in the curiosity for sex for men and women and the lack of sexual satisfaction would surely lead to broken marriages and separation. Since biologically men are at a disadvantage position and they cannot provide the needed satisfaction indefinitely, the consumption of Viagra-like products will increase with the passage of time and the sexual quacks and sexual *gurus* would make tremendous business. The demand for traditional healers will increase exponentially.

In addition to it, the Human Rights activists emphasise that as the girls are coming newly in the field of education and employment, they are serious in their studies. Consequently, they are getting better grades and better jobs. Employers also prefer girls over boys due to several reasons which are resulting in unemployment among boys compared to girls. It appears that over a period of time the greater number of women would work in the government offices, factories and farms and there would be feminisation of men and they would sit with their mothers and look after the kitchens and the children. Men caught in their new *avatars* will grow at slower pace. Their ambitions would tone down and they would pass their times in organising male kitty parties and attending religious functions. The world would face a civil war of genders and the sanctity of the family as well as the bonds between mother and child would break. Domestic life will be more conflict-ridden and boring. The consumerism would make women more innovative, and hungrier for life and more imaginative. They would take possession of public space. It is presumed that by 2020 the world will become a place of submissive men and aggressive women and it would face the crisis of middle age which will lead to gender battle. Women at that point of time would become more professional, more career conscious, more caring for their bodies and more sexually demanding. Freedom for women by that time would become a reality in true sense.

My Countrymen! Incidentally, if this theory proves correct it would surely and certainly turn the whole existing social and cultural milieu of the society upside down which our people have preserved over centuries.

**Decent Rearing Scheme for Children**

My Dearest and Nearest! Another peculiarity of our ancestors was that they were extremely cautious in rearing, nurturing and upbringing their children in the light of their conventions, culture and moral and spiritual values. It appears that many Indian parents have been influenced so much by the prevailing atmosphere in the country that they have allowed their wards to do anything and everything which they like irrespective of the fact whether such activities are legal or illegal, moral or immoral, permissive or non-permissive and religious or irreligious. They have allowed them to break dress code, food habits, family ties, civilised etiquettes, social practices, cultural norms and moral fibre of the society which the country had preserved for so long. Most of the parents have no control over the daily routine of their children. They know very little when they get up, when they go to schools, colleges or universities, whether they attend their classes or not, where they take food, in whose company they move, what they do and when they return home. Several parents despite not liking their dresses allow them to wear branded jeans, shoes, shirts, tea shirts, skirts, pants, mufflers, knickers and shorts and skinny and transparent dresses which neither suit to our culture nor to the local climate. Their misfortune is that their children bother least to cover their vital parts and those parts of human bodies that are likely to arouse passions and lust. Besides, the parents have no control over their food habits and their children eat every type of food, vegetarian or non-vegetarian, continental or occidental without realising the impact of different types of foods on human body, mind and soul. They eat pizza, shwarma, tandoori chicken, burgers, chilly chicken, lavishly in the food joints and restaurants of the city. The parents also do not mind when their kids take rum, whiskey and foreign liquor. Many of these lads make experiments with hashish, ganja, brown sugar and other intoxicants and stimulants. The tragedy with the country is that the nourishing and tasty vegetarian and non-vegetarian diets that Indian families had developed over years have been discarded by the children one by one. Not only this, the children too have become independent in their decision-making. Parents are not sure where their children would marry, whether they would consult their parents at the time of deciding their partners or tie the knot before the Registrar of marriages. Nobody is sure whether they would live with their parents after marriages or settle in new apartments. No one can predict whether they would maintain any relations with their members of family or forget all the obligations of the family members for all times to come.

Children are the gifts of God. Lord has given us children to test us, to enlarge the dimensions of our hearts, to make us selfless, sympathetic and considerate. He wants to develop all our faculties by giving our souls higher aims, so that we may bring smiles on the bright faces, joys in the tender hearts and love in the pious souls. Children are also in the shape of loan which the nature has given to mankind, one can employ them usefully or else one would have to pay with heavy penalty. Good parents feed their children with rich loaf but look with the eyes of lions. They make it sure that their children develop a balanced personality by following a golden mean between various extremes. They want them to spare some time for the worship of their creator and also strive for character building and building of healthy and well-rounded personality. Parent's eyes are always on the movements of their children. They know where they go and whom they meet and what they do. They command them to get up early in the morning and go to school well-prepared. They ask them to come home in time and take meals with them. They converse with them, try to know their problems and help them in solving their tricky matters. They do not do anything before their children which is likely to cause adverse affects on their development. They keep their private life private and do not allow them to venture into it. They allow their children to take most of their decisions by themselves but in decisions which are vital and of far reaching consequences, they intervene and intervene firmly and decisively.

**Parents are Financing their Children Instead of Nurturing Them**

My learned countrymen must have seen that how many of us are guiding our children on the right path? Is it not a fact that many children of neo-rich and lenient families rise late, bother least to go to the classes in time and pass their time in gossiping, idle talks and merry-making? They use shabby clothes, consume junk foods and spend extravagantly. Their time is mostly passed in Western music, robust dances and dating with friends. They use their college and university time as the best time for making friends and meeting people. Their dresses, addresses, gestures, postures and body languages are not befitting to the culture to which they belong. They are often noticed in late-night parties where alcohol and drugs are frequently served. If they come late in the night drunk and shattered, there are few elders who can rebuke them. If they are seen in the company of undesirable boys and girls, few can dare to scold them. Most of the lads decide their own pattern of living, they want no interference in matters of the selection of their life partners and they pass practically no time in the company of their parents. Divorces within few years of marriages have become very common among them.

Many parents do not know how to bring up their children. They spoil their children by making them too much happy. Most of the parents try to please their children rather than doing things for their betterment. If it pleases the child to rise late, go to school unprepared, gossip with friends, move in bad company and come late in the night, they keep mum. They do not give time to their children which they need most but spend money on them to show their love and compassion towards them. They provide them various types of toys, costly clothes and hefty pocket money to compensate the pains of loneliness which their children suffered while their parents were engaged at their work places. In order to let them to pass their time and to keep them busy the parents do not disturb their children when they watch cartoons or children films though watching of the television for so long affects their eyes, kills their time and affects them adversely. It has been estimated that in advanced countries by the time the child gets out of high school he has already watched more than 25,000 hours of television, witnessed 20,000 murders and observed 120,000 alcohol related cases.

The role of consumerism is immense in spoiling the children. The multi-national companies spend billions of dollars in promoting the sale of their products such as toys, toffees, chocolates, Chiclets, ice-creams, cold drinks, chips, shoes, clothing and gift items. The television programmes and the advertisements convey the message that drinking, smoking and drugs are a fun. Nearly eighty per cent rapists in developing countries admitted that they were the regular users of pornography and fifty per cent of them admitted that they experienced the pornography scenes. There are some parents who never stop their children in doing what they are doing. In order to enjoy the programme of their liking, if the children snatch the only remote from the hands of their grandparents watching the serial of their choice, they do not annoy their children but try to arrange a new television set for the parents. Mostly on holidays or after coming from offices, they take their children to food joints, cinema halls and try to please them by satisfying their genuine or non-genuine demands. A surest way to make your children miserable and unfortunate is to satisfy their all demands expeditiously and promptly. Children get flattered with every gratification and when their all the greed are not satisfied and parents have to stop at some point, it is too late because by that time the children become obstinate. We forget that when we try to please our children, we basically try to please ourselves rather than pleasing the children.

## Children do not Want to be Idle

It is in the very nature of the children that they want to keep busy and they generally hate to remain idle. We seldom bother to see how they pass their leisure time when we know that 'an empty mind is the devil's workshop'. We should make use of their costly time in games, sports, literary and cultural activities, hobbies and useful leisure. We also bother least in what company our children move for the child is known by the company he keeps. Happiness of the children demands that we should show patience with the tempers of children, understanding with their problems and appreciation with their progress. We are supposed to be gentle and not harsh with our tender ones; we are expected to keep a constant watch over them but not to spy; we are required to reprove them earnestly and not in anger and we are intended to work as models and not as critics. Of nine out of ten things in children, the parents should take no special notice because children make mistakes and it is out of their mistakes that they acquire wisdom.

However, if, as to the eleventh, they should give them direction or command and see to it that they are obeyed. See to it that if you have taken any firm stand in the interest of your child, you are obeyed at all costs for if you yield your authority this time you will hardly get it again. The children must not always have their way. There must be some point where they should be told that enough is enough. If you never have headaches through rebuking your children, you should be ready for plenty of heart attacks when they grow up. We should also not always discourage our children but encourage them wherever they are right. We should mix gentleness and politeness with firmness and strictness. When the child sheds tears not because of the fear of punishment but from repentance from his offence, he needs no other cure. It is irony of fate that instead of children fearing their parents, the parents are afraid of their children. The child can say 'no' to the parents at the slightest provocation but the parents seldom utter 'no' in extreme circumstances.

## Children are Sensitive

We know very well that the children are very sensitive. Their little grief of losing a ball is as painful as losing millions of dollars by adults in horse race. Similarly, their pleasure in kite flying gives them the same delight which a politician gets in his victory in the election. Children live in a world of imagination and feeling. They invest their time and energy in whatever they consider appropriate and rejoice in that accordingly. Beware that children are very nice observers. They feel injustice, they have a sense of right and wrong, they feel humiliated when they are insulted and they have liking for compassion, kindness and generosity. They observe our good and bad habits equally and place us on their scale accordingly. If we ask them to tell a lie to our visiting friends at our door-step by communicating them that we are not there, they would obey us in disgust but abhor us in their hearts and if the practice remains continuous, they too become liars one day. It is a fact that the minds of the children become developed even at the very early stage of their development. Whether it is for good or evil, the children mainly learn from observations of actions, words, voices or looks of those with whom they live. They watch every private activity which their parents commit in secrecy or dark or light considering them immature but the same is repeated by them at the slightest opportunity. Children usually desire that their parents look towards their problems from their point of view and the parents want their children to identify things from their view point which generally create misunderstanding and heart burning.

It has been seen parents generally complain that their children do not care for their love. They do not heed their advices and they do what they like. Many of them even begin to believe that they are not their worthy children. Some parents in disgust begin to disown them, a few develop disliking for them, many shower abusive language upon them, several use stick and multitude repent in solitude. The real fact is that the children generally do not know how much their parents love them, how sincere they are for them, how intensely they feel for their safety, security and growth. The cruel joke of life is that the children will never know the depth, intensity and purity of the love of their parents towards them till the grave stones would cover them forever or they have children of their own. When their children would grow old and become parents and have their children and bend over the cradles of their own children, they would know the sacredness of their mothers and fathers and realise how much they loved them. In the later years when their parents would have gone beyond this world in eternity, they would confront an extreme sense of loss. The sense would dawn upon them having seen their own children that they could not do anything for their loving parents when they were living, and could not tell them how precious they were to them when they were with them, and could not perceive their true love which was selfless, boundless and incomparable.

## Children Suffer due to the Follies of Parents

It has been generally observed that the conducts and styles of parents and the relationships which they had with people and the errors and follies of life committed by them penalise their children for no fault of their own. Their children suffer facing the stream of life whose fountain has been poisoned by their parents. The parents also suffer when they realise that their children were suffering due to their adverse behaviour committed in the past. In the same way, very few people realise that their children are rewarded for the parents' well-spent life, good principles, exemplary character, nice upbringing and the whole outfit that they provided to their children and which enabled them to lead a successful life. The legend say that if we want to be remembered for our good works, instruct our children to do good and nice things in life for all the good acts committed by them would be associated with us.

Usually, we do not find that love in our eyes as parents which we saw in our parents. It appears that someone has snatched our real and genuine affection for our children. In the past our parents showered their infinite smiles upon us, never minded our shortcomings and follies and guided us on the right path as friends, guides and philosophers. They played with us even when they were busy, lifted us in their lapses when we were dirty and gave us sweets which we liked most. They arranged for us monkey shows, they took us to the picnics and they enjoyed festivals in our company. Our parents were offended the least when their own grand children urinated upon their costly clothes, made them horses, rode on their shoulders, naughtily pulled their moustaches and smilingly hit on their cheeks. They fed them when they were hungry, took them in their lapses and moved around when they were not sleeping and changed their clothes when they were dirty. They did not mind when they disturbed them when they were intensely busy. They felt comfort when in their sound afternoon sleep they awakened them by throwing water on their faces with a view to play with them. They laughed when they spoiled their books by pencil and colour marks. They resisted the least when they forcibly took them to play ball game and they gladly ate the half eaten chocolates which they put in their mouths half bitten. When they demanded the toy gun or Barbie they presented them at short notice, when they ordered for ice-creams of their choice they quickly provided them and when they requested for special types of dresses they were placed at their disposal within no time. They took them on long drive to please them, they jumped in the swimming pool at their direction and at their command they ran after them to catch them. They could not sleep for many nights having seen them sick, they ran after doctors to see them fit and they went to saints, prayed at tombs and graves for their health. They took children's benefit schemes and invested substantial amount for their education, they made plans for their wedding and honeymoon and they left no stone unturned in making their future safe and secure. They did all these things knowing fully well that they would get nothing in return for by the time their grand children would become worthy, they would have gone too far.

It is the considered opinion of the experts that most of us are perhaps not aware of the consequences of what we are doing with respect to rearing of our children. The way many ignorant parents are bringing up their children on alien traditions which are repulsive to our culture, social norms and ethos should know that they are bound to face rough weather. The experience of Western countries is before us. We should not forget that soon a day may come when many of us too may become unneeded and thrown in old age homes where we would neither live comfortably nor die peacefully. We have not lost much. Still there is time to mend our faults. The sooner we do better it is in our interest.

**Affectionate Security Structure for Parents**

We must appreciate and give full credit to our ancestors for giving due respects to their parents. They considered parents as the miracles of the Lord and their voices as the voice of God. Parents are indeed a unique gift of nature. Only those know the utility of the parents who have lost them. They act as the mighty shield when the clouds of misfortune hang around over the heads of their beloved. They care least for their lives, honour and possessions when any eventuality struck their kids. They nurse them when they are in the cradle. They help them to move when their legs are feeble. They persuade them to speak when their tongues falter. They arrange for their food, clothing, comforts and entertainment as best as possible. They toil on farms in scorching heat, labour in factories day and night, manage petty shops throughout the day, participate in art, crafts and governing structure to earn money. They arrange tiffin for schools, send them for education in the colleges and finance their studies at university and higher levels. They run after door to door, pillar to pillar and place to place without caring for their reputations to settle their wards. They approach people, knock the gates of organisations and institutions to get them absorbed without caring for their health and comforts. They select the life partners for them and solemnise their marriages and equip them for the life to come. They act as comrades, consultants and advisors. Sages command the children to honour their mothers and fathers. They also ordain that the children should bestow their tender care upon their parents when they are old and feeble just as they showered their love and affection upon them when they were weak and helpless. They remind that how troublesome was it for the mother to keep the child in her womb for too long, how painful was it to give him birth, how inconvenient was it to up bring him and how difficult was it for her to look after him when he was sick, infirm and immature? The Holy Men told the children to look towards their parents with smiling faces, pleasing looks, helping gestures and affectionate hearts. They warned them not to object them or annoy them by uttering even 'oh! in the wake of their misadventures.

Tryon Edwards states,

*"Honour thy parents, those that gave thee birth, and watched in tenderness thine earliest days, and trained thee up in youth, and loved in all. Honour, obey and love them; it shall fill their souls with joy, and shall bring down God's richest blessing on thee; and in days to come, thy children, if they're given, shall honour thee, and fill thy life with peace."*

**Many Parents are Suffering Despite Legislative Measures**

Years of experience shows that the story at the grassroots level is quite different. The concepts of mother, father, brother, sister, cousin and aunt, etc. have become redundant in most of the parts of the world especially in such areas where there is supremacy of Western civilisation and culture. The family is confined to the extent of husband, wife and the minor children. The moment children become adults; they leave their parents and settle in their own nests as independent birds. They manage for their education, marriages, health-care and up keep and parents normally do not take any active interest in their private affairs. Naturally, when the parents become old, the children do not take any interest in their health, well-being and up keep. The parents are mostly left at the mercy of their past savings or on charity or state helps or sent to old men's homes.

In recent times, we have heard numerous complaints about the neglects of the elderly parents in Indian homes. The problems start when the parents are financially weak and they put some demands of financial assistance before their earning children for themselves or to meet the demands of their dependent sons and daughters and those demands are not met. The parents then begin to complain by leveling charges against their daughters-in-laws as well as calling their sons henpecked husbands. If the conditions of the earning sons are not better and they are not in a position to spare enough money for their parents, pressures begin to mount in favour of not sending money because the sons and daughter-in-laws know that it would be at the cost of the education of their children as well as the welfare of their families.

If the earning sons are financially well off, such matters seldom arise though a few unreasonable wives often call their husbands as 'the babies of their parents' for adhering to their demands. In some families, the quarrels begin to start between mother-in-law and daughter-in-law on petty matters concerning the management of the households. Sometimes these quarrels take the shape of the tussles between daughter-in-law and sisters-in-law which later on involve the males and even the children. Finally, the bickering goes to this extent that if the property is in the name of father and father is slightly strong the children leave the homes of their parents and settle elsewhere. Many a time it has been observed that a few self-centered and misguided children not only neglected, insulted and rebuked their parents but also turned them out of their houses. If the parents reminded them about their sacrifices, they ignored them replying that they had not done anything special for them since every parent did for his children. It is because of the atrocities committed upon the unfortunate parents by their wicked children that the Government of India had to bring an Act in the Parliament for the protection of the distressed parents but despite this the situation has not improved much.

**Loneliness of Parents**

The complaints of not providing supports to the parents generally come from poor parents especially in cases where their children are not well off or uneducated. Mostly people in India care for their parents due to Indian customs, ethos and practices. There are many obedient and loving children both boys and girls of sterling qualities who love their parents, care for them and adore them like anything. Besides, there are many brilliant children who are well to do, educated and meaningful and love their parents from the core of their hearts but they are handicapped as they had to leave their parents at the mercy of the servants in important cities like Delhi, Mumbai, Kolkata, Chennai and various other metropolitan cities because they had to go to America, Europe, Australia and Gulf Countries for lucrative jobs. They make it sure that they keep contacts with their parents on phones daily or very often and visit them regularly in order to know their well-being, health, welfare and safety. They very often lament that they could not live with their parents and could not serve them during the days of their weaknesses. They suffer in solitude having seen their parents lonely and alone, they curse their lust for money and wealth that detached them from their parents and they pray God for their safety and security. Many a time they express their desires to come to India to serve them after leaving their jobs but their parents in the interest of their children never allow them to do so. Several times one hears about the cold blooded murders of these old couples at the hands of their servants or unscrupulous persons for the sake of money.

The misfortune of these couples is that they have to do everything by themselves which they cannot do due to age factor and hence they have to rely and depend on their domestic servants who seeing them helpless but resourceful exploit them and one day wipe them out from the scenes. The elderly people could be helped by their grand children had they stayed with them during the period of their education or seeking jobs but it seldom works because in many cases the grand parents do not want to take the responsibilities of such children because of their age factor and more over the grand children too prefer to stay at the places of their likings. It is heartening to note that a new and healthy change has emerged on the Indian scene with respect to the help rendered by girls to their elderly parents. Indian girls were considered as helpless and weak. No parents could ever think of taking any help and support from them. Thanks to the modern education that they have boldly come in front to help their helpless and weak parents because of their strong educational back ground and earning capacity. In many cases, they have surpassed their brothers in providing moral and emotional support to their parents. They too visit their parents very often, arrange for their treatment, keep touch with them on phones and make it sure that their parents are safe and secure. It is a good omen and would go a long way in filling the gap that has been created by the absence of sons within Indian environment. It is the good fortune of many Indian parents that they do not want any financial help because they themselves are well placed. They simply need the help of their children when they are sick or in trouble. However, one thing is sure that there is no substitute to the presence of children when the joints of their parents begin to crack and they hopelessly look at others for help. It is nothing but the curse of modern civilisation that merely for the sake of few pieces of money, few doses of power and a little charm of name and fame loved ones have been separated from those whom they love most.

### Sound Joint Family System

The most important social institution that our elders had designed to preserve our culture and distinctiveness was the Joint family system which remained in vogue in the country for centuries. Essentially, it was the first form of church on earth and was the binding force that united all the members of the family into a composite whole. It not only protected the members of the family from going astray but also protected family customs, ethos, cultural traditions, moral conventions and spiritual practices. There was hierarchy in the joint family and the place of every member of the family was safe and secure. Respect for the elder and love for the younger was the motto of every family. Head of the family was the Chief Executive and his dictates prevailed upon all the members of the family. He made important decisions in consultation with family members. The role of grandparents and parents as well as husbands, wives, sisters, brothers, sons, daughters, uncles, aunts and nieces and cousins, etc., was well-defined and there was no anomaly in it. Parents and grandparents occupied highest respects in the family structure and no member could dare to show slightest disrespect towards them. It was considered pleasure and privilege to serve the elders and the parents physically, emotionally, mentally, spiritually and worldly. To displease father or mother was not only the unpardonable crime but it was also considered as a greatest sin in the eyes of Lord. Parents were looked after with grace, glory and comforts and their protection, safety, security, happiness and comforts were considered as the significant aspects of the religious duties for every citizen. What to talk of disobeying them, nobody could dare to speak in loud voice before them. Younger ones hesitated to come before the elders.

## Role of Females in the Management of the Joint Family

The management of the family was handled by the elderly ladies in consultation with other members of the family. What would be cooked and who would cook what, was decided by the mother-in-law. Similarly, the requirements of the daughters and daughters-in-law must be taken in care after by the elderly ladies. Bulk purchase of clothes, ornaments and other materials was made on festivals and important social and religious occasions. Younger members of the family especially the daughters-in-law took every care to look after the requirements of the family members. They participated in cooking food, serving meals, cleaning houses, washing and stitching clothes and preparing for festivals. Children and the younger ones also contributed in the welfare of the family in their own ways. However, girls were mostly not involved in the household activities. Every lady including the adolescent girls were obliged to cover their heads and private and sensitive parts of their bodies. When they went out they were supposed to cover their bodies and faces by their *saris* or *dupattas.* In the same way, they could not come before the senior members of the family with heads uncovered. Mothers-in-law were whole and sole in matters pertaining to dealing with daughters-in-laws. Their decisions were final in cases of inter-personal differences and disputes between younger and elder daughters-in-law.

In an extended joint family, there were several members and they were looked after by their uncles and aunts. Many children did not know who their parents were for they were generally looked after by the senior members of the family. Many a time the children used to call papas or fathers to the elder brothers of their fathers and *chacha* or uncles to their own fathers because other members of the family too called them likewise. Similarly, they took their mothers as *chachis* or aunts and the elder ladies as their mothers. It was not considered appropriate to mingle exclusively with one's own children or mix openly with ones wife in the presence of the elders of the family. The family system was so well-nit that the physical, emotional and all other needs of the younger ones and the elder members were met meticulously.

**Children were Taught Manners**

The children were taught etiquettes. It amounted to bad manners to point out the mistakes of the elders. Similarly, it showed poor upbringing to poke nose when two persons were talking. Likewise, children were taught to convey the pleasant news to the concerned persons aptly but were restrained from communicating the adverse ones because it was the cuckoo which brought the good news of spring and the owl was the carrier of bad news of the autumn. They were trained to keep their secrets to them only for leaking the secrets to dearest friends amounted to communicating it to all for their dearest friends too would have their dearest ones to communicate the secret to them. The children were also warned not to tell their important and personal matters to their dearest friends for per chance if enmity developed between them, the friends would exploit them to their advantage. In the same way, they were informed that in the wake of severe enmity with the past friends they should not cross the limits of decency for per chance if the bond of friendship revived, they would feel low before their friends. They were also trained in the art of conversation. It was pointed out to them that it amounted to lack of wisdom to be silent when it was proper to speak and speak when it was expedient to keep quiet. Similarly, they were advised to speak only when they found that others wanted to hear them and stopped speaking, before it that people said "enough". They were also instructed to "never answer" except when people questioned them and when the wise-men spoke to them, they were asked not to object even if they knew better than them. Actually, the early training ground for the children was the family. It was within the bounds of the families that the conducts of Indians were shaped.

All decisions about marriages of the sons and daughters, brothers and sisters, nieces and cousins were mostly taken by the parents and elders after careful consideration taking into account the family background, qualifications, beauty, health, aptitude and suitability of the brides and bridegrooms. Love marriages or marriages outside the castes or religions were considered taboo. Adult males and females of different families were not allowed to mix freely in order to minimise the chances of love affairs. Likewise, the head of the family was the custodian of the wealth and treasure of the family and all financial and property matters too were decided by the elders of the family. At the time of sickness, accident, civil or criminal cases or eventuality faced by any member of the family, all the young and old of the family stood like a rock. Old age was not a barrier to the elders and the parents. In their old age they participated in all the activities and were looked after with much care and caution and their last journey to eternity too was solemnised with grace and piety.

Marriage was considered as a contract as well as the sacrament. The couples entered into the wedlock for life assuring each other complete love, sincerity, devotion, help, compassion and shelter. Wife was sure of the integrity of the husband and the husband could never doubt the loyalty of the wife. Both of them cared for each other and worked as the two wheels of a cart. Extra-marital relations at school, college and university levels were unthinkable. Divorces, separations, elopements, etc., were extremely rare. Misunderstandings or family discords were amicably settled at family level by the elders of the family. They never allowed their children to know any differences among them if there were any and never quarreled or showed any disrespect with respect to each other before them. The secrets about the private life of the elders or the differences between them were kept secret from the children. Once the children reached the adolescent stage, the parents took every care not to utter or act or behave in any manner prejudicial to their development and consulted them on important family matters.

## Care of Children by Parents

Parents took every care of their children once the conception took place and never did anything untoward which could harm the growth of the child within the womb. The children were breast-fed by mothers and mothers used to nurse them by sleeping with them, looking after them and caring for them till they were mature enough to stand on their own feet. The infants were never kept aloof save in very rich families where they were looked after by the nurses. Mothers took every care that they remained with them and they also took interest in teaching good manners and *sanskars* to their children and fathers saw to it that their children were behaving nicely and were in safe hands.

Parents tried to provide their children with all the possible comforts of life but looked at them with critical eyes. They did not hesitate to give them physical punishment if the situation so demanded. They did not try merely to please them but tried their best to do what was in the interest of their children. Children were not pampered by giving them costly toys or commodities of their choices that could have adverse and hazardous affects on their personalities. Parents cared very little about the moods, reactions, stubbornness; insistences, etc., of their children but did that which was within their means as well as in children's interests. They were not moved by their crying, not taking food and repeated requests but tried to convince them of their inabilities to yield to their demands. However, if they persisted mild force or harsh words were used to set them right.

Parents were not afraid of their children. Instead their children feared them and could not dare to disobey them. The spirit behind the training of the children was to make them enlightened and disciplined citizens. Etiquettes pertaining to taking food, wearing clothes, maintaining cleanliness, meeting people, getting blessings from the elders and the teachers and facing different situations and mixing with people in and outside the houses were taught to improve their personalities. They were warned not to quarrel, not to use force or violence, not to use abusive language and not to indulge in the habit of smoking, *pan* chewing or moving in bad company. They were discouraged from taking part in backbiting, spying, slandering, nicknaming, ragging and indulging in unhealthy activities. Children were persuaded to take part in games, sports, literary and cultural activities, quiz competitions, hobbies and other creative activities. They were asked to pray and read the scriptures daily to keep their body, mind and soul clean. They were obliged to come home before sunset and complete their home work after taking food with their parents. They had to get up early morning for getting bath, took breakfast and went to schools in time. Very little pocket money was given to them, so that they might not develop bad habits but meet their genuine requirements. Parents kept watch on the movement of their children and ensured it that they were going to school regularly and were in good company. Feedback was often taken from friends, elders and school teacher about the behaviour pattern of the children. The essence of family life was the spirit of give and take, cooperation and peaceful coexistence. Children were taught to tell the truth, to help the needy, to honour the commitment made by them, not to deceive any body and not to indulge in any immoral, illegal, criminal or sinful activity. They were guided to wear decent clothes to protect their physical bodies, behave nicely to be called civilised citizens and perform good deeds to purify their souls. In those days parents did not hesitate to say anything to their children below 18 years because Indian children had not become conscious of their rights and stringent laws were not framed to make child abuse a serious offence.

**The Atmosphere within Joint Family**

The joint family was generally a male dominated unit where the males of the family had preference over the females. In matters of providing education, clothing and other facilities and comforts of lives, the males were mostly gainers. Generally, the sons and daughters lived in same rooms and independent rooms were provided only to the married couples and elders of the family. In many cases even the books, dresses and utility items were shared by different members of the family. The atmosphere of living in a joint family created among the members the spirit of sacrifice, tolerance, patience, give and take and cooperation and co-existence. It ironed out the problems of egos, self-interest, vanity, hatred and wickedness. Only those members acquired respect and honour, who were tolerant, conscientious, hard working and considerate for others. Many members of the family were known for their specialised arts and expertise. For instance, some were famous for their art of conversation, a few in doing household chores, rare ones being the toppers in the class, many for gossiping and whiling away their time. There was inter-rivalry and bickering among different members of the family. For instance, there was a hidden and concealed clash between the mother-in-law and the daughters-in-law and a mild heart-burning between brothers and brothers, sisters and sisters and brothers and sisters but it could rarely take any ugly turn.

The festivals and social and cultural ceremonies were also meant to strengthen the bonds of families. For instance, on *Rakshabandhan* the sisters tied *rakhis* on the hands of their brothers and brothers went to the houses of their sisters on *Bhaiya Dooj*. Similarly, the wives kept *Karwa Chauth* for the longevity of their husbands. *Diwali* and *Holi* too were celebrated with great fanfare. *Dushera* depicted the fall of satanic forces and *Diwali* revealed the victory of virtues over depravity. Similarly, Eid, Christmas and festivals of Sikhs, Jains and others also enriched the composite culture of the country. Festivals and the cultural functions provided the opportunities to clean the houses help the destitute and mix with the members of other families spread over villages and cities. When the joint family became too wieldy or unmanageable it broke down and gave birth to nuclear families. Many a time the partiality, insincerity or incompetence of the head of the family or the grudges of the wives, sons and daughters of earning members led to the fall of joint family system.

**Emergence of Nuclear Families**

The major cause of India's social, cultural and moral decadence is the creation of nuclear families. Nuclear families are the product of modern civilisation. However, they were encouraged by several vested interests such as the builders were interested in selling their flats in the cities, property dealers wanted to raise the value of the plots ,the business units were interested in boosting the sale of their refrigerators, air conditioners, sofas, chairs, dinning sets, crockery, cutleries, cars and consumer durables. Similarly, the interior decorators wanted their presence to be felt in each house and the modern education had made each individual independent in thinking and the state too had ensured protection to every family. All these factors plus the role of family serials or televisions showing contradictions of the joint families as well as the conflicts between *Saas* and *Bahus* or mothers-in-law and daughters-in-law led to the growth and development of the nuclear families in the country. When such families were created, brothers were separated from brothers, sisters from brothers and parents from children. The bread earner sons established their own families along with their wives and children leaving the parents and the young and minor brothers and sisters with their aging parents. The parents struggled hard to feed, educate and marry their dependent children though they were occasionally helped by some of their obedient elder sons. The dependent members developed bitterness in their hearts against their brothers and the wives of their brothers for deserting them which ultimately turned into rivalries and hatred between different members of the family. The new pairs settled mostly in rented houses in the cities and big towns where they got jobs. In such places, they faced a completely changed atmosphere because they found themselves surrounded by so many nuclear families having varying social, cultural and religious backgrounds. There was no communication between various nuclear families with diverse backgrounds which made them lonely and isolated. It also minimised the social pressures on such families which were bent upon moral misadventures since there was none to check if they dared to do anything repugnant to family traditions, cultural norms and religious practices. People became care-free and gradually and gradually forgot all the nice values that they had inherited from their families. The changed situation arising out of the settlement of different people from several places with diverse backgrounds created Cosmopolitan atmosphere which was the amalgamation of various cultures and social traditions. However, wherever people of a particular caste or religion or area were numerically and otherwise in dominant position, the culture of such people got precedence over the cultures of others.

Living in nuclear families created fear psychosis and inward looking attitude among the members of such families because the individuals of these families very often felt lonely, without friends and in minority. In joint families they were strong because of their manpower. Even today wherever the people live in groups in old cities, their family members come to their help on slightest provocation compared to the individuals of the single families who have to face music by their adversaries in the wake of any misadventure. Thus, before taking any bold step or facing any eventuality they have to think ten times because they are sure that in case of any proactive deed on their part they would neither be helped by their neighbours as they were aliens to them nor by their brothers, sisters and relatives as they were too far from them. This feeling of being lonely and helpless made them over cautious and even coward. They feared resisting against the excesses of their bosses at the work places did not raise their voices against corruption and tolerated silently what happened around them. Besides, the life of the individuals in nuclear families became troublesome. The joint families worked as the shock absorbers. There was none in such families to salvage them, to console them and to help them.

Consequently the psychiatric cases and cases of suicides increased immensely. The experience shows that Japan confronted the maximum psychiatric and suicide cases after the break of joint family system. Moreover, there was none to look after their children, none to help them in cooking and other house hold activities and none to look after their homes in their absence when the husband and the wife were on work places and the children were in schools. The nuclear families thus created the needs for baby-sitters, domestic servants and watchmen etc. who were not so reliable as the members of the joint family and experience shows that many of them caused immense harm to such families in the shape of thefts, murders and black mailing. Moreover, living in cosmopolitan atmosphere developed in them a new culture which was contrary to centuries old customs and practices. Over and above this, since there was none to watch the perverted activities of the members of nuclear families, the unscrupulous people took the advantage of the freedom given to them and crossed the limits of piety, sanity and good moral conducts. Furthermore, since there were no set standards for dress code, diets and behaviour pattern among such families, the youths blew with the wind and did what others were doing. There are many families in biggest cities which are perturbed due to lawlessness around them and are reverting back to joint families. Thus, many people conclude that it was the fall of joint family system that led to the fall of family values and the abandonment of our various social, cultural and moral systems.

## Viable Neighbourhood

Just see my countrymen! Our ancestors, gave too much prominence to the neighbours because a good neighbour doubled the value of the house and it were the neignbours who could be approached in case of emergencies. Neighbourhood was a cohesive unit which shaped the destiny of the residents of the city. It was an extended form of the joint family. People of various castes, creed, class, colours, and religion and belief systems lived together with peace, harmony and brotherly feelings. Neighbourhood acted as the strong fort for the safety, security and protection of the neighbours as well as their cultures, social customs and moral practices. Aliens and undesirable elements could not dare to enter the neighbourhood. They were easily spotted by the neighbours and pushed out. Once in the neighbourhood, everyone felt safe and secure for there were many committed elders, uncles and brothers to provide them protection and help and assistance. The relations between the immediate neighbours were highly cordial, better than the bonds between the relatives. Being in close touch they were aware of each other's problems, needs and eventualities. If any neighbourer was going to the market to buy household goods others never hesitated to give him the list of their products which were readily and smilingly accepted and goods were delivered to them according to their likings. People left their valuable belongings, ornaments and cash in the custody of the neighbours while going to other places to meet their relatives or accomplishing any ventures and their trusts were safely returned to them on their return. Neighbours helped one another by giving them interest free loans and other moral and material support.

It were they who were always available in the wake of problems, and it were they who used to come to the rescue of their neighbours before the arrival of the kith and kin. Quarrels between the neighbours were peacefully settled with the help of the elders and nobody felt the need of knocking the doors of law courts. Males of every caste, community or religion were respected irrespective of their economic status, educational qualifications and social background. Likewise, the females too were loved by all the sections of the society transcending all barriers of professions, vocations, business and trade. Women of every family were given highest respect and regard and nobody could dare to show slightest disrespect to them. They could freely move with costly ornaments on their persons. Eve-teasing, molestation or taunts could take bloody shape. One could take the risk of life in the wake of protecting the dignity of the woman of the vicinity. People helped each other in seeking employment, constructing houses, seeking brides and bridegrooms, nursing the sick and sorting court cases. The child births, marriage ceremonies and festivals were observed with gay and gaiety. If any boy or girl committed any untoward act anywhere in the city or if anything adverse happened to anyone of them, the information could reach the parents of the concerned boys or girls through the medium of their alert neighbours.

Nobody could dare to do any immoral or illegal activity within the vicinity due to the pressure and fear of the neighbours. Since people of different faiths and belief systems lived together in amity and peace; there was unity in diversity, communal harmony and peaceful co-existence. Neighbourhood being a vibrant and the dynamic force helped in preserving the rich cultural heritage of the country. The neighbourhoods worked as the shock absorbers because there were several witty and expert neighbours, who were masters in the art of pleasing people by cutting jokes, reciting couplets from Hindi, Urdu and Persian poetries, creating laughter by their satires and other expertise. Thus, many diseases, shocks, worries and anxieties were solved then and there without resorting to the psychiatrics. In the nights especially in winter the grandmothers used to tell stories of the kings and queens, *tota* and *maynas* and fox and monkeys which were heard with rapt attention by the children with their bodies covered with shawls. The stories were so long that they were never finished and children used to sleep while replying her in 'yes' and 'yes' and they were taken by their parents to their homes in late nights. The neighbourhood was a lively place. It was visited by beggars in stylish dresses wearing black clothes and rosaries around their necks singing beautiful songs. Likewise, the snake charmers, mimics, monkey and bear masters, jugglers, palmists and *Nats* charmed people with their masteries. Idle people gossiping at the street corners, barbers shaving their clients and sweet venders frying their *jalebis* mesmerised the onlookers.

**Neighbourhood Lost its Charms**

Unfortunately, with the passage of time, the charms of the neighbourhood too became the casualty. Presently, the position of two neighbours is like that of strangers, if one asks the name and address of any neighbour, even the immediate neighbour expresses his ignorance. Neighbours seldom greet each other, hardly meet on festivals and other important social occasions and never help their neighbours when they are in distress. On the contrary, there are jealousies, hatred and ill feelings as well as altercations, quarrels and litigations on minor matters. They would feel happy in the wake of the fall of the wall of their neighbour no matter their calf got crushed in the process.

*One day an angel appeared in the dream of a neighbour and told him that he could grant him a wish if he so desired. The neighbour was immensely happy. He said that he wanted that whatever he desired must be accomplished. The angel said that he could grant his wish from tomorrow morning if he accepted his condition that whatever the neighbour would have, his immediate neighbour would have double of it. The neighbour readily agreed to the condition. To make it doubly sure the angel asked him, "Are you sure?" The neighbour replied in yes. When he got up early in the morning he demanded that a beautiful house made up of pure gold be provided to him. To his great surprise not only he got one but his immediate neighbour also got two. The next time he wished for a magnificent car, lo! The car was there. When he looked at his neighbour's house, he was amazed that two cars were standing on his doorstep. He could not sleep for many nights due to extreme jealousy and decided that he would not wish for anything as his neighbour would get double of it. His wife advised him not to do this foolish thing but demand that his one eye is blinded. To his great surprise his one eye became blind but his happiness was doubled when he observed that his immediate neighbour had lost eye sights in both of his eyes. The wife then asked him to demand that one deep well be constructed before his gate. In no time one deep well appeared before his house and double of that before his neighbour's houses.*

This type of situation is found practically in every neighbourhood. The neighbours have lost all sympathies for their adjacent fellows and they have no soft corners for those who are living in their vicinity. They do not mind people doing legal, illegal or moral or immoral activities and many a time undesirable neighbours harbour criminals and anti-social elements which cause immense harm to the society. It is the misfortune of the society that it has lost its valuable treasure which protected the neighbours for centuries and which saved their vibrant and dynamic social, cultural, moral and religious systems for so long.

## Vibrant Educational Arrangement

The education system left by our elders was the main system which moulded the personalities of the youths and made them enlightened citizens. After the families and neighbours, it were the schools, colleges and the universities that taught people the etiquettes, behaviour patterns and do's and don'ts. Along with providing education these institutes also brought about changes in their cultural baggage, work ethics and ways of living and rounded the sharpened corners of their personalities by developing in them the spirit of introspection, live and let others live and transcendental perception. The teachers of those days were indeed teachers in the real sense of the term. They considered their students as their own kith and kin and took immense interest in their growth and development. They did not mind even going out of the ways to help their pupils. Their salaries were meager and it was difficult at times for them to meet their two ends but despite this they never exploited their wards.

They took several classes in a day without minding time limit, took tutorials and gave homework. At the time of examinations they took extra and special care to see that courses were not only completed well in time but they were also revised and important guess papers were set and solved for the benefit of the students. Weak and poor students were often called by them at their homes without charging any fee just to provide them extra teaching. They kept sharp and piercing eyes on the dress code of the students, their diets, companies, conducts and behaviour patterns and did not hesitate in reprimanding them. They did not create any difference between students and students on the basis of castes, religions, riches and worldly distinctions. They also encouraged the students to take parts in games, sports, cultural and literary activities and supervised their activities by their presence at the time of debating, sports, literary and cultural competitions. They took interests in the progress of their students even after they left their institutions and kept their keen eyes on them till they were absorbed in some jobs or settled in their own ventures for earning their livelihoods. Such teachers always left the lasting imprints on the mental canvas of the students and they were remembered for ever as their ideals, guides and well wishers.

## Lengthening of Educational Time

In those days, if anybody passed high school, he was competent enough to work at subordinate and middle levels and on completion of BA, B.Sc or B.Com one could do any important work of government at any level. Mostly, the District Magistrates and the Superintendents of Police were BAs or BScs. Many educationists of the country are not happy the way our government, moved by the educational practices elsewhere, made our education system lengthy. First of all two year BA, B.Sc and B.Com courses after intermediate were converted into three years BA, BSc and B.Com honours courses. Recently, a prominent university of the country has introduced a four years degree course after intermediate which has become the subject of public discussion. Subsequently, MA, MSc and M.Com became minimum qualifications for getting higher jobs. Soon M.Phil was added for joining Ph.D course and gradually and gradually Ph.D became the required qualification for getting lecturer's post. As time elapsed, Net was also included as one of the essential qualifications for obtaining any teaching post. This happened in every sphere. Previously a simple MBBS could do any medical practice with success but there also MS and MD were introduced and as time passed DM and super specialties became the required qualifications for working as a successful medical practitioner. Likewise, LLM was added in LLB; M.Ed in B.Ed and MSc engineering after BSc engineering. Not only this, the qualifications obtained in one segment were found lacking hence they were supplemented by other segments such as MBA was supplemented by BE, LLB and computer engineering.

In this process not only the time and money of the community became the casualty but the students too became shaky. A simple MA, MSc or M.Com degree holder despite spending huge amount of money in obtaining his higher degrees found himself hopeless in the job market. The lengthening of education period proved boon to the government for those students who could demand jobs from the government after high school and BA, B.Sc could not do so till they obtained their highest degrees. Besides, they did not blame the government for not getting jobs but cursed their own lucks for not obtaining the super specialty degrees. Over and above this, since their whole youth was passed in colleges and universities, they became docile after leaving the universities and could not agitate or behave actively with a view to put pressure on government for securing jobs. Moreover, the government did not face the ire of the youth as it was faced by the Principals of Colleges and the Vice-Chancellors of the universities. The government did not take part openly in controlling the law and order situation within the campuses but left the matter at the disposal of the Principals and Vice Chancellors. It assisted the colleges and the universities during emergencies. The greatest loss due to the lengthening of education process was to the country for the energetic power of the youth which the country could use during their hay days was lost in involving them in search of better and better degrees. In addition to it, the period which the students should have passed in their homes in leading married life and rearing their children after completing their education, they passed in the colleges and the universities which affected their life cycles adversely.

**Quality of Education is not Rich**

If we now look at the educational sector and literary problems of our countrymen, we feel highly disgusted and dejected. The misfortune of the country is that despite knowledge explosion in the country, people could not avail the benefits of quality education. In 2004, there were nearly 311 universities and 15,600 colleges in the country. After liberalisation and privatising of education innumerable schools, colleges, universities and institutes have been opened in every corner of the country during the last decade but the misfortune of the country is that quality of education provided to the students is not up to the mark. One can find the sign boards practically on every corner of the city for MBA, PGDM, BBA, B.Com, M.Sc, BCA, BSc, Engineering, medical and dental courses. Save a few private universities, colleges and institutes most of them are third grade. Their buildings are beautiful but the teaching is below average and the faculty is below marginal. Consequently, the product which is coming out from such universities is third class. Similarly, in the government sector too, we have hardly a few universities and institutes of excellence when Japan has several world class universities and China, United States of America, UK and Germany are far ahead of us. Besides, education for us is simply an ideal method to earn livelihood. We find a great rush of students in professional and technical courses where students acquire skills with a view to secure lucrative jobs in multinational companies. There are very few students who join the courses in arts, humanities, science, theology, comparative religion, aesthetics and astrology. Moreover, education has become a profession and the commodity approach has developed a professional relationship between the teachers and the taught with the result that the very purpose of education has been defeated.

It is the misfortune of our universities that many healthy traditions and good customs which enhanced the status of our Universities in the past are in bad shape. The cheap and feudal work culture in which many unscrupulous persons participate is in much vogue. The mediocre with the help of flattery and back-biting acquire the patronage of men in power and repel the efficient, qualified and excellent people from the main stream as the debased currency removes the new currency from circulation. Many universities find it difficult to appoint highly qualified and competent persons on the top positions due to pressure politics with the result that many incompetent people find their way. It has been generally observed that in administration the same poles attract and the opposite repel. For instance, if the head of the department is competent, he would attract the competent persons and repel the incompetent and *vice versa*. Besides, in the present scenario the respect for an individual, like anywhere else, is confined merely to his being an administrative head or occupying the prestigious chair or being a part of any power centre and not due to excellent performance, honesty, commitment, meritorious acts and good moral conducts.

It is generally claimed that in some low grade universities, colleges and institutions many teachers develop close affinities with the Heads and Deans and many Deans and Heads and Provosts, Proctors and others become the intimates of the Vice-Chancellors. The non-teaching staff too does not lag behind. Such people become the favourites of their patrons and go to any extent to please their bosses. In turn the bosses too are compelled to go out of the way to help them at the cost of others. The favourite teachers are appointed in the universities by following short cuts. Initially ad hoc appointments or appointments as guest lecturers are made, later on they are introduced through local selection committees and finally with the help of the external experts they are absorbed on permanent vacancies by the strategies of the respective officials. The pet Lecturers and Readers are also appointed as Readers and Professors artfully by their bosses. The general impression in the third grade universities is that either "owns" are appointed or failing this the "known" are introduced. Many unscrupulous people help in inbreeding and regionalism by appointing the relatives and friends of their colleagues and in lieu of it they get their friends and relatives appointed by them. The interesting thing is that most of these favourites remain loyal so long as their bosses are in the chairs. The moment they are out, these opportunists also erase them from their memories. They criticise them after their retirement, talk ill of them and never visit their sympathisers after their retirement.

It is also said that many undesirable teachers in the third grade universities do not take their classes regularly. If they take any, either they do not go well-prepared or talk upon personal and general matters or teach on the basis of their old notes which they had prepared many years ago. Many of them give them higher sessional and other marks and behave with them nicely. They hang around their bosses and try their best to please them. They seldom complete the syllabi over a period of time and rarely take their tutorials and scarcely give them any home assignment. At the fag end of the examination they hurriedly complete the syllabus and give important questions for the guidance of the students. The research scholars including the girl students too are exploited by many irresponsible teachers. They hardly help these scholars in completing their theses. The students themselves try here and there and submit their research work but these teachers help them in getting their degrees. Similarly, for appointments and promotions many crafty people take the help of the internet or approach the professionals who come to their rescue in lieu of money.

**Corruption in the Third Grade Institutions**

It is irony of fate that Indian Universities were immune from corruption but today it is alleged that the corruption has spread in many universities in all directions. Many people openly say that many admissions in the important courses are given in lieu of money, some allege that payments in the finance departments are made after receiving cuts, several claim that contracts in the building departments are mostly given violating tender rules and there is no dearth of people who say that there is tremendous bungling in the purchases of equipments, furniture, machinery and instruments as well as commodities of every day needs. Several people alleged that money is generally taken for giving licenses for canteens, cycle stands, buying liveries and for giving appointments to daily wagers such as peons and cooks, gardeners and others. The finger of suspicion is also raised at the University Libraries where books and journals worth crores of rupees are purchased every year. It is also stated that several people in the non-teaching staff too have become corrupt. The complaints regarding the sale of fake marks sheets and fake degrees are received in many institutes from time to time. Many people allege that the palms of some of the clerical staff have to be greased for processing the cases of the university employees or for providing them important information or for expediting their files.

It is highly regrettable that despite receiving higher salaries and non-practising allowances some university medical teachers carry on their private practices openly without any fear. They have opened their clinics and diagnostic centers and are minting money. They ask the patients to come to them in their clinics for operations and other important consultations instead of directing them to come to the OPDs. Likewise, several teachers run tuition classes and many attend private coaching centers and earn substantial amount of money. Besides, there are some families in the universities which are influencing the politics of the university being in dominant positions. Their members are spread in many departments and at several levels and they help each other in promoting their family interests. It is pertinent to note that many shortcomings in the Indian universities are perpetuating due to the lack of competent and efficient vice chancellors. Generally vice Chancellors are appointed either on the basis of their administrative experiences or academic qualifications. Those who are administrators are found hollow in academic aspects and those that are academically sound miserably lack in the field of administration. If there is an academy for providing proper training and background to the vice chancellors about academic administrations it will go a long way in improving many evils in the university. Similarly it has been observed that the MLA's and MP's are appointed ministers and occupy important positions but they lack political acumen and they have to depend upon the bureaucracy. An academy for such people giving them proper education on the functioning of the parliament, assemblies and the government would certainly help in minimizing many ills in the political lives.

It would not be out of place to mention here that privatisation of education has created knowledge explosion in the country but in the name of privatisation many innocent, poor and ignorant people have been exploited immensely by the vested interests. Thousands of private colleges and institutes as well as hundreds of private universities have been opened practically in every city of the country but the quality institutes are not many. They are those which are being run by big corporate houses or by the philanthropists or committed teachers and dynamic young men. Mostly, the private educational institutions are below standard and the teaching is also below average. It is most unfortunate that thousands of students are spending their costly resources but the education that they are getting in most of the below average institutions is not helping them in getting jobs in job markets. Consequently, there is a vast bottleneck between demand and supply. At one side millions of unemployed graduate and post-graduate students are standing in search of jobs on the road side with degrees in their hands obtained from below standard private institutions and government agencies while on the other hand there is a tremendous shortage of experts, technical know-how and efficient, competent and experienced persons. It is highly regrettable that neither efforts were made in the country to improve the conditions of the below average colleges and universities, nor schemes were devised to produce the technical know-how nor solutions were found to absorb those students who nether find jobs in the cities nor find them fit to join the professions of their parents. It is most surprising that instead of doing something for raising the quality of education, efforts are being made to open new institutes to fish in troubled water.

**Effective Governing Mechanism**

It is a fact that our elders believed in good governance because an effective government machinery plays a dominant role in preserving and protecting the diversities of the nations and bringing people to sanity and righteousness. It is only when there are conflicts, natural disasters and upheavals that the peace, progress and the cultural distinctions of the countries are dented. The British Government had left an administrative system in India which was colonial in nature but still it was effective and deterrent as far as the law and order was concerned. People feared the police since it was under the commands of the tyrants but crimes of thefts, murders, lootings, rapes, etc. were solved within a meaningful time horizon failing which the concerned officers were taken to the task. Likewise, the District Administration despite being pro-British was alert and cautious in ensuring to it that the social, cultural and religious sensitivities of Indians were not hurt. In the same way, the judiciary also was serving the cause of justice save in cases where the interest of the British Government was at stake. When India became free, our bureaucracy, judiciary, legislature and the media too became free along with people and institutions. Some of the legislators took government officials as their subordinates and compelled them to oblige them at every cost. Due to excessive interference of some of the Ministers, elected representatives and the higher ups, the police and Para-military forces became docile and lethargic. Many NGOs took administrative machinery to task in the wake of excesses. Several Government Officials had to face inquiries in connections with false encounters, custodial deaths and excessive use of force as a result of which many in administration became over cautious. The criminals and the mafia took the advantage of the leniency shown by the governing structure as a consequence of which crimes multiplied in the country. Besides, country's police and Para-military forces are generally employed in curbing communal riots, suppressing Naxalites and fighting terrorists. They are very often used in controlling processions, protecting guests and important dignitaries, managing traffic, participating in ceremonial parades and serving VIPs and VVIPs. They have little time to curb crimes. Over and above this, the ruling coalition governments are involved in saving their skins and the opposition parties are waiting for the opportunity to topple them. As a result of all these factors the whole structure of the country has become shaky. It would not be wrong to say that whatever little good was left in the sphere of governing structure, social customs, cultural practices, moral conceptions and religious notions is now at the verge of decadence.

**The Law and Order is Bit Shaky**

Law and order is the essence of every civilised society. No civilisation can survive without the backing of a strong law enforcing agency. Unluckily our internal condition is not very encouraging. We are facing sundry troubles in the shape of ethnic and caste troubles, farmers protest against the acquirements of their agricultural lands, demands for reservation, tussles between various segments raising the bogy of sons of the soil, demonstrations by various groups in support of linguistic states, protests by students demanding union elections and processions by house wives against rising prices. These are healthy signs because they reflect the agility and dynamism of our democratic system. Our trouble, however, is that our police and other law enforcing agencies are under heavy strain. Many cases of suicides have been reported among Para-military forces due to excessive pressure. It has also been noted in recent days that people are not joining police force in large quantity due to professional hazards. There is an acute shortage of trained and efficient police personnel as a consequence of which law and order has become a bit shaky. The news channels and the local papers are full of murders of the senior citizens committed by their domestic servants, kidnapping by friends and relatives to get ransom, suicides by depressed and frustrated people and elopements by lovers of different castes and religions. Criminals are seldom caught and punished at right times due to police laxity and political interference. Besides the conviction rate of the crimes too is insignificant. The crimes are also flourishing because the cases are decided in law courts in years due to the large number of pending cases and the shortages of the judges. Besides, money power, muscle power and political power play an important role in the multiplication of the crimes in the country. We do not have a proper law to protect the whistle blowers hence many people are not coming forward to expose the mafia and the musclemen. Those RTI activists who tried to bring unsocial people to book had to lose their lives. We have heard about blatant violations of election codes during the recently concluded parliamentary elections, 2014 in the country. Everybody in the country realise that our administrative system is virtually at the verge of collapse. The basic problem with our country is that our police force and governing structure have not been designed for a democratic system. They have been designed on colonial patterns and hence they do not suit our democracy nicely. Many hot-headed officers treat Indians as if they are not worthy citizens. If one happens to go to a few police stations where Station House Officers are autocratic, one is considered a criminal unless and until one proves ones innocence. During British rule it was difficult to enter the government offices because it was said that one should not dare to knock the doors of government officials without acquaintances else one would either be welcomed by the barking dogs or caught by the alert guards. The same is more or less true even in democratic India. Many government officials are living a stylish life at government expenses. They enjoy high class travel and hotel facilities and live in posh bungalows. They keep themselves away from general public as the British Officials used to keep people at arm's length and behave as if they are superior. They are followed by guards and army of subordinates to give the impression of their dignity and grace. Gandhiji impressed upon the public that in Free India the government officials shall be the servants of the public and the general public shall be the sovereign body. He emphasised that they would work in simple offices, their lifestyle would be unassuming and they would be honest, just, bold and transparent.

Alas! We are too far from the expectations of the Father of Nation. Our governing structure has no will to streamline its functions compatible with the requirements of the democratic state. Besides, Indians too have discarded their inherent qualities and viable systems one by one which sustained them for so long as progressive and prosperous people. In such a situation, the need of the hour is that we should develop in *Aam Aadmi* the liking for simple living and high thinking, reverence for the elders, love for the younger, respect for women, usefulness of the joint family system, utility of the viable neighbourhood, charms of the indigenous ways of living, sanctity and purity of our educational system and importance of sound governing structure. Besides they should also be made aware of the relevance of social system, significance of cultural norms, solemnity of moral values and gravity of spiritual practices which strengthened the foundations of Indian society since time immemorial. It is highly regrettable that under the impact of new values and new challenges brought about by New World Order the solid pillars upon which our country was firmly based are falling and there are no signs that things are converging towards a philosopher's stone that will cause all the pieces to fall neatly into place.

# 5 The New World Order is Impacting Us

It appears that our learned countrymen are not fully aware about the New World Order. It is so devastating in nature that wherever it triumphed it flattened the age-old social and cultural systems and time-tested practices and heartfelt values. It destroyed many cultures; civilisations and ways of living, ruined many customs, traditions and ethos and dented several people, groups and nations. Even the Christianity has lost much of its grace and glory due to the onslaught of this monster. Since our culture and style of living are posing a formidable challenge to the liberal and permissible ways of living, produced by the New Order, the vested interests are bent upon to make our culture, systems and values irrelevant and redundant. We should not forget that we belonged to that group of civilised people who were highly cultured and had an appreciation for arts, literature, painting, sculpture, music, religion, technology, sciences, politics, psychological perspectives, behaviour patterns as well as to the promoting of development and to the totality of society's achievements. We were highly cultured and civilised and our culture and civilisation were all-pervading, all-embracing and all-encompassing. It is only very lately that most of us have adopted materialistic and narrow concepts of culture under the influence of New World Order. We have generally begun to call those people as cultured who are highly educated, rich and famous forgetting the fact whether they are economically, politically, socially and culturally enlightened or not. We too have chosen to define human life as a mere physical entity in the corporal world and values it in terms of only material satisfaction and hence our culture too has become primitive and rudimentary regardless of how economically, politically and technologically advanced we might be.

We should recall that our Indian Order was rooted in principles and it pertained to higher moral, spiritual and aesthetical values of life. We had faith in Supreme deity, we believed in authenticity of the scriptures, genuineness of the *Avatars*, saints and holy men and had conviction in the Philosophy of *Karma.* We claimed that the divine truth prevailed in every corner of the world including India, China, Africa, Australia, America and every part of the world. We were convinced that it could be unthinkable that human beings were left unguided. We emphasised that the same Inexpressible and Unthinkable Reality which different people call by different name was perceived in some form or the other by different people following varied customs, traditions, religions, belief systems and life styles as well as possessing different cultural backgrounds, conceptual frameworks and historical perspectives. We also affirmed that the world without a sound value system would be a void. It would be impossible to govern the world without all pervading governing principles for man can be controlled only by man himself and by creating in him the love for truth, justice and equity. The whole social, economic, political, moral, spiritual and cultural order of ours was based on above premises. Unfortunately, under the impact of the invasion of New World Order we are forgetting most of our precious heritage.

## The Invasion of the New World Order

Our countrymen should know that the New World Order is highly enticing, hypnotising, mesmerising and appealing especially to the younger generation. It attracts the younger minds in the same way as magnet attracts the iron. It would not give them much but take away everything from them. We should not be ignorant of the fact that the West has lost much of its glamour under the influence of this order and it is a spent force. The New World Order corrupted the Western Civilisation based on time tested values and created a new civilisation which is materialistic in nature and which produced a climate for Western type of economic democracy within *Laissez Fare* frame of reference and a liberal and permissive mind-set along with faith in reason and science as the vital means to understand the world. The whole idea of the so-called modern civilisation and culture is based on the theme that believing in reason and science is the only solution of making sense of the realities of the world which means that those matters which reason and science cannot explain are senseless. This horrible concept of rationality not only posed a great challenge to the traditional and religious authorities of Judaism, Christianity, Islam and Hinduism but also denied any Biblical, *Vedic*, *Quranic* or spiritual basis for truth. The rationalists held that faith and belief systems were based on a very shaky foundation since they revolved around some inexpressible and unexplainable matters that could not be established by senses and thus could not be established by reason. Likewise, they were grounded on the notion of Almighty which could not be seen therefore could not be proved by science. They thus, replaced the religious and spiritual concepts by the materialistic and universalised ideas which in effect were the ancient forms of perverted religions without God. The followers of the contemporary version of the New Era or Modern Era which was shaped by European exploration of the non-European world, Italian Renaissance, Reformation and the scientific exploration of the natural world, tried to create a global and universal civilisation or global and universal empire based on universal human rights called universal religion without God both at home and abroad which subjected people to reason and science and not to higher and absolute truth brought by the Holy Men and taught by the scriptures. The new religion of the Era was being popularised by the liberals, academia, media and globalists as well as the liberal democrats of America and Europe. The New Era or Modern Era or the post-modern era also saw the decline of the Classical and Western traditions both in Europe and America as well as in the rest of the world. The Post Modern Era saw the emergence of Information Age supported by intellectual and technological developments together with the massive increase in the number of the students in the American and European universities and the huge expansion of popular culture assisted by the liberal media. The liberty and equality of individuals, individual freedom, concepts of human rights and human dignity and the entry of women in large number in the co-educational institutions and their seeking jobs in full time ventures as well as the availability of contraceptives and legalising of abortions led to the emergence of strong feminist movements which changed the entire perspective of the world. Various judgements of the Supreme Courts of America and Europe created massive conflicts between the church and the state and removed Christianity from public domain. The spread of liberal democracy, emergence of human right activists, and prevalence of free-markets led to the development of several secular institutions supported by so-called neo-religious democracies and neo-religious commercial markets which were not only independent of church and state but were also independent of each other.

Thus, the New World Order with its newly-created denominations and the institutions has produced a modern belief system which asks the enlightened secular and liberal elites to bring about human betterment on a global scale by tempting or even forcing the people of the world to form a single community enjoying universal human rights without involving the faith. This new system suits the interests of the American and European corporations which have moved in non-European and non-American markets with diverse cultures and ideologies for fresh business. In societies like India, China, Middle East and North Africa, they cannot succeed without flattening their cultures and religions. These multi-national and multicultural business magnates, therefore, want to link them with progressive, global and universal ideas and ideals and not with traditional and religious concepts. Instead of Western civilisation which was based on faith, they have created a global civilisation in which the multi-cultural and business magnets would create a unique empire in the shape of powerful governing structure and universally acceptable religion without God supported by universal human rights. The Western society has justified and even legitimised many irreligious, immoral and unethical notions which were the basis of traditional and old belief systems. It has also redefined objectives of educational policy, the philosophy of human conducts, the sphere of morality and ethics and the domain of social, cultural, and political systems in the light of corporate spirit, liberal democracy, individual freedom and human rights which have enough potentials not only to flatten Oriental civilisations but also destroy the cultures of rest of the world.

## The Salient Features of the New World Order

The New World Order is a beautiful trap. It has been based on rationality principle, separation of church and state, man-made criteria for right and wrong, individual freedom, liberal democracy, *Laissez Faire*, human rights, equality of genders, materialism and modern education. If our children are not made aware of its shaky, untenable and faulty foundations there is every likelihood that they would be caught on the wrong foot with disastrous consequences. We should therefore ponder over some of the Fundamental Principles and the determinants of the New World Order in the following pages.

## The Principle of Rationality

The World Order is based on the premise that only that is true which can be felt by five sense organs and which can be established by reason and scientific inquiry. According to this notion since universal creator, *avatars,* after-life, etc., can neither be felt by any of the sense organs nor proved by empirical enquiry, they are mere conjectures. Needless to say that the above description is absolutely fallacious because there are innumerable realities of life which can neither be seen by us nor felt by our senses. Besides, we do not see and perceive many things in the world but still we believe on the basis of the sayings of others. For instance, we believe in atoms, dark matter, negative energy, etc., on the basis of the claims of the scientists that they had observed them and found them to be true though we have neither seen them nor can we perceive them by our senses. As against this, the scientists and the rationalists do not believe in unknown realities on the basis of the claims of the theologians, philosophers and the religious thinkers when they say that they had observed and experienced the eternal and spiritual truths with the help of their special senses and special techniques and found them to be correct. We forget that just as an individual can perceive many scientific truths with the knowledge of science, scientific training and scientific instruments similarly, the ordinary people too can conceive the immaterial objects and eternal truths with spiritual knowledge, spiritual training and spiritual methods. Just as there are special instruments to perceive special scientific objects and phenomena so also there are special senses in human body and special procedures in the realm of spiritualism to conceive immaterial and religious truths and phenomena. Over and above this, see the damage that has been caused to humanity by such ideas and ideologies. It is because of the principle of rationality that Europe, America and several countries which are under the influence of the superiority of science and reason over theology, religion and philosophy have become faithless. God has been mostly banished from their day to day affairs, Christianity has taken back seat, churches have become empty, papal authority is merely in name sake and the ancient forces of pride, rebellion and eat, drink and be merry have resurfaced in the garb of materialistic philosophy.

It is irony of fate that despite the intellectual advancement people are not perceiving that we cannot create any superstructure of science, culture, morality or philosophy without an unfailing belief in some system and without uniting mankind on a common plane as an extended family and without believing in Scriptures laying norms as well as without accepting holy men, *avatars* and guiding principles and without recognising the sacred places for convergence. All important religions and belief systems of the world have been based on belief in some deity, faith in some scripture, recognition of some guide and the existence of some religious centre. For example, Judaism has Javeh as Lord, Old Testament as scripture and Moses as a prophet and Jerusalem as a religious centre. Likewise, Christianity has Trinity to represent God, Bible as scripture, Jesus as prophet and Jerusalem as a centre; Islam has Allah, *Quran,* Holy Prophet and Mecca; Hinduism has *Om, Gita,* Krishna and Virandavan and also Ishwar, *Ramayana,* Ram and Ayodhya and Sikhs have Wahe Guru, *Granth Sahib,* Guru Nanak and Amritsar. Unity in God binds people across the world into the fold of one big family. People begin to consider the entire humanity as the sect of brothers and sisters created by the same Lord with variations in colour, sex, and place of birth or other physical, economic, social and cultural differences. They can think of a common structure of the society based on common bondage. They can frame their rules and regulations in the light of their scriptures and guidance's of their warners. They can share the resources of the world among themselves as equals considering the world resources as being the trust bestowed by Lord. They can boast of forming one world government or one civilisation or one culture for human betterment. History testifies that all fountains of knowledge, wisdom and intellect sprouted from the religious centers and the main sources of education, training, upbringing and ethics, morality, spirituality, contentment, salvation as well as peace, progress, development, harmony and co-existence were the synagogues, churches, monasteries, mosques and religious places. Man could not learn by his own efforts all the secrets of nature, mysteries of human body, cures of diseases, qualities of vegetations, minerals, liquids, gases, fruits, flowers, medicines and food articles without guidance from above. Thus, the world culture, civilisation and world order have emerged mainly from religious sources rather than the secular streams.

The world has seen that people can be temporarily united on the basis of emergencies, personal interests or common fears but such bonds break down on the slightest cracks. As against this, the blood ties, family and social bonds, cultural affinities, religious affiliations, national loyalties are relatively more stable as they have strong backings of parents, families, society, culture, religions and nations. Those intellectual elites or multi-national and multi-cultural business magnets who are trying to shape Global Civilisation or Universal Empire or Universal Religion without God or Global Governance or Olympian World Order by forcing people to form one community at global level for human betterment based on universal enjoyment of human rights would fail miserably because the democratic and commercial spirit would not be able to sustain such structures for too long. The emergence of the Soviet Union as an alternative system to Western culture and civilisation shook the political and economic foundations of Europe and America. It created two world blocks and led to the Cold War for a considerable period of time.

However, since the Socialist block too was based on atheism, materialism and anti-Christ values, it collapsed due to the weight of its own superstructure. Cracks have started appearing in the family system, social structure, cultural and moral connotations, and the institutional frameworks of the faithless, materialistic and eat, drink and be merry type New World Order based on narrow and parochial considerations. Negation of God, disrespect to church, disregard to moral and spiritual values and excessive reliance on material and worldly considerations would shatter the so-called New World Order of the Western World in the near future. The world would soon realise the need of guiding principles and if they did not exist, they would invent them.

## Separation of the State and the Church

The scientists and the rationalists also emphasised that religious and worldly lives should be separated. The day to day life should come under the purview of the state and the religious one under churches, temples, mosques, synagogues, monasteries and other religious sects. The concept of dividing the religious and worldly lives in water tight compartments is based on wrong notions. Life is a composite whole and it cannot be divided into parts, sections and segments. It is true that bread, butter, clothing and shelter are highly essential for human beings but equally important are his social, cultural, moral, aesthetic, political and spiritual needs. Man also requires the compassion of blood relations, support of family system, sanction of social customs, need for political authority, and help of the moral principles and the guidance of the spiritual values. Besides, every act of mankind has multiple aspects such as secular, political, social, economic, moral and religious. For instance, to acquire bread for the family is a physical necessity but it is not immune from emotional considerations because it is obtained for kith and kin. Likewise, it cannot be devoid of legal, moral and spiritual connotations because bread has to be secured through legal means as well as without exploiting and hurting people and without violating moral and spiritual norms. Actually divisions and water-tight compartments cannot be made between the Church and the State. Just as all human actions whether they pertain to faith or worldly matters are interlinked so also the functions of the state and the church. The state should be as much involved in religious values of people as the church should be mindful of the worldly affairs of human society.

Thus, for a healthy functioning of any system a harmonious blending of the secular authority of the State and the religious powers of the Church are highly essential. Merely, by finding out certain faults in the functioning of the religious authorities and highlighting the contribution of the state neither we can undermine the significance of the church nor over estimate the role of the state. The Church and the State both are the integral part of the society and they shall have to play their roles in tandem for the betterment of mankind and any effort to create divisions between them would lead to the disastrous consequences. We have a beautiful blending of faith and worldly affairs in our Constitution. The State guarantees Freedom of religion, worship and conscience and side by side performs all its secular and worldly affairs without any hindrance. Such a nice blending of secular and religious matters is the need of the time.

## Basis of Moral Norms

The rationalists also claim that right and wrong and good and bad are the creations of man and not the super imposed concepts. They hold that customary values, moral norms and spiritual ideas were not conveyed by the higher authority but they were evolved over time through the process of consensus between the stake holders and as such they are not sacrosanct but flexible and changeable over time. History testifies that these concepts are eternal. They have existed since time immemorial. Different societies possessing different paraphernalia, varying ethos and unique legends and separated through acts and events had such notions engraved on their mental canvases. We find such concepts practically among all the societies across the world whether they were primitive or advanced ones. How different segments of human society possessed common moral and ethical norms when they were not known to one another and there was no contact between them. It can be explained only when we believe in their common source and common origin. Save this we cannot explain why we have been guided and cajoled by our consciences since time immemorial. It appears that humanity got them through their saints, guides, gurus, *avatars* and warners in the form of epics and religious books. The man-made criteria could not satisfy all the stakeholders with diverse perceptions and contradictory interests. The superimposed criterion of good and bad is the only criterion which humanity has followed since eternity and it is the only standard which should determine our course of actions. We should not be led by the modern concepts which are based on wrong premises and as such they are biased, defective and untenable.

## Basic Unit of the Society

The modern thinkers also believe that the basic unit of any civilised group is an individual and not the group or society. According to this concept the freedom of the individual in secular and religious matters as well as his equality before law irrespective of his society or national considerations should be guaranteed. This principle too is misleading because man being an integral part of human society is subject to social constraints. We have seen that there are several countries in the world such as USA, Europe, and Norway which in the name of freedom of individuals panalise even parents for punishing or threatening to punish their children below 18 years. Recently, Chandrasekhar got 18 months jail term and his wife Anupuma 15 months in Oslo court for ill-treating their seven year child. In such countries there is none to control the misdeeds of children and spouses for the parents fear to question their sons and daughters and the husbands are afraid of their wives due to the stringent laws. We have been hearing since unknown times that man is a social animal. We cannot conceive him apart from the society. He lives in the families, converses with the neighbours, interacts with friends, colleagues and well-wishers and participates in religious, social, political and cultural functions in groups with others. His interests lie in the welfare of the group and not merely in his own personal well-being. The society affects his behaviour pattern and his action too affects the society. He cannot absolve himself from the responsibilities of the society. The story goes like this;

> *Several people were sitting in the boat which was crossing the river. When the boat reached the middle of the river one of the occupants decided to blow a hole in the boat under his feet thinking that it was his prerogative. Having seen him doing that people rushed to him and stopped him from doing that. He insisted that he was not making holes under their feet but under his own which should not worry them. The occupants replied that he could not be given that liberty because if he was allowed to do so others would also get drowned in the water along with him.*

A man cannot be permitted to move without clothes through localities that are frequented by females and children. He cannot be allowed to play with loud music in the middle of the night when others are sleeping. He cannot be provided freedom to light his house when there is general black out due to the fear of enemy attack in the night. Admittedly, societies are the basic units and the individual liberties and freedoms are always subject to social, cultural, moral and spiritual considerations because human beings live in groups, societies and countries and the individuals have to adjust themselves within the constraints of these organisations. We are finding that the unrestrained freedoms of the individuals are causing havoc in the society. The concept of individual liberty has broken many families, destroyed several homes and uprooted many institutions.

**Liberal Democracy**

The rationalists accepted the liberal democracy as the most acceptable form of governance and rejected all the authoritarian types of regimes such as kingship, individual or party dictatorship, religious rule and aristocracy. Liberal democracy has surely benefitted many nations being the government of the people by the people for the people. However, many experts suggest that it is a *Laissez Faire* concept. It benefits only haves at the cost of have-nots or those who are numerically or otherwise strong. History shows that when it is converted into the rule of the majority segment, it harms those sections that are numerically weak. When it becomes a mob rule it breaks all the standards of governance and when it is converted in oligarchy or the rule of few stalwarts, the people suffer immensely. Experience teaches us that in developing countries too much emphasis must not be given to the word liberal but the social aspects of the democracy should be highlighted. Mere numbers are not enough to run the government. Behind the numbers there must be some corrective mechanism so that those who have no voice may also be heard. The capitalist type of economic democracy does not suit the marginalised sections of the society. The democracy should have checks and balances so that it may benefit even the downtrodden and the handicapped sections of the society. Facts reveal that as far as the interest of general public is concerned, that form of government proves better which is run by all the segments of the society for all the sections of the people through just and transparent governing mechanism controlled by the elected representatives.

### *Laissez Faire* Economy

It is a fact that free-market economy or *Laissez Faire* type system or globalisation as suggested by the modernists cannot be regarded as the most ideal form of instrument for growth and development across countries and regions. The concept of globalisation is based on the rule of jungle or the principle of survival of the fittest. It benefits those that are strong and destroys those that are weak. The humanity has seen that once upon a time there was free-market economy which mostly benefitted the rich at the cost of the poor. The capitalistic economy was dented by Soviet type of Communist economy but it has resurfaced. This system works well if all the participants are equally strong and powerful otherwise the balance of trade and payment will always remain in favour of mighty countries at the cost of weaker nations. Moreover, in modern days, wherever globalisation has been imposed upon the weaker countries they have suffered immensely.

### Human Rights

The concept of Human Rights is dominating the world scene. It is alleged that it is the invention of the Super Powers to impose their culture and ways of living upon traditional and religious societies with a view to flatten them. Experience shows that the conventional social, economic, political and cultural systems of various countries have been uprooted in the name of human rights by these vested powers. It is the belief of the human right experts that enlightened intellectuals can bring about human betterment on a global scale through human rights by forming a single community or universal empire or global governance or universal religion without God. They believe that various societies possessing varying customs, values and belief systems cannot be united on a common platform. They can be brought at par only when their social, cultural and religious differences are ironed out and they are equipped with new concept of human rights. This approach of the liberals is defective in the sense that social, cultural, moral and religious connotations are so strong that they cannot be flattened by transitory concepts like individual freedom etc. It is stated by several experts that the concept of human rights is a wonderful idea, if it operates within limits but when it is extended to extreme limits it proves harmful to the society. It is very difficult for the ancient and conservative societies to tolerate the interference of the state or governing structure or third agency in their religious, domestic, social and cultural fields. They cannot tolerate any interference in matters of rights and duties of their women, children and elders, meddling with their marriage and social customs and bungling in religious and ethical matters. Likewise, these societies can hardly allow their members to live life as they desire violating all the established norms of the society. Conservative and the traditional societies allow human rights within the constraints of their established systems, conventions and practices. They claim that one cannot become a good Human Right activist and observer without the support of clean conscience. No power or philosophy on earth can make us just, honest and conscientious without the support and basis of belief systems. In a faithless system one can be compelled to honour human rights by the deterrent power of the state but if the state becomes weak or its dictates are not obeyed, the whole idea of the human rights becomes redundant.

**Feminist Movement**

My countrymen! Modern society has strengthened the feminist movements by giving women equal rights vis-à-vis men in economic, social, political, sexual, spiritual and religious and personal matters with a view to stop their discrimination. However, several Indians believe that the notion of equality of sexes is also based on misleading notions. Nature has not made men and women equal but made them different. It created women more powerful in love, emotions, patience, tolerance and sacrifices since they were destined to become mothers and made men rough and tough for they were to build houses, earn livelihood and protect the families. Thus, instead of equal rights, it gave them equitable rights according to their needs and necessities. It gave them what was due to them. In some areas it gave more powers to females and in other areas it equipped men with greater authority. If equal benefits, facilities and rights were provided to all created beings there would have been chaos in the society.

The story says,

*Moses was once upon a time highly worried and perturbed having seen the inequality between rich and poor. He prayed Lord to make all the people of the world equal in riches as well as other aspects. The prayers of Moses were heard and all the people became equally wealthy and resourceful in all respects which gave immense satisfaction to the Prophet. Once Moses had collected enough load of important material which he wanted to carry to his home. It was so heavy that he could not carry it by himself. He called every passerby and requested him to help him to carry his weight up to his house in lieu of money but nobody responded. Moses prayed Lord to send some labourer to his help. The Lord expressed His inability telling him that nobody was willing to work as a labourer since everyone was well off. Lord reminded Moses that He himself was responsible for the mess for it was on his behest that all people were made equal in riches and comforts hence he should bear it. Lord further told him that He in His Wisdom did not make all people equal in all respects. To some he gave more wealth but loaded with excessive worries, to a few he gifted with better health but confronted with hard work, to many he provided sound sleep but kept them in extreme poverty and to many he bestowed with comforts of governance but imposed diseascs. Moses prayed Lord in extreme anxiety to restore His previous order to make the world functional.*

Thus, interfering in nature's Plan with reference to the rights and duties for sexes too would lead mankind to chaos and confusion. Man should be equipped with those rights that they need most and they are extremely useful to them and women should be blessed with those rights and duties that are conducive and beneficial to them. Indian society has beautifully blended the rights and duties of males and females. It made the man lord of the house being the earning member and the protector of the family and made the woman queen of the house to manage the household affairs and to rear children and to look after them. Likewise, it bestowed rights and duties upon fathers, husbands, brothers and sons suiting to their needs and temperaments and upon mothers, wives, sisters and daughters according to their requirements and mind-sets.

**Materialistic Fervour**

Most of the rationalists believe that human beings should enjoy the worldly life as much as possible by using physical and material means optimally. Nobody can deny the importance of material prosperity because wherever materialism has succeeded it made people rich and prosperous. Material well-being is highly essential for every being for without money the mare cannot go. The problem arises when we give it importance beyond what is due to it. Money is good so long it is in our pocket, it becomes bad when it pockets us. Money can certainly provide us comforts but not necessarily happiness. Too much importance of material prosperity mostly destroys the sanctity of family life, separates children from parents, create mistrust among spouses and increases divorce rates. Experience teaches us that in wealth worshipping countries it made their religious places empty, shattered their social and cultural institutions and shook their moral and spiritual beliefs. It gave many people blood pressures, diabetes, heart attacks, cancer and dreaded diseases. It debarred many from sweets, rich protein diets, and oily substances, and delicious fruits, comforts of cushioned beds and benefits of luxurious life. In a sense, man got prosperity but lost relations, neighbours, friends, well-wishers, peace of mind and the charms of harmonious life and the benefits of composite culture. Today he is alone in the crowd of people, dejected and frustrated. No sensible man would plead for this type of life for the human beings.

Man is a social, cultural, moral and spiritual being. He needs a holistic concept of life covering all phases of life for his meaningful living.

**Modern Education System**

Secular education was considered by the modern society as a suitable means to develop the physical, mental and aesthetical calibres of the individuals and groups and to make them enlightened citizens. Ironically, modern education in India was introduced by Lord Maculay in 1835, to form a special section of anglicised Indians who were Indians in blood, colour and origin but English in taste, culture, opinions, morals and intellect and who could be used as interpreters, facilitators and helpers between British rulers and Indian masses.

However, the fact is that the modern education which had flourished in Europe after Renaissance, French, English and American Revolutions as well as Reformation, Counter Reformation, Enlightenment and Industrial Revolution certainly exercised a constructive influence on Indian society. From eighteenth century onward elites and intellectuals in India were exposed to the ideas and philosophies of thinkers like Rousseau, Voltaire, Spencer, Burke, Locke, Mill and several others. It has made the present generation aware of what is happening around them but Modern education based on colonised British Grammar School type mode made Indians crammers, imitators and unfit for original work, innovative ideas and inventive thoughts. It put heavy strain upon their time, energy and resources and deprived them from their rights and disassociated them from their classical roots, cultural traditions, value systems, ways of living and philosophy. Many educated Indians developed apathy for the primitiveness of Indian society and developed in them the inferiority complex about the efficacy of its value system. They lost faith in Indian identities and began to consider Indian social customs and practices and ways of living as impractical, indefensible and out of date.

A revolutionary and drastic change is visible in the attitudes, values, thinking, behaviour pattern, conducts and etiquettes of neo-rich youth of elitist and rich class which has emerged in Metros and urban areas. They are alien in their own country and have not only lost faith in their families, neighbours and colleagues but also in themselves. They follow mostly the Western style, foreign value system and American and European ways of living. Their primary aim is to fully enjoy sensual pleasures of worldly and material life at any cost without any hindrance, restrictions, social bondage and comment on their doings. Many of them have become undisciplined, intolerant, aggressive, violent, selfish, self-willed, arrogant and corrupt. Thus, we can neither depend upon modern education nor consider it as our saviour since it has given us material prosperity but has snatched from us many things including our precious heritage.

The author has highlighted the various salient features of the New World Order and it is hoped that they would help the learned readers to come to the conclusion that the pillars on which the New World Order is based are not only fragile and feeble but also infirm and shaky. They would fall down one day along with the whole super structure with disastrous consequences.

**The Strategies to Impose the New World Order**

It is a fact that Europe and America especially the whole Christendom was highly perturbed due to the emergence of Communism in Europe and Asia since it was posing a challenge to Christian culture, Christianity and Christian ways of living. The forces supporting Christian civilisation tried their best through wars and Cold Wars to topple communism. However, when they succeeded history took a curious turn and globalisation, Christian culture and Western ways of living triumphantly penetrated into the bounds of emerging nations. The non-Western Nations which were following their own patterns of development had no options but to follow the Western modes of democratic governments and human rights and aspired to achieve the latest technology, market driven economy and irresistible mass culture. Many developing nations in fact reverted back to free play of market forces, abandoned controlled and mixed economic models and indulged in high mass consumption along with adopting democratic means of governance and showing commitment towards the utility and the usefulness of human rights. The impact of commercialisation, opening of the economies to private domestic and foreign segments as well as restricting trade union practices and curbing public sector undertakings damaged much of the socialistic and classical ideas and ideologies. Even the Communist Parties in sheer disgust brought about tremendous changes in their outlooks and molded their strategies according to the needs of times. Along with achieving excellence in the field of science and technology and removing poverty, diseases and hunger from the masses and providing them progress and prosperity, there was a strong desire in the emerging nations to mark their presence in each and every field at the global level as equal participants even at the cost of their past heritages, value systems, indigenous cultures, ways of living and religious notions.

The vested interests also created much chaos at global level and caused heart burning and misunderstanding by floating the idea that there was a mighty clash between civilisations. The clash of civilisation theory suited the vested interests and fitted in well with the geo-political interests of certain super powers. The aversion towards Muslims was understandable for until the emergence of Soviet Union there was none to challenge the Western ideology except Islam. Islam was not only posing military threat to Europe but the Arab World was intellectually and culturally superior to the Christian philosophy and provided an alternative model for emulation. It was because of this reason that a climate of enmity was created and it was supported by senseless acts of violence by some radical Muslims in some countries. Even the political and cultural conflicts within Muslim countries too were not only projected as the byproducts of radical Islam but they were also shown as the chief threats to global peace. Actually, it was not Islam but the ghost of faithlessness and the urge of the vested interests to impose their culture upon others that were haunting Europe and America.

Just as the West tried to impose its culture through dubious means upon Islamic countries, in the same way, the Western nations want to contain India, China and other African countries because they are thinking that these regions would emerge on the world scene in near future after the decline of the West with revenge for the atrocities committed by them in the past. They are, therefore, taking the help of globalisation to flatten these countries. The West believes that globalisation would make the world identical and the market forces, keen competition, emergence of new products and new technologies would make the national borders redundant and diminish the power of national governments by increasing the demand for foreign goods and services. The demand for branded goods, fast food, luxury cars, entertainment units, fashion items, alcoholic products, casinos, mighty mansions and quest for individual prosperity would outstrip every other demand and eventually diminish the importance of religion, ideologies, ethos, customs, traditions, cultural values and nationalistic fervor.

Certainly, the demand for foreign goods and services has increased in the developing countries during the last few years even at the cost of national products causing lack of effective demand and leading to unemployment as well as inequality of incomes. However, these countries have not fully succeeded in their ventures. The adverse affects of globalisation, unfavourable terms of trade against the weaker countries and the weak bargaining position of Afro-Asian countries have put their national governments on the defensive. Consequently, the state intervention, restrictive trade practices, protectionist policies and the authoritative political segments have raised their heads to minimise the effects of *Laissez-Faire* forces. Even the advanced countries were not immune from manipulating their ailing economies. Despite the fact that the markets and the technologies have been integrated through the process of franchises, market forces and transfer of technologies, the backlash of globalisation has been very severe and brutal. The world, in place of becoming similar and homogeneous, has become differentiated and divided in camps, regional groups and political alignments.

## The Game Plan has not Suceeded So Far

It is clear from the trends of history that so far the vested interests have not succeeded in their game plan. They are playing the game of chess at world level with a view to protect and promote their personal interests. It is true that after the failure of Russian Revolution, most of the countries abandoned their ideologies and replaced them by pure nationalistic passions. Their quests for identities, individualities and uniqueness forced them to think about whom they were and what was their role and place in the world. There is clear-cut divide in the United States of America, Europe and Australia. The Western World as a whole is under the grip of fear psychosis. The fear of coping up with non-Western citizens in their midst and the fear of losing ground to Asians and Africans especially Indians and Chinese are haunting them beyond redemption. They are apprehensive of the emergence of Asian Power since the Asians are aspiring to carve out their place in the world history. It is the fact that hope, fear and humiliation are playing an important part in shaping the new world order but in themselves they are not enough to mould the world history. Actually, in the modern world, perceptions are more important than facts. The media is reflecting and magnifying perceptions resulting in fear, hatred and humiliations. Besides, the emotions rooted in faith, belief systems, religion, culture and ethnicity count more than reason to understand geopolitics and to shape the conduct of nations and peoples.

It is also worth noting that the West has understood the fact that with the unfolding of globalisation in the 21st Century, four competing civilisations would emerge on international scene and the new contest of these civilisations would surely and certainly dent the Western Civilisation and culture for generations to come. They believe that the Western civilisation can save it despite its all round decline provided it continues to influence the global policies through its culture and technology. They are certain that the rise of China would lead to a powerful Confucian counter-civilisation rooted in history with its influence extending from the Pacific to Africa. Similarly, the next major civilisation with strong roots in history and culture will thrive in India. The world's third largest economy would be backed by India's hard and soft power, strong demographics and a far-flung Diaspora. It would play a global role and influence the course of world history as it did during the past one thousand years between the 5th century BC and 5th century AD when the country produced two great geniuses namely Buddha and Mahavira, the two great epics—the *Ramayana* and *Mahabharata* and the two great emperors Asoka and Chandragupta. Lastly, the civilisation which would compete for space and significance would be Islam. There is resurgence of Islam from Morocco to Indonesia and it is expected that the moderate Islam with its influential culture and value system would shape the destiny of many nations and regions in the world.

They know that West equipped with American and European value system can contain China, India and Islam with its strong world-wide influence and rapidly growing stature provided its culture and civilisation are embraced by these emerging countries with zeal and enthusiasm. They are afraid that as the time is elapsing, the reverse process is accelerating due to stagnation in Europe and the vibrant growth in India and China. They are certain that in the new scenario the West with its declining man power and its dwindling resources would remain globally shaky. The only way they can salvage their position is through its strong technology and vibrant culture. Thus, they earnestly feel that before it, that India and China and Islamic countries would be restored to their past glory, they should corrupt their cultures and civilisations and flatten their social, cultural, moral and religious differences so that the West may resemble with East, South and North as gold resembles with gold and silver with silver. They have partly succeeded in damaging us and our heritage but so far not much damage has been done and still there is time. If we awake we can save our golden past as well as surge in the race for peace, progress and prosperity and leave the lasting imprint upon the annals of history.

Our distinctiveness is in our unique ideologies, strong belief system, vibrant culture, rich heritage, marvelous architecture, modesty of our ladies, melody of our music, grace of our manpower, sweetness of our language, charm of our customs, piety of our religious institutions, harmony of our peaceful coexistence, grace of our dress code, beauty of our etiquettes, purity of our diets and humility of our character. With our unique identity we provide an alternative vision before the world which is highly appealing and challenging. The world is anxiously looking at us as one of the most important prospective pioneers and the champions of the new world order. Our tragedy is that the world wants to see us on the top but we are dragging ourselves towards the lowest of the low. We have become like Joneses and there is little difference between us and the rest of the people who are drifting towards chaos and confusion. However, we should not forget our glorious past, the contribution of our splendid ancestors, the role of our culture and civilisation in shaping the destiny of the world. If we forget that we shall lose everything.

In this context I would like to quote Nehruji from what he wrote in Discovery of India,

> *"We can never forget the ideals that have moved our race, the dreams of the Indian people through the ages, the wisdom of the ancients, the buoyant energy and love of life and nature of our forefathers, their spirit of curiosity and mental adventure, the daring of their thought, their splendid achievements in literature, art, and culture, their love of truth and beauty and freedom, the basic values that they set up, their understanding of life's mysterious ways, their toleration of others ways than theirs, their capacity to absorb other peoples and their cultural accomplishments, to synthesise them and develop a varied and mixed culture; nor can we forget the myriad experiences which have built up our ancient race and lie*

*embedded in our subconscious minds. We will never forget them or cease to take pride in that noble heritage of ours. If India forgets them she will no longer remain India and much that has made her our joy and pride will cease to be."*

Finally, I would like to conclude this chapter from Rabindranath Tagore's "Gitanjali."

"Where the mind is without fear and the head is held high,
Where knowledge is free,
Where the world has not been broken up into fragments by
narrow domestic walls,
Where words come out from the depth of truth,
Where tireless striving stretches its arms towards perfection,
Where the clear stream of reason has not lost its way into
the dreary desert sand of dead habit,
Where the mind is led forward by thee into ever widening
thought and action-into that heaven of freedom,
My Father, Let my country awake."

# 6 Indian Economy could not Benefit *Aam Aadmi*

The greatest worry to the people of India is that nothing substantial is being done for man on the street. They assert that poverty, hunger, diseases, ignorance and superstitions are widely prevalent. Inflation, adulteration, black money, unemployment have snatched the sleep of common man. Infrastructure, transport, railways and health sectors are in bad shape.

*Dalits,* urban poor and marginalised sections of the society are facing terrible days of their lives. Rural economy is starving, inequality between rich and poor is increasing, and FDI and foreign goods have dominated Indian markets. It has become difficult for an ordinary man to meet the two ends. He is perturbed and has begun to question the men in authority about the health of the economy and his future. It appears that we have faltered somewhere in properly managing the price policy, fiscal and debt management policy, monetary policy, import and export policy and employment and investment policy of the country for the benefit of common man. We have not fully succeeded in raising the real per capita income of the people substantially and failed in reducing the gap between the rich and poor to the satisfaction of our people. We also could not prevail in maintaining regional and sectoral balance, stabilising Indian currency and creating surplus in the balance of payment. Besides, in providing job opportunities to people, giving impetus to industry, agriculture, service sector and infrastructure and maintaining its viable social customs, cultural practices, moral norms and religious practices we did not do that which was expected of us.

## Geological Layers in Indian Economy

Thinkers and philosophers are in a dilemma because the moment we ponder over the economic prosperity, social stability, cultural maturity, moral soundness and spiritual viability of India, several India's come before us. We observe an ultra modern India in the wake of Film Festivals, Beauty Contests, Television Shows, Cultural Evenings, Indian Premier Leagues (IPLs), and various pomp and shows organised by the rich and famous as well as the celebrities throughout the length and the breadth of the country. The type of gentry we see there reminds us of Hollywood, Las Vegas, Paris, Singapore and Hong Kong and we feel highly elevated. When we happen to pass through New Delhi, posh areas of Metropolitan cities and state capitals, modern India is projected on our mental canvas and we get immense satisfaction. We observe beautiful high ways, magnificent flyovers, majestic Malls, attractive shopping centres, splendid cars and wonderful hotels. Our delight is slightly dented when we confront Medieval India emerging before our eyes in the shape of Chandni Chowk, Bhindi Bazaar and Hazrat Ganj. We are dented when we confront rikshwa-pullers plying two to three people on their rikshwas, old cars moving in by lanes and labourers perspiring with heavy load on their backs. We pity when we observe the heaps of dirt in the corners of the streets, the leaking municipal pipes in plenty and the hawkers spreading their goods on roads. We begin to think that we are where we were. We are shaken when the ancient India emerges before us in the shape of bullock carts laden with bricks, herds of a stray cows sitting on road sides and the dirty children loitering here and there. We cannot bear when we glance at the miserable condition of old people sitting on the broken cots, women in tattered clothes carrying cow dung on their heads and merchandise of iron age hanging in petty shops. We are broken down when we face women running miles and miles in search of water, farmers watching helplessly their barren fields without rains and the unemployed destitute sitting with their heads sunk under their knees in villages and huts. We lose our complete patience when we enter the Stone Age India where we observe tribal's dazed, half naked, shy and curiously gazing at the strangers. Our conscience questions us which India we wish to build and project before the world, the India of arrows and bows of Bheels of Udaipur which has not confronted the trains and trams for centuries or the India of huts and clusters of Orissa which has not seen sky-scrapers since unknown Times or the India of Panchayats and Chopals of Madhya Pradesh which has not solved the problem of drinking water or the India of Chandni Chowk and Johri Bazaar that tell us the stories of Moghul and British times or the India of Parliament, Sansads and Media which is buzzing with scams and juicy news or the India of rich and famous which deals in gems, jewels and diamonds. Alas! we have perhaps no answer.

The child in us asks. Are these country's gems, jewels, diamonds, pearls, sapphires and the heaps of gold and silver only for the famous actors and actresses, renowned celebrities and men of prominence? In whose accounts have been credited these mountains, rivers, plains, springs, valleys, deserts, forests, farms, meadows and herds of cows, buffalos and horses save some of the perverted politicians, business magnates, fraudulent builders and anti-social mafia? Is the claim of big business magnets, influential bureaucrats, famous technocrats, successful professionals and meaningful intellectuals on country's magnificent mansions, malls, food joints, cars, high ways, bank balances and health centers and educational institutions justified? What has fate destined for the farmers, peasants, artisans, petty shop keepers and labourers from the wealth and treasures of India? What portion has been assigned for the poor, needy, hungry, and destitute and the downtrodden? What has been left for *adivasis*, tribals and the people of far-flung areas? The time has come when we shall have to give the answer of this vex problem.

**The Need to Salvage the Marginalised Segments**

My inner voice says that till the tears are hanging in the eyes of the depressed farmer, lines of frustrations are lit large on his aging forehead, torn *dhoti* is around his lean body, rain water is leaking from his worn out hut, thorn is piercing in his bare leg and the fear of snake bite is haunting him while sleeping on the ground, prosperity would not come to India. Till he sleeps on grass bed in dim light, remains empty stomach most of the day and his wife cannot cover her full body, till his children die in infancy, the creditors knock his door very often, the future of his young daughter shatters him and he looks helplessly at the sky, progress would not dawn upon India. Till the poverty coax him, ignorance and superstition assault him, malaria attacks his mother, TB consumes his father, his sister remains unmarried, son does not go to the school, India cannot see happiness. Till he sinks between his knees having seen his crop destroyed through famines and thunder bolts, till he is broken by the loss of harvest due to heavy rains, cajoled by insects and pests, exploited by *dalals* in *mandis,* compelled to sell his crop to pay loans and become dazed, progress would remain away from India. Till he ploughs in scorching heat, his wife plucks weeds in noon, his kids graze buffalos in barren lands, younger daughter brings bread and onion from home and he eats under the shade of the tree half- hearted, good days would remain away from our country. Till the heaps of dirt would be mounting at his door step, mosquitoes would be hovering around, bacteria would generate in drain waters, pathways would be bumpy and slippery, village ponds would be filthy, animal caracara would rotten in the neighbourhood and the peasants would be frustrated and commit suicide, the destiny would not smile upon us.

So long as a *Dalit* remains landless, works as bonded labourer, lives in clusters of huts, insulted, humiliated and tortured, affluence would not see the face of India. So long as a downtrodden *Dalit* woman carries bricks on her head, her daughter is molested, sister is raped, husband is beaten and children pick up rags, opulence will be conspicuous by absence. So long as he is isolated, considered out cast, untouchable and unwanted and not treated equal harmony would evade the nation. So long as he earns his lively hood with broom in his hand, scavenger on his shoulders and dirt scattered around his whole body and he does not become a professional, bureaucrat and technocrat, the Indian society would suffer. So long as he would be discriminated at schools and colleges, debarred from performing his traditional and cultural ceremonies and remains handicapped in social circle luck would not laugh upon us. So long he is not visible in industry, trade, commerce and media, the nation would remain draw backed. So long as he would depend for work upon the landlords, safety and equity upon state, livelihood upon others and health and old age security upon none, the health of India would be dented.

Likewise, If some numerically small segment of the society feels discriminated, unsafe and insecure or any section of the society fears neglected, marginalised and humiliated, the country would not progress. If there are frequent riots, burning and looting of shops, murders and rapes and hatred and ill-will, the heaven would not shower its blessings. If there are custodial deaths, people are falsely implicated, innocent are sent behind the bars, the faultless and guiltless are encountered to get awards, and misery would dawn upon the country.

Similarly, when the poor and helpless are driven from villages and cities and they are compelled to live in thatched fabrications, dirty surroundings, fowl atmosphere, criminal areas and unsocial neighbourhoods of the *ghettos* and slums, the heaven weeps bitterly. When in their canvas covered bamboo houses they face heavy rains, scorching heat, biting cold, suffocating moisture, punching odour, the destiny curses us vehemently. When they neither succeed in stretching fully, nor sleep nicely, nor leisure peacefully nor live comfortably nor entertain guests respectfully, the fate laughs at us. When their huts are burnt by anti-social elements, they are thrown out of their dwellings, their belongings are scattered hither and thither and there is none to speak on their behalf, the sun, the moon and the stars drop tears. When their girls work as dancers in cabarets, sons as vagabonds, youths as criminals and elders as beggars, the country sinks to the lowest of the low. When the unfortunate parents notice the urchins peeping their half naked girls bathing at Municipal taps, goons molesting their ladies, unscrupulous police men searching their dwellings, creditors threatening their earning members, the whole environment gets dumb-founded. When they fall sick and cry for help but find no response, no money, no helper, no supporter, the nature laments badly. Despite the presence of thousands and thousands of such unfortunate Indians among us if any one claims that Indian is shining, we would call it a cruel joke.

There are millions of artisans, petty shop- keepers, lower government officials, private sector employees, hawkers, labourers, workers and ordinary people who are living in Indian cities. They are not so fortunate as the urban haves are. Many of them do not have their own houses and live in rented or government or in the outhouses. Those who have their *kachha* or *pucca* houses have no drawing, dining, guest and servant rooms. Many live in one to two bed room houses attached with kitchens and toilets. There are several houses without kitchen and toilet facilities and without electricity, gas and water connections. Many houses are without plasters, without white wash and without proper doors and windows. One would be amazed to see goats, hens, cats and men living in the same apartment with coir curtain hanging on the outer doors. On an average five to six persons live in one house and hardly there is any permanent source of income for them. All the members of the family work to meet the two ends. Children work on shops, hotels or factories or move astray, women folk either work as artisans on nominal rewards or take sub contracts or work as domestic servants and few men get occasional jobs on an average for a week or so in a month and few remain unemployed. There are some who ply rickshaws or act as hawkers or petty shop keepers and employees in government and private sectors but such people are not too many. The family expenses are met by the combined earning of the family members.

On the occasions of festivals, emergencies and marriages and sickness they face tremendous pressure and mostly resort to borrowing, the payment of which sucks their blood. Most of the members wear shabby clothes, eat course food and sleep on the floors. They can be recognised by depressed faces, lean structures and frustration appearing from their eyes. They too aspire for cars, bungalows, comforts and luxuries and pomp and show as they observe people around them with such facilities. Besides, it is they, who take part in the construction of the houses of the rich, decorating their interiors and serving them as drivers, cooks, peons, gardeners and washer men. Their misfortune is that they can neither provide adequate education to their children, nor construct their houses nor enjoy any specific entertainment facilities. Many of their members develop the habit of alcohol, drugs and gambling due to extreme frustration and cause immense harms to children and women folk. One can see chunks of such clusters in every city. No country can boast of its greatness where millions of unfortunate people suffer from birth to death and die unsung.

We have also seen miserable people in plenty like widows, orphans, divorcees, handicapped, aged, destitute, unemployed, shelter less, beggars and what not. When we notice them struggling for few loafs of bread, to partly satisfy their hunger, for few yards of clothes to partially cover their bodies and a small place to cover their heads we begin to wonder whether they are our own people living in a greatest democracy of the world which claims to be the government of the people by the people for the people or they are aliens? Alas! Nobody can deny that they are our own, our part and parcel, our kith and kin, our dearest and nearest and our hearts and souls. Their fault is that they remained behind the rat race of material prosperity for they were handicapped and were not born with silver spoons in their mouths. Besides, neither they had rich parents to look after them nor the well to do philanthropists to support them nor the governing structure to help them perhaps because they remained in the shadow areas of obscurity. When we see them begging, struggling or lying helpless at bus stands, railway stations, public parks, city crossings, our inner-self questions us whether they would remain in the same state for years to come or there would come some *Messiah* who would salvage them from their perpetual doom?

When a hungry orphan questions her mother why the fire is not on in the kitchen, mother clings him to her bosom and burst into tears. There upon the child consoles her by saying that he was not at all hungry, he merely asked her casually and assures her that he would remove all her difficulties when he would become young. After seeing this we certainly praise the genius of the child but curse our helplessness. Likewise, having observed well to do parents buying balloons of different colours, ice-creams of several varieties and chocolates of many types for their children when the child of a separated mother asks her about the whereabouts of his father and the mother fails to satisfy the child, the unfortunate child weeps and weeps and finally slumber overtakes him. We pity the child and question the separated parents: why they punished the child for what crime? Similarly, when we notice an exhausted beggar eating old and dry pieces of breads after softening them in the water, the Fundamental Rights of Indian Constitution come before us and tears role down from our eyes. In the same way, when the poor and shelterless people die in extreme heat or cold and they are buried or cremated in wilderness, we begin to question the wisdom of the people at the helms of affairs. We have read the worries written on the face of a seventy year old rickshaw puller pedaling the rickshaw with intense pain. We have watched gloom covering every inch of the existence of a girl who remained unmarried throughout her life after the death of her father. We have heard shrieks of grief and pain on the death of the earning member of a family in a destitute home. We cannot forget the agony which we observed lit large on the foreheads of the anxious parents when they were told by their unemployed son that this time also he remained unlucky and could not get the job. Our eyes have seen a minor child carrying a heavy load on his head which was virtually breaking his neck. We have not forgotten the agony of the young girl carrying a grass bundle on her head and covering her bosoms repeatedly from the piercing eyes of the vagabonds.

There are innumerable stories of the unfortunate people of India which the pen cannot portray because when it dares to write about true things which are stranger than fiction it too begins to bleed. We too cannot muster courage to highlight the misfortunes, anxieties and torments which our people across the country are facing in silence. We wish to ask our well-wishers: Can we as Indians prosper or boast of prosperity merely on the basis of the successes of a minor segment of the society when the two third population of our nation is in trouble? Do we have any responsibility towards them? If yes, then what have we done so far and why the situation is persisting?

**Neglect of the Rural Economy**

My fellow brothers! Our conscience very often cajoles us and asks us awkward questions. It asks us pointedly why our planners instead of developing the rural economy which was providing livelihood to majority of people gave more emphasis to the production of automobiles, consumer durables, fashion goods and entertainment items. When the agriculture was providing grains, pulses, oil, butter, milk, ghee, vegetables, cloth, mutton, chicken, eggs, sugar, timber, cooking fuel and all the commodities of our daily use, why did we not develop it? Why it was not strengthened when it was the greatest employer of the country? Why was it destroyed by enriching cities and making villages dependent upon them? Why they planted all the offices of the Central Government at Delhi and not in various state capitals, the Departments of the States in the state capitals and not in different districts and the governing structure at districts at district head Quarters and not at suburbs and villages? Our inner voice interrogates us who is responsible for one-way flow of manpower and resources from villages to cities at the cost of villages? Who can own the responsibility for creating favourable terms of trade in favour of the cities leaving villages neglected? Who has left villages without police force, revenue departments, schools, hospitals, markets and sanitation facilities and compelled village folks to leave their houses and settle in the slums and *ghettos* of the cities in search of livelihood when they were at ease at their sweet homes? The solution to this vex problem was the decentralised pattern of growth. Only decentralisation was ideal for the economy as a whole for in the wake of dispersal of government funds and resources at both levels there could be ideal balance of trade between rural and urban sectors. We can also say with some force that there was no logic in overcrowding cities by multi storey buildings, army of city buses, trams and metros when the clusters of beautiful suburbs well equipped by all the modern facilities could be established between the cities and villages by following the reverse model of growth. However, we keep mum because there are no takers of the reverse model of growth.

**Nerve–breaking Inflation**

An adolescence in us coax our inside time and again by saying what was the necessity of abandoning the mixed economy which we had adopted after much thought and which was most suitable for a populous country like that of ours? Why we opened Indian markets under the pressure of WTO, World Bank and other political sources when we knew that neither our agriculture nor industrial nor service sectors would be able to compete with advance countries? Is it not a fact that due to globalisation our internal prices have come up to the international level but our income levels are far behind the world standards? Consequently, with low incomes but higher prices it has become difficult for two third of Indian population to meet the two ends. The prices of vegetables, mutton, chicken, fruits and dairy products are sky rocketing. Pulses, oils, sugar and items of daily use are consuming larger portion of the budget. Cooking gas has become costly, petrol and diesel prices have gone up, electricity charges have been enhanced and the dry fruits have gone beyond the reach of many Indians. Besides, the prices of medicines and life-saving drugs which were lowest in India and which were somewhat within the reach of some commoners are touching the peak. The school, college and the university fees have gone up, donations have multiplied, restaurant charges and the cost of consumable durables have broken the backbones of the house wives and the withdrawal of subsidies given to *Aam Aadmi* under the poverty removal programme in the garb of reforms is proving the last nail in the coffins of the marginalised and downtrodden sections of the society. If one looks at Indian markets one would be surprised to see that Indian markets are full of foreign goods mostly the Chinese, Japanese and Korean products. Indians feel proud to purchase imported goods without pondering over the fact that Indian factories would be closed down one day and unemployment would increase and there would be no taker of these goods in the long run due to fall in effective demand of the people. The foreign franchisers would run away with their profits leaving the machinery and the unsold goods with their Indian counterpart. China is exporting from pin to everything of daily use to India.

Consequently, the lock industry of Aligarh, carpet industry of Bhadohi and Murshidabd, the silk trade of Banaras, Assam and Andhra, brass wares of Moradabad, Hosiery trade of Ludhiana, paper massy of Srinagar, Zari business of south, consumer durables of Ghaziabad and Noida and innumerable items produced by our petty artisans have been lying unsold. It appears that governing structure has accepted its defeat in controlling the prices. Inflation is the single most important item which is the subject of discussion of every household. It is such an acute problem that has perplexed every individuai. The history is witness to the fact that prices of onions have brought tears in the eyes of many politicians. It is feared that the rising prices will cause the fall of many politicians and political parties in the ensuing elections.

**The Problem of Adulteration**

After inflation, the next most horrible problem that is perplexing people is the problem of adulteration. Adulterating goods and services is not only heinous crime but also the greatest sin and evil. It is worse than the wars, for it kills silently more people than are killed on battle fields. Indian epics, legends and *Rishis* have always abhorred it. The whole world knows that India was one of the unique countries where people never adulterated any item of necessity, comfort and luxury due to their clear consciences. Only a few years ago our water was uncontaminated, our rivers were pollution free, our forests were refreshing, our mountains were clean, our deserts were spotless and our oceans were unviolated. Our milk was nourishing, our ghee was full of nutrients, our butter was delicious and our oil was unadulterated. Our grains and pulses were full of proteins, our vegetables were immaculate, our fruits were tasty and our flowers were full of scent. We enjoyed clean air, drank pure water, ate bacteria free food and breathed in the smoke-free environment and slept in healthy atmosphere and moved on pollution free routes. Alas! With the advent of modern civilisation and the culture of mass and extravagant consumption and demonstration effect as well as the electronic era and the rat race of becoming quick rich we have become acquisitive, pro-active and money-minded. The quest for material prosperity and the desire to become famous and rich quickly has compelled us to do everything fair or foul as a consequence of which the country is suffering from various maladies.

It has been aptly remarked that 'the healthy body possess healthy mind and healthy soul'. If the nation is healthy and robust, it produces smiling children, happy youth, brave soldiers, sturdy workers, studious students and energetic citizens. However, if its residents are sick, weak, under nourished and unfed, the country is bound to suffer in the race for growth and development. Healthy environment, clean surrounding, pollution free atmosphere and healthy infrastructure are highly essential for every civilised country. History testifies that adulteration is the biggest silent-killer of the people and it is because of this reason that in almost all the developed and advanced and civilised countries the adulteration is practicably conspicuous by absence. The citizens of those countries have controlled it by rule of law and through social awakening. We should know that adulteration is a serious matter it ruins the nation as the white ants destroy the old trees. It is not hidden from us that in every sphere the adulterated goods are being sold openly and without any check or hesitation. Our people are consuming such products knowing well that they are not genuine but fake, adulterated and injurious to their health. When they go to the market to buy vegetables, they buy even such vegetables which are grown in the gutter water and are produced by using poisonous insecticides and pesticides. Many vegetables are coloured to give them the look of freshness, several are increased in size by giving them injections and so many are preserved in the cold storages with a view to sell them at higher prices when their seasons end. Likewise, they consume adulterated fruits many of which are ripened by artificial means, some are polished by shining material, various are coloured to look bright and many are stored in the cold storages with a view to bring them in off seasons.

**Practically Everything is Adulterated**

What has happened to the consciences of the people that they are not hesitating from adulterating every conceivable item of consumption be it fruits, vegetables, milk, oil, ghee, butter, pulses, grains, flour, sugar, soaps, tooth pastes, honey, sauces, jam, drinking water, cold drinks, medicines, paints and what not. Colour is added in the chilies, refuse in the coriander powder, dust in grinded turmeric, and poisonous liquids in cooking oil, animal fats in ghee and urea and soap in milk. Petrol is adulterated by mixing kerosene and diesel by substituting other combustibles. Similarly, the soaps, tooth pastes, colours, paints, distempers and polishing items are adulterated by mixing inferior quality material. Banana is ripened by artificial means, apples are provided shining by wax, watermelons are sweetened by piercing sweetening materials, cucumber is increased in size by inserting medicines, ladies fingers are coloured to keep them green, and buffalo milk is enhanced by giving injections. In the same way, there is adulteration in the food grains and pulses. Various types of inferior materials are mixed in food grains and pulses in such a way that they may not be easily detected.

There is no limit of adulteration in medicines. Fake and adulterated syrups, tablets and life saving drugs, injections, syringes and cottons etc are openly sold in the markets. Besides, duplicate clothes, watches, toys, cells, cameras, cell phones, furniture, music items, consumer durables are available in plenty and it becomes difficult to distinguish between the fake and the real. Every year we hear several people dying by consuming spurious wine, adulterated sweets, stale food and fake medicines. Government agencies become alert for the time being but ultimately the result turns out to be zero because mostly the unscrupulous agents investigating such matters are bought with money. The government has advertently or inadvertently given the impression as if it is not very serious in the matters of hoarding, adulteration, under weighing, cheating, frauds and misrepresentations. Likewise, there is no awakening on the part of civil society to fight these menaces. It seems as if Indians have accepted their defeat at the hands of unscrupulous elements and accepted the problem of adulteration as the fact of life. The misfortune of the country is that there are NGO's and other civil agencies who could raise their voices against the government officials who have been deputed to control adulteration, under weighing, pollution and fake items but they too have become indifferent.

A genuine question can be asked to us as to why have we surrendered before the unsocial elements? We give the impression that they are more powerful than the whole nation. Our tragedy is that the government has yielded before them, the governing machinery has bowed down, our elected representatives are unconcerned, NGO's are helpless and our meaningful people who could do something are silent. There is none to give the boycott call of adulterated goods, none to cajole the consciences of the ant-social elements and none to assure us that the problem is not at all serious it can be solved with strong will, tact and firmness. Practically, all the developed and sensible people in the world have controlled this problem to their entire satisfaction. The problem with us is that we have mastered the art of making compromises and it has become our second habit to yield to those forces which we deem beyond our control. Everywhere, we have yielded considering ourselves lonely and alone in the crowd of people. We sit within the boundaries of our houses repenting, abusing and cursing but in doing nothing because we know that our relatives would not help us, our friends would not come to our rescue, our neighbours would ditch us and the government agencies would never oblige us. This helplessness of ours is making us further weak and we are gradually and gradually drifting towards the vicious circle of weakness and helplessness. There is *Aam Aadmi* uprising in the country simply because the existing paraphernalia has completely failed to put a permanent dent to such problems.

**The Transport and Insfrastructure Problems**

Transport and infrastructure problems are such problems that affect all people in one way or the other. When we look at the means of transport in the country, we get amazed having seen millions of cars, scooters and motor cycles of different models, various designs and varying costs. We can certainly boast of owning largest number of vehicles in the world compared to those possessed by several countries in Europe, Asia and Africa. Many families have a fleet of cars of various types such as luxury cars, sports cars, pick-ups, cars for picnic parties and outing and robust and sturdy cars for plying in deserts and on mountains. Likewise, several families have cars for husbands, wives, and daughter-in-laws and for sons and daughters. When we see Indian cities bursting with glittering vehicles and the young and the old sitting in air conditioned cars we feel proud as well as happy because millions of youths like us had passed major portion of their lives during fifties, sixties and seventies without scooters and cars. We were told by our leaders that we had limited resources which we needed to buy petrol for laying the solid foundation of the country rather than for using them in buying cars, scooters, motor cycles and other luxury items. We were told to sacrifice till every Indian was freed from the clutches of poverty, diseases, hunger, superstition and ignorance. The country allowed merely a few types of cars such as Ambassador, Fiat and Standard Herald and limited number of scooters such as Lambretta and Vespa. Over and above this, the employment and income position of the country was such that only a few people could afford cars and scooters. History testifies that it was due to the sacrifices of the elder generation that cheers on the faces of innumerable families could be brought within four or five decades.

When we see millions of people without bicycles and even shoes in their feet and find the rich and famous people as well as many of the middle class families who have joined the upper middle strata buying costly cars and motor cycles for their families and kids and wasting costly petrol like water just for fancy driving, enjoyments and pomp and show, we begin to wonder whether our previous leaders were right or the present ones are rightly guided. An inner voice in us asks us: Have we succeeded in providing sufficient food, decent clothing, reasonable shelter, fresh water, stable electric supply, pollution free atmosphere and comfortable life to our millions of people living in the villages and cities? If the answer is yes, then we are certainly justified in enjoying the luxuries of costly cars, scooters, motor cycles, and petrol and consumer durables.

However, if the answer is in no, we find ourselves defenseless because our conscience cannot justify the extravagant expenditure of national resources on the purchases of so many cars, scooters, motor cycles and luxury items when our innumerable people are below the poverty line, our numberless children find it difficult to get two times meals and we have miserably failed to provide the required necessities and comforts of life to our two third population. Our conscience provokes us by saying why our leaders are not asking us to sacrifice our passion for glittering cars, beautiful scooters and shining motor cycles and attractive means of comforts and luxuries till our have-nots and downtrodden sections are brought at par with others? Alas! we over hear demands from our grandsons and grand-daughters compelling our sons to order for them magnificent motor cycles and cars which keep our lips closed and our consciences succumb under the heavy pressure of emotions and we become dumb founded.

**Inadequate Infrastructure**

It appears that we are the victims of circumstances but nobody can deny that we committed the folly of jumping in the automobile age without providing necessary infrastructure with the result that each family is facing transport problem from morning to evening every day. Despite the phenomenal increase in the number of trucks and cars and tremendous increase in road traffic, we have not been able to chalk out an effective transport policy. The manner in which licenses are given to some of the unscrupulous people by obliging the officials and the way in which some of the police constables collect money openly from the drivers of the heavy vehicles and the tone and temper with which a few proactive road inspectors check the army of trucks causing road jam are worth noticing. See the conditions of roads in the cities of India with water logging, pot holes, bumpy spots, broken patches at regular intervals and congested routes damaging tires, delaying traffic, depreciating vehicles and increasing the travel cost. The public faces traffic jam on every crossing of each city leading to the blocking of school buses, causing anxieties to the patients, raising pulse rates of office-going people and resulting in immense fuel loss. So also is the state of the national high ways. Unfortunately, the high ways of world standard are very few in India. The existing ones have been encroached everywhere and mostly they are narrow, and unsafe. Old and depleted and overcrowded buses ply and in the process of overtaking several accidents take place. Many a time the rash driving youth dash with the coming cars or buses at very short intervals which not only cause accidents and result in loss of limbs but lead to heavy traffic congestion here and there. The passengers are never sure that they would reach their offices in time, the attendants fear that their patients might not see the faces of the hospitals and those who have to reach the airports always look at their watches in anxiety. Besides, there is very poor patrolling by the police resulting in looting and murders at lonely and isolated places. If accidents take place the patients mostly die on the spots for there is no arrangement to take them immediately to nearby hospitals. The situation is mostly compounded due to the lack of traffic clearing agencies and trauma centers and near absence of monitoring and patrolling authorities. The national high ways have been mostly damaged by the heavy trucks which ply day and night. Since railway takes much time and there are chances of pilferages, businessmen mostly use heavy trucks for plying goods across the country, though they are risky. The most interesting aspect of the road development is that generally important national high ways are repaired and improved every year but after every rainy season they get spoiled. One can see patches of water ponds on the roads and at times it becomes difficult to drive the vehicles due to big and deep holes. The traffic moves at very slow speed and it takes hours to reach homes. If by chance there is any road block it takes unthinkable time to clear it.

Besides, several roads in the country have been built through toll tax. They appear very nice. People willingly pay the exorbitant toll tax but within few years they become problematic. The manner in which the roads are repaired by filling the pot holes by mud and grass is deplorable since after the first rain the pits again reappear. Our country has constructed several kilometers roads and has also laid many high ways still we are not nearer to many African and Asian countries which have laid a chain of beautiful roads and high ways. The problem in our country is that whenever the land is acquired for high ways there is tussle between the farmers and the government. The farmers complain that government pays them pea nut price and sell the land to private builders at exorbitant rates and the government justifies its action. The tussle between the government and the farmers usually takes the ugly shape. Mostly there are agitations, strikes and *gheraos* in which many people are killed in firing. Besides, several times the environmentalists put their foot down and thus the process of laying new high ways is dented badly.

If one happens to go to the bus stands one would find that mostly they are situated either in the congested areas of the cities or in the peripheries. They are generally occupied by beggars, leprosy patients and the wayfarers. Leaking water, torn papers, layers of dust and pieces of leftover are spread here and there. The poor passengers sleep on the grounds without shelter and the *dhabas* and hotels that provide food items are in a miserable condition. There is a great rush on the windows where tickets are distributed and in the process several pockets are picked by the picketers. There is hardly any place to sit for the waiting passengers and no proper arrangement for keeping the luggage. The law abiding authorities too take little interest as a consequence of which many hawkers of dubious character befool the passengers by selling them fake drugs and duplicate materials at high rates. Mostly the buses are old and depleted. Their seats are uncomfortable, glasses loose and body parts noisy. They have been plying since long and there is no scientific method to repair, renew or discard them. They are sent to workshops only when they confront some problems. Consequently, accidents and breakdowns are very frequent. It is heartening to know that some states have wonderful high ways and their road ways too are nice. Beside, one is bound to give credit to our road ways and Taxi services that through their mediums one can at least reach one's destination in the wake of some urgency because it is next to impossible to travel by railways at short notice.

**Indian Railways**

It will not be out of place to mention here that despite the fact that our Railways have been functioning nicely since

British times, the condition of the passenger and goods trains and the traffic is not satisfactory. The platforms have practically no sitting arrangements for the waiting passengers. The waiting rooms are mostly overcrowded, untidy and generally occupied by non-deserving elements. The halting rooms at the railway stations are mostly untidy and uncomfortable. The children, ladies and the aged lie on grounds facing scorching heat, heavy rains and extreme cold as they do on bus stands of the road ways. There is no proper drinking water facility and toilet facilities for such poor passengers. The hawkers also exploit the passengers by supplying them substandard material so also the coolies extract money due to their strong trade union and unity. The chronically sick, the fortune tellers, the beggars and the unsocial elements mostly occupy the platforms of Indian railways. There is no proper system of disbursing information pertaining to various aspects of travel. Consequently, people are seen running after the railway officials. It is difficult to get reservation in most of the trains due to heavy rush throughout the year even on *tatkal* tickets. One has to apply much more in advance which is not possible for those ordinary people who have to travel due to emergencies on short notices such as to see the sick relatives or to attend demises or to attend religious or social ceremonies. It is the tragedy of the country that despite having a chain of Railways people cannot travel by railways due to lack of reservation.

The elected representatives, government officials and high ups have no difficulty since they have reserved seats for themselves. The problems arise for middle class people who can neither take the risk of entering the congested unreserved bogies nor can afford to get reservation. Most of them have to travel by buses which take much of their time and cause too much inconvenience. Many of them become the victims of the picketers and the unscrupulous agents. The students who move to face interviews or to search jobs or to meet their parents due to emergency too suffer immensely. Such passengers travel in inhuman conditions. One is shocked having seen them travelling on the roofs of the compartments, hanging outside the compartments and suffocating in the compartments without water and without attending toilets. Only those travel with ease and comforts who have their quotas or who can manage to reserve their tickets in time or who can manipulate by greasing the palms of the ticket checkers. On many routes one is not sure whether one would get ones seat despite reservation because many people especially the students and daily commuters occupy their seats and nobody is there to help them. Besides, many daily travellers sit in the reserved compartments, many milk vendors move in groups and they occupy the reserved compartments. At many places people pull the chains and get down wherever they feel necessary. Over and above this if any train is late then it goes on becoming late and one is not sure when one would reach the home. Needless to say, that the tracks, bridges, railway crossings, railway signals and railway equipments are very old and depleted so also the compartments of the passenger trains and bogies of goods trains. The result of overusing the tracks, bridges, compartments, engines and other facilities is that accidents take place at short intervals.

When any accident occurs at odd positions such as on the bridges, rivers, during floods or in thick forests, the passengers have to suffer at the hands of the nature as well as unsocial and unscrupulous elements of the society. Their chains, ornaments, watches and belongings are snatched leaving them crying but if it happens near some cities or villages, they are generally helped, assisted and treated nicely by the residents. However, the disaster management or crisis management proves cumbersome. The sick and the injured have to wait for too long for proper help. The passengers that are entangled within the compartments suffer immensely due to lack of proper rescue instruments. The dead lie unattended and the care and treatment of the passengers at the hospitals raise many eye brows. Important dignitaries express their condolences, charges and counter charges are levelled at the level of the Parliament.

Railway Minister and high ups visit the spot meet the injured in the hospitals, make the arrangement for the relatives to meet their relations, rescue the stranded passengers and compensations are immediately announced for minor injuries, seriously injured and the dead. Alas! When the time comes for the payment so many queries are put forward as a result of which only those benefit who are resourceful. Railway Minister announces various innovative measures and assures the nation that such ugly events would not be allowed to happen but as time elapses history repeats itself. As day is followed by night and night by day so also accidents are repeated in short intervals.

It is a fact that our Railways, High Ways and Transport System have failed in providing the necessary facilities to our passengers. We have not succeeded in managing our productive Railway Corporation when other smaller countries like France have managed it nicely generating enough surpluses. We have also failed in laying world class High Ways when tiny countries like Nigeria, UAE and Malaysia have succeeded in laying a splendid chain of high ways in their countries. We do have enough funds and can also spare or generate sufficient resources to lay new roads, new high ways build proper tracks, produce new engines, new compartments, new bogies and new bridges, proper railway crossings, scientific signals and a suitable scientific crisis management system. However, our problem is that we do not adopt the need based lucrative system but follow the populist policies and take undue credit for running Railway Ministry without increasing railway fares for several segments. We do have enough experts to man various branches or departments of the railway ministry and the Indian Transport system on scientific and commercial lines but we have none to raise questions about so many free tickets, reservation quotas and other facilities to elected representatives, politicians and government officials when the general public is finding it difficult to travel by trains. Our NGOs and the media too have failed to raise such questions at national level to awaken the interest of the general public. We are at the mercy of fate. It appears that till conscientious people from among the common men take the reins of the country in their hands, we would be be fooled by assurances that everything will be all right in the long run when in the long run all of us would be dead?

**Health-care**

Have we ever observed that when we return to India after visiting America, Europe and Australia the first impression that we gather after seeing Indians around the airports is that India is a very poor country, a country of sick, weak and downtrodden people. Our observation is based on the relative socio-economic conditions of Americans, Europeans, Australians and Indians. In comparison to the residents of the above mentioned foreign countries, we certainly find our people lacking in all the parameters of health and well-being. We have made much progress in our health sector after 1947 still much needs to be done. The condition of our government and some of the private hospitals, medical and dental colleges and the diagnostic centers is miserable. We have utterly failed to provide medical and health-care facilities to most of our countrymen. Several unlucky and unfortunate infant girls in the backward families die before coming in this world, many poor kids perish after taking birth due to lack of proper medical care, innumerable indigent and impoverished do not survive as a result of mal nutrition and those who survive among the multitude are mostly weak, sick and undernourished. Our elderly and poor, paupers and handicapped die every year in large number due to the lack of medical care. Several dreaded diseases like diabetes, cancer, typhoid and heart attack kill many young and old and several children become defunct because of polio. We do not have enough hospitals, nursing homes, diagnostic units, medical colleges, super specialty segments and health care centers commensurate to the need of the country's population. Those that are there are ill-equipped, poorly managed and starve due to the funds.

**Malpractices in Health Sector**

The most perplexing thing in our health sector is that like other segments of the country this segment too is the victim of corruption and malpractices. Many of those who are directly or indirectly associated with this sector, be they physicians, surgeons, technicians, pharmacists, druggists, medical practitioners or those manning medical colleges, nursing homes, diagnostic centers or others have mostly become money minded. Up to 1990 when the country pursued the mixed economy, all the medical colleges, major hospitals and important diagnostic centers were under the control of the government and they were mostly run on social considerations rather than on profit motive. However, after adopting liberal policies under the influence of globalisation various segments of the health-care were thrown open for the private sector. Consequently, there was mushroom growth of medical and dental colleges, private hospitals, clinics, investigation units and others. Seven star, five star and three star hospitals, super-specialty units, clinics, diagnostic centers and medical colleges were opened in the capital, metropolitan and important towns of the country. Being glamorous in nature and content they provided the seven, five or three star facilities to the patients and charged the seven, five and three star rates. These medical institutions are spread on a large tract of land and have a wonderful infrastructure. One is bound to be influenced after having seen the buildings, equipments, operation theaters, rooms for the patients, dresses of the attendants and the service conditions. Only those can afford to go to these institutions that are rich, influential, famous and resourceful. It is alleged that the infrastructure, equipment and service conditions in these institutes are wonderful but the quality of physicians, surgeons, experts and technicians is not generally to that standard. It is also claimed that some of these rich and famous institutions indulge in unfair practices such as charging higher rates from those government officials who are to be compensated by the government and those patients who are insured by the insurance companies. There is no dearth of people who complain that some of these institutes that have higher overhead costs and who are unscrupulous generally prescribe costly medicines and high priced injections. Sometimes they unnecessarily detain the patients for more than the required period and charge for such treatment which is not necessary. As soon as the patient enters these hospitals, their meters start running fast and end up in the payment of exorbitant medical, operational, hospitality and miscellaneous charges as well as charges for injections, drugs and other tests. These institutes are believed to be secretive and not transparent. They have a highly developed marketing, advertising, publicity and public relation net work. Ordinary people and those who cannot afford seldom go to these areas. However, if they venture to do so, they are overburdened for life.

Besides, there are some posh private hospitals, splendid clinics, glamorous medical colleges and wonderful diagnostic centers that are serving the health sector of the country nicely. However, the condition of many government hospitals is pathetic. They have been mostly located in old and depleted buildings around congested areas. There is shortage of qualified and technical staff and free medicines are seldom given to the patients due to the financial crunch. The dishonest officials do not hesitate in buying cheap and out of date medical instruments, expired and adulterated medicines and recycled syringes and cotton and used bed sheets. If one visits these institutes one is confronted with dogs, cows, crows and dirty surroundings. The wards are unclean, the beds are dirty, the furniture is sordid, the floor is broken, the walls have broken patches and the whole atmosphere appears depressing and gloomy. The poor and helpless visit these hospitals since they cannot afford to go to the private clinics. It is alleged that even in these hospitals one has to pay for the medicines and grease the palm for getting admitted and operated. Government hospitals serve with some sense of urgency to politicians and government officials or those who are resourceful. Charges of corruption, miss use of government funds, embezzlement and scams involving high officials are very common. In a sense these government hospitals and institutes have become redundant in the days of globalisation because even the poor and the downtrodden have started going to private practitioners or medical college hospitals.

The people are also fed up by the exploitative practices of many unsocial practitioners of private hospitals which have become the substitute of government hospitals. As the nice government hospitals are conspicuous by absence, people have no alternative but to go to the private practitioners many of whom charge astronomical amounts from the patients. The physicians sit in a set up of two to three rooms with stethoscope around their neck and the blood pressure instrument before them. They generally sit from 8.00 am to two pm and seven pm to nine pm and examine nearly 50 to 60 patients daily and charge abnormally per patient which they cannot earn in any government or private office.

In the same way, the surgeons, dentists, ophthalmologists, pediatrics, orthopaedics, gynaecologists, radiologists, micro-biologists and pathologists start their ventures in five stars type buildings by investing their savings or taking loans from banks. They employ juniors and earn huge amounts through operations and consultations. Patients are impressed having seen their infrastructure, their advertisements, latest instruments, army of employees and the rush of patients. These people form a coterie and promote one another. The well to do among them buy ornaments, landed properties, flats in multi-stories and invest in shares and gold. There is no limit to their earning for their charges per operation are very high and the patients pay them anyhow. These medical practitioners get cuts for recommending various tests or sending the patients to their fellow brothers. The medical representatives also provide them incentives in cash and kinds for recommending their costly medicines. They arrange for their conferences and foreign travels to promote their products. Besides, they have their own medical shops which are the sources of their earnings. There is nothing wrong in earning money provided it is reasonable because these persons had spent much of their time in learning the art of medicine and had spent huge amount in the establishment of their business concerns. They should know that the tax payers' costly resources were spent in providing them medical education. By themselves they could not succeed to become experts in the area of modern medicine. Thus, they too are duty-bound to serve the nation and the taxpayers by charging the sums which they could otherwise earn in the alternative sources.

**The Adverse Effects of Privatisation in Medical Profession**

It is worth noting that government of India allowed the private sector to start dental and medical colleges, training centers for nurses, diagnostic units and pharmaceutical courses to meet the shortages of the medical personnel which proved counter-productive. Ironically, only those capitalists could start such courses who had abundant money for the cost of land, buildings, medical equipments and expenses on salaries of the teachers and staff and the expenditure on infrastructure and miscellaneous items crossed crores of rupees which the medical men could not afford. Motivated by profit motive the big businessmen and influential politicians jumped into the field and employed medical people to man their institutions. Just as universities and colleges in the private sector should have been started by university and college teachers and not capitalists, so also these medical institutes in private sector too should have been started by medical practitioners and not by the capitalists. If efforts were made through providing finance and lands to teachers and medical practitioners at concessional rates the situation in the country would have been quite different. Unfortunately, the beginning of such institutions was laid on shaky foundations. Presently, a chain of dental and medical colleges, nursing training centers and similar medical institutions has spread throughout the country. The owners are charging astronomical sum in the form of tuition fees, donations, development money and excursion charges etc. Mostly, these institutes run on profit motive. It is alleged that they charge nearly Rupees forty to fifty lakhs for admitting students into MBBS courses and nearly a crore of rupees for MD courses. Similarly, the dentist colleges too charge exorbitant fees for their graduate and post-graduate courses. Many of them do not have competent and qualified staff in adequate number. Teaching in many institutes is below standard, training of the students lack penetration and the quality of hospitals supporting the teaching is far from satisfactory. Several students adopt unfair means in the examinations and some of the observers adopt lenient attitude to please the owners and in turn they are rewarded handsomely. Only those students join such institutes who are rich and do not find admissions in the main stream or those who belong to the reserved categories and are provided scholarships or loan facilities. Many a time some spoiled children from ultra rich or influential families join these institutes not for the sake of degrees but to pass their student days in merry-making. These institutes in real sense suit those mediocre students who by themselves cannot compete the medical examination tests but find the entry due to their parents who being in medical profession and running their own clinics, nursing homes or institutes can spare huge sum of money in the hope that their wards would inherit their professions. Besides, there is a large chunk of students who has acquired their medical degrees from East European countries and former Soviet Union Republics much of which are not recognised in the country. Only God knows, what would happen to these medical students when they would enter in their practical life and undertake medical profession?

Medical profession has become somewhat suspect in the eyes of general public. A few medical personnel are involved in the illegal transplant of human limbs. Poor and helpless people are the victims of loss of limbs at the hands of unsocial elements. We often hear the sale of blood, kidneys, eyes and other vital limbs fraudulently by unscrupulous surgeons. Many irresponsible gynecologists very often perform the surgery to deliver the child in order to get more money when the delivery could be obtained normally. Several persons dealing with ultrasound tell their parents about the conception of female children and the cruel parents get them aborted through anti-social gynecologists. Many physicians and surgeons prescribe costly medicines to please the medical representatives when cheap medicines can serve the same purpose and they also suggest numerous tests which are unwarranted. These unrequited tests are prescribed simply because they get substantial cuts or commissions on every blood, urine, sugar and other tests as well as on X-rays, cat scans, ultra sounds, etc. They cleverly put certain marks of identification for the required test or tests to be done through proper procedure and for the rest they ask them to give the normal report. Thus, in real sense the investigators conduct merely one or a few tests but charge for all the prescribed tests, the booty of which is distributed among all concerned accordingly. Likewise, it is alleged that many deceitful people do not conduct urine, stool or blood tests but give their reports based on their commonsense and charge exorbitant fees from the innocent patients. Besides, there are so many fake physicians and surgeons who are carrying on their profession since long and there is no check upon them. Many clever and cunning people take the help of print media, television and press conferences in befooling the general public that they have discovered the cure of dreaded diseases like cancer, diabetes, Aids, leprosy, epilepsy and impotency. Many produce several meaningful men and women before the audiences that they had immensely benefitted from the medicines of so and so. The misfortune of the country is that it is the victim of inaction. There is extreme form of adulteration in the medicines including the life saving drugs, injections, syringes, and medical instruments but one can easily escape the attention of the law enforcing agencies by greasing their palms.

It is a fact that we have failed to solve the health-care problem of our citizens during the last six decades. It appears that in real sense we are not so serious in solving our health problem though there are some exogenous and endogenous factors that have constrained us. Apparently, it looks that with the existing scenario as mentioned above we would hardly succeed but if new and viable and useful government hospitals are opened in cities and towns and nearby villages, private medical and dental colleges and private hospitals and clinics and nursing homes are revitalised and some foreign, famous and dynamic hospitals are invited to compete with our existing stuff much can be done, If unscrupulous adulterators and fake medical practitioners are penalised, strict vigilance is exercised on diagnostic centers and price structure of the private institutes is streamlined, our health care system can come on rails. Similarly, if our private medical colleges and super-specialty centers become society-oriented, our famous, competent and efficient physicians, surgeons and technicians follow the age old medical ethics and we can assign responsibility upon some person, group or organisation in governing structure for in action much improvement can be done in shortest time, Likewise, if our elected representatives in Panchayats, Zila Parishads, Municipal Corporations, state assemblies and Parliament become pro-active, Media come in the forefront, NGO's get activated, we can think of better future for our posterity. Despite all these, if we find it difficult, we can change the laws of the country by democratic, constitutional and peaceful means and make health-care a fundamental right so that the state is duty bound to take appropriate actions well in time.

### Senseless Introduction of the FDI's

When we meet our elders who are learned and more experienced, we face a volley of questions from their sides about the Foreign Direct Investment (FDI) policy of the country. They ask us why India allowed FDI in those areas which were not of much importance for the nation and where we had the required technology, necessary manpower, adequate resource base and the much needed expertise? Why did we not take lesson from the countries like China which did not permit such FDIs in those areas where they were strong? Certainly, we cannot justify FDIs in cold drinks such as Pepsi, Coco Cola and others because save the formula water, sweetening material, working force, bottles and everything from production to distribution was ours. Not only every work was done by our people but our people were their clients. How much foreign exchange have we lost in the form of Gold simply for drinking our own sweet water when the thirsts of millions of people suffering from water shortages could be extinguished by the gold that we lost in buying Pepsi or Coca Cola? Likewise, there was no logic of FDIs in food joints, branded clothes, fashion products and consumable items at the cost of huge foreign exchange when these items were not very vital from national point of view. Over and above this, from raw material to expertise and from production to distribution and consumption our people were involved in all processes. Similarly, there was no need of the FDIs in retail trade which will not only drain out our costly foreign exchange but also increase our imports and damage our millions of petty shop keepers and traders who are involved in selling agricultural and industrial products produced by our own country. When these foreign Marts would come initially they would sell cheap goods imported from foreign countries damaging Indian economy and displace millions of people but once they are settled, they would increase their prices and reap huge profits. In the same way, many sincere people ask us the logic of opening such stores in India when our own people can do the same thing. Besides, lands would be ours, buildings would be ours, manpower would be ours, commodities would be ours, they would be manned by us and we shall be the buyers. Moreover, save money which is not lacking with our people, the foreigners would bring nothing but carry away tremendous foreign exchange from our country. They also ask us the logic of allowing all types of sundry cars and motor cycles when problem could be solved with a few types of models only.

Everyone in the country is in favour of FDIs in the excavation and exploration in oceans, deserts, forests as well as in increasing the productivity of agriculture in arid and barren zones. Many support FDIs in constructing roads and bridges and tunnels in hilly and tough regions, in connecting rivers, in constructing mighty dams, in generating electricity, in improving infrastructure and in those areas where we do not possess the necessary expertise, raw material, technical know-how and funds. However, they abhor FDIs in drinking water, in cold drinks, in snacks, in chips, biscuits, food items, branded clothes, fashion items, alcohol, gambling and consumer durables. They also do not approve that the franchises are given in those areas where we possess the necessary technical know-how, raw material and the markets. Besides, all sundry goods produced by these foreign companies in India should not be allowed to be sold in our country. Only those goods should be permitted which we cannot produce efficiently and easily, the rest they should export elsewhere.

It appears that we have been perhaps hypnotised by the massive advertising campaigns of these multinational companies which they undertake by paying astronomical sums to our celebrities to popularise their products. Besides, the manner in which they promote their products through organising one day's, 20-20 contests, beauty shows and music nights spell bound our people and they forget to perceive their designs. Moreover, since these multi-national companies absorb our young talents at very high salaries there is much craze for such companies in the country. These companies employ our youngsters as CEOs and they fight the cases of these companies in government offices and elsewhere. The Indian counterparts also help them considering them their owners without realising the fact that they are merely the employees and these companies are being governed by the remote controls. Furthermore, there is a very strong patronage to these organisations by some of our rich, famous and influential sections of the society for many of them have franchises with them and several of them are the important partners with them. In addition to it, the internet's, mobile phones, i-pads and modern style of living and the impact of Western culture have created a mind-set which suits high mass consumption, extravagance and materialistic ways of living. As a consequence of which the products of these foreign companies in quick earning areas such as food, clothing, fashion and consumption items are thriving. Over and above this, there is an assured market for them which has been created in the country due to the emergence of rich businessmen, builders, politicians, professionals, government servants and neo-rich within the country which is supporting the demands for cars, consumer durables, fashion items, jewels and eatables. However, it is certain that the optimism would not last long. With the spread of education in the far and wide of the country the two third population of the country which is sleeping under dogmatic slumber would awaken. The villagers have spent huge amount of money for the education of their children in third class colleges opened by the private sector at every corner of the city who have degrees in their hands but are unemployed. This huge unemployed army of newly educated rural people is feeling cheated since the job market is closed for this segment due to poor academic background and they cannot fall back upon their ancestral professions after getting higher education. This frustrated group of young men is watching prosperity, extravagance, high mass consumption and plenty of money in few segments of the county on one hand and extreme poverty, hunger, misery, helplessness and exploitation on the other. One day it would rise to the occasion and change the balance of power through its voting power democratically, constitutionally and peacefully.

### Astronomical Salary Increases

It is highly regrettable that he who got the opportunity to obtain benefits from the country and the government did not lag behind. It is alleged that the politicians raised their salaries, allowances and other fringe benefits to the maximum, the government officials increased their salaries and benefits to the highest levels forgetting the fact that general salary standards in the country were at the very lowest side. The President of India was to get the salary of Rs 10,000 per month which was the highest salary in the country. Now a peon in government office gets more than what the President of India used to get. This shows that either the country has made extraordinary progress or the efficiency of the people has increased tremendously. When the ground reality is that neither people have become more efficient nor the economic conditions in the country have been improved tremendously. The government servants and the politicians have taken the advantage of the weakness of government and by showing the higher salaries in the mult-inational companies they too have succeeded in enhancing their pays and allowances. They did not bother about the fact that the jobs in multi-national companies were temporary and the qualifications were very high and the work load too was tremendous compared to government offices. Besides, a peon in private sector is working at Rs 2,500 per month and that job too is not available to many. Likewise, Professors in the Universities are getting more than one lakh rupees when a PhD is working in private colleges at Rs 10,000 per month and many of them are not finding even that job. The condition of efficiency in government offices and elsewhere is that people mostly do not work unless they are paid extra in the shape of bribe. Over and above this, the government servants have increased their age of retirement. This has not only blocked the careers of many young people but created inefficiency in the offices because many aged people find it difficult to perform their duties effectively. The states are in trouble because most of their budgets are spent in paying salaries to government officials and very little is left for developmental projects. A new pay commission is at the corner and the new salary scales would touch the sky. If this remains the state of affairs only God would save the country from doom.

**Sundry Issues**

We observe that many of us have lost the sense of direction. We are running fast but on the wrong track. We have discovered our own standards of dignity and glory but in reality they reflect our weaknesses and immaturities. We feel that by spending money lavishly on material things we can earn name and fame while the truth is that these things strengthen merely our egos and make us proud and arrogant. People are never remembered for their extravagance, they are loved when they do something for others rather than for themselves. We have seen that our marriage, birth days, house warming, victory and other ceremonies and festivals in the past were very simple. Although a large number of people were invited by the villagers at such functions but the items of food, decoration, entertainment, clothes and ornaments were not only simple and few but also less costly. Likewise, in cities very few people were given the invitations and the eatables as well as other paraphernalia selected for the purpose were deliberately kept simple, cheap and just the minimum. As against this, the modern ceremonies are very showy, costly and extravagant. People spend lavishly on dresses, ornaments, decorations, entertainments and pomp and show. Besides, there is tremendous wastage in the cities as well as in villages. Not only the food items are innumerable but they are very costly. People fill their plates but throw them after eating a fraction of it. Unfortunately, the extravagance is practiced in a country like India where thousands of people die every year due to hunger and due to lack of warm clothes in winter and numberless die in hot summer due to scorching heat and the multitude die due to the lack of treatment of Tuberculosis and other dreaded diseases. The rich and famous have only few family members but they are building palatial mansions buying several cars when the huts and ghettos are multiplying day by day in every corner of the country and multitude is moving on foot. Nobody is coming forward telling the rich and famous that they should spend reasonably on their various requirements but spare the rest for the marriages of the destitute girls, erecting shelter homes for the poor, providing medicines to the sick and improving the living conditions of those who are living in slums.

There is tremendous exploitation of some of our women folk, children and the destitute in the country in the name of *Nari Niketans*, women rehabilitation centers, women shelter homes, orphanages, destitute homes and shelter houses opened by a few unscrupulous agencies. Many a time, we hear about under nourishment, harsh treatment, mental break downs, suicides, molestations and rapes of the inmates by the unscrupulous elements. We often come across with cases of exploitation of female prisoners in jails, forced marriages of the innocent girls by their parents to foreigners, NRIs and others and the sale of poor girls to brothels by enticing them to provide them lucrative jobs in the cities. Similarly, a large number of girls are being exploited every year by the vested interests by employing them in fashion clinics, massage centers, boutiques, dance instructors, singers, dancers and actresses in film industry. Several sex rackets of call girls are operating in the big cities of the country in the guise of dance and music classes, travel agencies, gymnasiums and health-care centers. Mostly girls from small town are lured to run these enterprises and many of them finally face mental break down, several acquire Aids, few commit suicides and multitude end up in brothels. Likewise, we hear about the exploitation of boys in orphanages, rehabilitation centers and certain *madarsas* and *pathshalas.* Complaints of sexual exploitations, under nourishment and excessive hard work have been often received from many of these institutions. Employment of children in construction industry, industrial units, and domestic sector is very common and despite laws prohibiting child employment and child prostitution they are continuing unabated in the country.

Many manipulators have entered the Indian economy. Everywhere there are unions and cartels and pools that control prices and supplies. Vegetable sellers' union decides the prices of vegetables. The drivers' union decides the monthly salary of drivers and the union of daily wage earners decides the rates of daily wages, likewise, a powerful segment of the top class businessmen is controlling the country's commodity and the share markets by its bulk purchases and sales. Besides, every type of product legal or illegal, desirable or undesirable is available in the Indian markets. There is no dearth of contraband fire arms in the country. One can buy the same with ease in Indian markets. Many vagabonds possess pistols or guns and even the modern arms looted or acquired from foreigners or some of the unscrupulous army people and most of these weapons are used by the insurgents and the anti-social elements.

Recently, many cases of killing police personnel by these sophisticated arms have been reported in the country. Few are printing fake currencies to befool people, many are smuggling Indian currencies manufactured by our adversaries to sabotage our economy, several have opened bogus companies to harm people, multitude claim to have acquired the cure of dreaded diseases and innumerable are selling fake drugs for sex, diabetes, arthritis, cancer and vitality. Many loot people by promising them to send them to Gulf countries, several deceive people by *satta* business and lotteries and there is no dearth of people who are corrupting our young boys by selling them hashish, ganja and gutka. Many fake *gurus* have emerged on the scene and they are not only hypnotising innocent people by their sermons but are also exploiting their religious sentiments for their personal interests. Many *tantrics* have raped several women who approached them for getting sons and several of them have sacrificed their children who sought their help in getting the hidden treasures.

The agonies of the common man have no end. The Municipal Corporations do not leave them untouched. They increase house rents, water and drainage charges at short intervals without providing any facilities. Dirt and refuse mount on roads and the employees of the Corporations responsible to look after the affairs take least interest and there is none to control them due to their strong unions. A large section of the society including anti-social elements, musclemen, some unscrupulous industrialists misuse the electricity and many of them do not pay electric charges but the whole burden is being born by the honest payers. Generally, people are afraid of government machinery. They do not dare to challenge government officials even if they are wrong. Mostly, they settle matters by paying bribes because if they complain to the higher officers they get nothing as they support their own subordinates and if they approach the courts it takes years to decide the cases. There is a great bungling in the name of secrecy. Every department head has some kind of emergency as well as discretionary powers. Besides, there are some items of expenditure which do not come under the purview of audit being the secret ones. It has been observed that many irresponsible people take the advantage of the situation and usurp much of government funds under the pretext of secrecy. Alas! The country has innumerable economic and social problems but no effective voice is being heard from any corner to confront and solve them. There is complete silence in the country and a sense of loss among people. However, it appears that people have suddenly awakened from their long deep slumber after the victory of Aam Admi Party in Delhi and they are expecting that one day someone would rise and expose the blunders of the present system and set it right.

# 7 Emerging Scenario of Governance in India

*Aam Aadmi* proposes sweet dreams but our political leaders disposes. *Aam Aadmi* waited and waited for too long for seeing the results at the grassroots levels but got nothing. He asked the men in authority and the responsible people of the country to salvage the conditions of the country but no man, no leader, no political party and no social, moral and cultural organisation came to his rescue. Compelled by the circumstances he was forced to come on the scene. The signals of his uprising are coming from various sources and the political climate of the country too appears to be quite fertile for the emergence of such movement in the country. The basic reason for the emergence of people's movement is that the existing governing structure has lost its fighting and killing instinct. It is making compromises and getting out of the kitchen because it can't stand the heat. More or less the same is the condition of the civil society. We fear telling the truth and we hesitate taking the risk. We have forgotten the hard truth that success is neither an accident nor a destination but a struggle and a matter of choice. History shows that all successful people confronted a series of failures. They too failed but did not quit. They succeeded because they possessed the quality of bouncing back and did not deviate from principles. Our state in golden days too followed *Raj Dharma* and believed in the principle that "*Truth always remains victorious*" and never compromised with evil forces. Experience is witness to the fact that our eminent leaders never ditched the trusted friends of our country in their worst days, who shared our woes, regarded our sorrows as their own and helped us during our lean days. They cared least for their personal gains and losses while fighting for principles, values, ethics and morality. It appears that many of our political parties too have deviated from our age old principles; consequently we have lost many of our costly friends in hours and minutes, whom we had befriended in years and centuries.

It appears that as a group and nation all of us have lost our self-esteem and self-confidence and fallen from heights. The story of the lion would perhaps throw some light upon our state of affairs.

*Per chance a lion pounded on the herd of a sheep. It was dumb founded seeing the cub of a lion running along with sheep due to the fear of the lion with grass in its mouth. Having seen the condition of the cub, the lion understood the whole meaning behind its grazing grass. It took the little one to the nearby river and caught its neck and lowered down its face towards the mirrored water. The cub was shocked having seen its face in the water resembling with the face of the lion. He pondered why the sheep were running due to the fear of the big one and nobody bothered about the small one when both resembled with each other as cuckoo resembled with cuckoo. When the lion took the small one along with it and roared upon the sheep loudly, the smaller one also thundered like a lion. To its great surprise those naughty sheep which were punching the younger lion hither and thither were running in fear after having seen it roaring like a lion.*

The gist of the story is that we too need some Mahatma Gandhi like savour, who can revive our self-esteem. However, it is certain that as the things exist today no such thing is going to happen in near future though there are enough indications of the emergence of a bunch of conscientious *Aam Aadmi* on Indian political horizon. We are analysing various socio-political conditions of the country to see whether there is any possibility of a massive people's movement or it is merely a wishful thinking.

**The Dream of Mahatma Gandhi**

The Father of the Nation wanted a government for the people of India where there were neither rulers nor the subjects but equals and those that were at the helms of affairs were not superior to others but first among equals. The people on the top according to Babu were there not because of their money power, political backing, family background, oratory and geniuses but because of service motive. It was expected of them that they would be hard honest, sincere and committed and lead simple and meaningful life and would be easily accessible to the general public. They would be hard-working and duty bound to relentlessly work for the welfare of the people day and night and would be transparent in their dealings and accountable to people. It was believed that they would go among people openly and in disguised forms to find their problems and to know their reactions about the functioning of the state with a view to make corrections accordingly. They would not enjoy extraordinary benefits but would get that much which would be necessary to function efficiently without any financial or logistic constraints. He wanted to lay the foundation of state on truth, justice, equity, piety, peace, progress, harmony and rich and composite heritage of India. He wanted an India where even the *Dalit* could be the President of India; a minority candidate could think of becoming the Prime Minister of the country, an *Adivasi* could dream of becoming the Speaker of Lok Sabha. He also wanted that in his *Swarajya* anybody could stand and object boldly any functionary of the state, if he was on the wrong foot. Above all, he wanted to see a prosperous, progressive and strong India where all people live happily without any discrimination based on caste, creed, religion, sex and place of birth. The experience during the last six decades reveals that still we are too far from the dream of Mahatma. Certainly, we have a democratic system in the country and we are one of the largest democracies of the world but we cannot claim that our democracy is the government of all sections of Indians by all types of people for all kinds of citizens. Some claim that it is the government of the rich and powerful people by the politically and economically strong segment and for the benefit of the affluent and resourceful sections. Others claim that it is the rule of a few powerful and politically conscious families, dynasties, caste conscious leaders, ideology-based persons and political stalwarts run by their nominees for their personal benefits. It is not the government of the majority of poor, marginalised and neglected people as well as farmers, artisans, workers and petty shop-keepers and the less privileged high castes, downtrodden backwards, depressed minorities and the miserable *Dalits* by their representatives for the benefit of the common man. It is the considered opinion of the common man that country does not need the presently prevailing politico-economic democracy which is a government of the minority of Indians by a fraction of the society for a limited section of the country. We need a socio-cultural democracy which is the government of all the segments of Indians by all the sections of the society for all the subjects of the country.

Its our misfortune that we have a Western type of democracy which is supposed to be a government of the people by the people for the people. This is a capitalistic concept based on *laissez-faire* philosophy where there is free competition between the participants and those survive in this system that are fit and those perish that are weak. In this type of government, the power vests collectively with the people and it is administered apparently by peoples' elected persons, but in real practice the benefit is not achieved by the whole segments of the society but by those who are competent. This type of democracy functions successfully in situations where all people are more or less similarly situated or in other words where the society is homogeneous in nature, in the sense that the abilities and capabilities of the people are not materially divergent and there are no structured layers of inequalities in the society.

However, where the society has geological layers and diversities of all types, this concept creates Verna's or zones of powers and influences and *ghettos* of poverty and helplessness. In structured societies this type of democracy cannot work efficiently without creating abilities among the handicapped people through affirmative actions. The notion of equal opportunities is relevant where not only there is absence of disabilities but also there is presence of equalities. It is foolish to believe that a handicapped can compete with a normal athlete in hundred meter race in the wake of fair umpiring. This form of democracy is only democracy merely in the name because the opportunities are mostly usurped by the haves, privileged, competent and resourceful people. The weaker and downtrodden sections fail to compete in every sector. They not only suffer but also remain always at the mercy of the ruling and powerful groups. We know that wherever the Western type of democracy is functioning it is benefitting the privileged sections of the society at the cost of majority of the commoners. As the governance and the resources of the country vests with rich, mighty and powerful people, the ordinary people have no alternative but to tolerate their domination with a view to obtain their livelihood and patronage. Essentially, this concept of governance is exploitative in nature and does not suit the majority of the weaker, marginalised, poor and the downtrodden sections of the society. For a country like India, we need a democracy with checks and balances well defined and well-marked in the Constitution, so that affirmative steps may be taken to compensate the handicapped sections in the wake of competition between unequals.

**Apprehensions of the Father of Nation**

We are reminded of the prophecy of Mahatma Gandhi. He said that a time might come when the "*Gora* ruler would leave the country and in his place the *Kaala* administrator would rule the nation". It is the misfortune of the country that despite the fact that India is the only democracy whose foundations have been laid on sacrifice yet Indian democracy became a self-centric. The world can hardly show any example where a man who was the cause of obtaining freedom or who was in real sense the conquering king kicked the throne and did not enjoy the fruits of freedom after pushing out the aliens from his soil. He was none other than the Great Mahatma Gandhi. Instead of becoming the President or Prime Minister of India, he preferred to remain a *sadhu* or ascetic. He did not involve even members of his family in the governing structure. He wanted the Presidents, Prime Ministers, Ministers and MPs to wear *khadi* which was the dress of ordinary man or *Aam Aadmi* and live in simple houses, move in ordinary cars, get reasonable allowances and mix with people like ordinary human beings. He could never imagine that our elected representatives would become VIPs, VVIPs, His Excellencies, My Lords, and Sirs wear Western dresses, live in posh bungalows, move in imported luxury cars and earn huge salaries and allowances and get immense benefits and facilities. He could not dream that they would entertain their foreign guests with best types of imported wines, continental and world class food items and with fan fare instead of Indian foods in simplistic manners. He could never think that *durbars* would be held, buggies would be used and guests would come in wonderful attires. He could not imagine that it would be difficult for the ordinary man to meet the ministers and MPs and the VVIPs. Gandhiji must have been shocked having seen the army of body guards around the elected representatives. He must have been amazed having observed the elected people fearing those who had elected them. Thank God that during Pandit Nehru and for some period of Indira Gandhi the President, Vice-Presidents, Ministers wore *khadi*, moved in ambassador cars and kept the salaries and allowances at reasonable levels but later on the situation changed drastically. It is heartening to know that our present President of India Mr Pranab Kumar Mukherjee has directed that he be not addressed as His Excellency but simply Shri. It is a healthy sign for the country.

### Indian Politics Appears Feudal and Capitalistic in Character

The misfortune of the country is that Indian politics appears capitalistic and feudal in nature where the position of an individual is insignificant without the patronage of the peers. There are so-called capitalists and the feudal lords in the Indian politics who command the politics of the country from Panchayat to Parliament levels. They are there in the Parliaments, State Assemblies and other elected bodies for the last several decades along with the members of their families, friends and supporters due to their family influences, playing caste politics, supporting the *Dalits*, spreading certain ideologies and espousing the cause of the minorities and the weaker sections of the society. The heads and the important men on the top of each political party decide the fates of the candidates as well as the policies of the parties. There is practically no internal democracy in most of the political parties. If there is any, it is perhaps in the name sake. Be it the distribution of the tickets, selection of a minister, appointment of the Chief Minister or Prime Minister or giving any favour or settling any dispute the matters are mostly left to the discretions of the heads whose dictates are considered as the last words. It is also alleged that the countrymen mostly do not cast their votes in favour of the candidates on the basis of their credentials but they usually vote on the basis of the reputation, work, promises and assurances of the leaders. Ironically to get the ticket or to become a minister or to get any favour or any position in the party every member has to look towards the head of the party. Thus, it is claimed that loyalty to the person and not to the party or nation is the motto of most of the parties in the country. It is further stressed that many parties charge huge donations from the candidates in lieu of giving them tickets and for providing the blessings of the party heads. Since the major objectives of almost all the parties are more or less to secure power by hook or crook, they field candidates whose winning powers are better irrespective of the fact whether they are tainted or not. Most of the parties try to please the electorate by raking emotive issues. Questions pertaining to growth and development of the country, interest of the people and matters relating to cultures, values, principles and morals are seldom raised. Whether it is the forming of the government, joining a coalition, supporting the no confidence motion, opposing the issue of black money or horse-trading, each party generally keeps its interest in mind and usually behaves rationally, selfishly and pragmatically without caring for principles and practices. India's politics has become more or less a profession. Just as in any profession the children, wives, relatives and friends and acquaintances are hired similarly, in politics also sons, daughters, wives, daughter-in-laws, son-in laws or friends and relatives are preferred. Since these days the politics need more money, resources and manpower, everybody cannot enter into it. Only those join politics who can afford it and who have interest in it. Besides, as they spend astronomical sums in getting elected it is expected of them that they would recoup the same many fold consequently principles, ideologies, ethics and moralities get back seats and pragmatism and self interest rule the day.

The impact of some of the dirty and unconventional electoral practices is that from the stage of getting the party ticket till the expiry of their terms many crooked elected candidates too become pragmatic, selfish and self-centric. It is claimed widely that they try their best by any means to win elections. They use liquor to attract the votes of the addicts and vagabonds, pay hefty money to the poor for casting votes in their favours, hire touts, criminals and unsocial elements to deter their adversaries, invite film stars, celebrities, saints and religious people and men of eminence to corner the votes of ordinary people. It is also alleged that they perform *pujas, havans*, go to the tombs of the saints, pay lavishly to the religious institutions to win elections. They request with folded hands, raise sensitive issues, roar like the lion and do not hesitate to vitiate the atmosphere if it is in their favour. They care most for the party bosses and try to befriend or please the heads. They know their limitations and are aware that it is practically impossible for them to displease their bosses or leave the parties because for deserting the parties they need the support of at least one third members which is not easy. On the contrary, they could be expelled from the party and lose their position in the assembly or the Parliament in the wake of violating the whips of the parties. They continue to remain in the party despite being displeased with the policies of the party and wait for the opportune time when they are able to cross the floor. Since they have to pay huge money to get tickets and they also incur astronomical money and resources during electioneering, it is said that they too make it a point to earn as much money, favours, concessions, commissions and resources as possible. After getting elected many of the rogue politicians try for the ministerial jobs, failing which they struggle to get the chairmanships of the corporations or president ships or headships of some lucrative bodies. It is alleged that the anti-social elements among the elected persons earn substantial money out of their development funds and other state level or district level funds which are provided to them for the development of their constituencies. Besides, it is also said that they earn enough money in getting government officials transferred to the places of their choices, in getting the work done of their clients at police stations, government offices and at secretaries levels or at the stage of ministers due to their influences and connections. They earn huge salary, they are entitled to pension facilities, they can travel by air and railways, they have the telephone and internet connections, they can enjoy the hospitalities of government guest houses at concessional rates and they are respected everywhere. They are invited in every function, they have red bulb cars, and they are escorted by the police personnel. Many of them keep muscle men and anti-social elements with them to deter their enemies and it is also said that some capture unclaimed lands and disputed properties by force and become quick rich. Most of the political parties at the level of the centre, state, district or village generally does not go into the details of the reputation, criminal background, social status or moral conducts of their candidates but it sees to the winning positions of the candidates. If the candidate can win the seat by his social status or by criminal background or economic strength or muscle men or tongue power or communal image or nuisance, the party would generally not hesitate to give him the ticket. Irrespective of the proclamations of the political parties the fact is that, practically all parties have fielded some candidates against whose names there were criminal cases. The political scenario in the country is such that every elected person wants to become a minister and if he is not given a suitable birth he becomes a nuisance. Therefore, the political leadership has to constantly struggle to please their MLAs and MPs by providing them suitable positions and favours, so that they may not defect.

**Remote Controls in Politics**

It is also claimed that many political parties and governments in the country are governed by remote controls. There are several parties which depend upon their victories on the help and assistance of certain expert groups, business magnates, hard core segments social and cultural organisations, muscle men and mafia. Such groups, individuals, organisations provide them necessary manpower, funds, resources, guidance and favours at the time of electioneering. Those sections which have their base in public try their best to convince the masses to vote for the parties of their choices. Their cadres and manpower work at the grassroots level and their supporters try day and night to garner as much votes as possible. It is maintained that when such parties come in power, they generally yield to the advices, directions and requests of their mentors. These organisations, bodies and individuals are also provided land facilities, finances and other government favours in lieu of their services at the time of elections. The ruling governments promote their policies and ideologies, support their social and educational institutions, guest houses and cultural centers and look at them with respect and favour.

It is also claimed that several businessmen exert their influence upon the ruling governments to extract some concessions and favours for business community in exchange of the mighty funds and resources they spared at the time of elections for the victory of the parties. Their influence is so mighty that hardly any political party dares to go against them. In the same way, there are some influential families in the country which practically run the governments supported by them from their premises. They decide the Prime Ministers, Chief Ministers, Ministers and their port-folios. Their influence is such that they decide who would become the President and Vice-President of the country, who would be the Chairman of Lok Sabha and who will be what. Day to day directions are provided to governing structure by such bosses though efforts are made to convince the people that the real power vests in the party structure. Likewise, the muscle men and mafia too do not lag behind. They try their utmost to take as much benefit as possible generally in the shape of withdrawing criminal cases against them, getting room for manoeuver to carry on their criminal activities and exercising their presence at the level of governing structure which prove counter-productive for the ruling governments in the long run. Similarly, where some religious, caste or sectarian groups assist the governments they too expect *quid pro quo*. It is also alleged that the government servants, media and various segments of the society also try to see that their problems too are redressed in the manifestos of the political parties and It has also been observed that some government policies are also changed many a time due to the remote controls exercised by certain international agencies and the governments in lieu of financial, political, strategic or moral supports. It is a reality that in the days of electronic media remote controls have become a necessity and no organisation can escape from it.

**Some of the Misadventures of the Elected Representatives**

Time is witness to the fact that India was ruled mostly by Rajas, Maharajas and kings. Some amongst them were generally just, fair, truthfull and impartial. There have been a few renowned kings like lord Rama, Vikramaditya, Ashoka and Akbar the Greats. They followed *Raj Dharma* and treated all their citizens equal without any difference of caste, creed, colour, religion, sex or place of birth. By and large they were pious and meticulous and kept the sentiments and the requirements of the general public upper most in their minds. The *Rishis, Saints* and learned *Brahmans* guided them and also controlled them wherever they faltered. While selecting their ministers, courtiers and officials they fully ensured that they were honest, trust worthy, and devoted and corruption free. They visited various parts of the state in disguised forms to know the conditions of their subjects as well as to get reaction of the citizens about the functioning of their rule and the state. The criminals, corrupt and the wicked were dealt with sternly and the ordinary people were looked after with care and compassion. Several roads, forts and Raj Mahals or mighty mansions were constructed during the famines out of the Kings private properties to provide employment to the people. Taxes and levies were reasonable and subjects paid them willingly. One could travel throughout the length and breadth of the state without any fear to one's life, honour or property. Prices were affordable, commodities were adulteration free and there was peace, prosperity and tranquility among various sections of the society. The glorious period of magnificent Rama is known as *Ram Raj* or an ideal rule. History is also witness to the fact that most of the kings were moody, erratic and incompetent. They never bothered about the interest of the general public and mostly remained involved in wine, women and luxurious entertainments. They considered states as their personal properties and subjects as their slaves. Per chance if there were despotic rulers they were God's curse for the people. It was because of the atrocities of the kings that kingship was banished from the world and democracy took its place. Democracies being the governments of the people suited the mankind most. They functioned and are functioning efficiently throughout the world and benefitted mankind to the maximum. Incidentally, when democracies went in the wrong hands, they created severe heart burning.

Indian masses are generally not satisfied, the way their representatives behave with them after being elected. They allege that several of them came to their doorsteps at the time of elections with folded hands, made huge promises and assured them of their fullest help and support but when they got elected they minted money, benefitted their dear and near ones and lived beyond their means and bothered least for them. Their main grudge is that many of them do not visit their constituencies after getting elected, care least for those who elected them and do not solve the problems of their constituencies. They also allege that many of them do not attend regularly the Panchayat meetings and assembly and Parliament sessions but indulge in horse-trading and involve in illegal gratification. They also complain that a few among them have many criminal cases against them, some of them used criminals, anti-social elements and rogues at the time of their election rallies and innumerable offered liquor in abundance, paid huge sums of money to touts and spent unaccounted sums to win elections. For argument sake if we believe it to be true then the question arises why they elected them? Were they not aware of their background and antecedents when they elected them? Did the candidates force them to vote in their favour? Did they threaten them of dire consequences in the wake of not electing them? If their answer is in yes then the question arises as to why did they not complain to the election officer or the officers on duty? Actually the fact is that they knew everything about the candidates but there tragedy was that they had no alternative. They had tried practically all political parties and found them more or less the same. They had to select the lesser evil that they did.

It is a fact that many of them did not take any interest in the elections because they knew that it was of no consequence for them and they were the last to benefit. Besides, they considered no party and no candidate of any significance. They also knew that they would miserably fail if they faced elections themselves due to lack of their muscle power, money power and lung power. They also knew that all peace loving citizens abhorred the type of elections which were being fought on Indian soil. They were also knowing the fact that fighting elections usually resulted in bickering, enmity and bloodshed. The Indian masses, therefore, provided their hidden support and gave them leeway believing that those who spent millions of rupees, time and energy would like to earn as much as possible. They were sure that whoever would be elected would behave as others have behaved. Many of them found it an opportune time to earn money by acting as touts and agents, several wished to enjoy the luxury of free liquor and many of them asked the candidates to help them in their police cases and internal disputes. These politicians tolerated all their unreasonable demands and spent money, time and energy with the vengeance that they would teach them a lesson after being elected. The above situation shows the highly frustrated state of Indian democracy where neither the elected representatives seem serious in their tasks nor those who elect them. Both are equally responsible for the mess.

### Worth Seen Moments in Parliament

Strange and curious scenes are observed in and around the Assemblies and Parliament. Mostly the known faces are found sitting on the specified front seats near the familiar faces. Some faces are observed smiling, some calm, some serious, some anxious, some pro-active and some docile. Here and there are found sitting gorgeous, smart and famous personalities from the women section adding grace and glamour to the Parliament or Assemblies. The attendants in their neat dresses and imposing turbans move in between to add beauty to the whole scene. Sometimes the legislators speak with great emphasis, many a time they thunder in high-pitch and several times they raise their voices in increasing tones and innumerable times they speak with projected lines on their foreheads, anger in their eyes and hands moving in all directions. From one corner comes the noise of thumping of the desks and from the other the loud noise of shame and shame. Sometimes people recite Urdu poetry to attract the attention of their colleagues, at other times some cut jokes, a few take the help of satires. Many a time some interesting personalities with their stylish accents and typical tones spread laughter. It also happens several times that when the atmosphere becomes surcharged the whole surrounding gets disturbed. There starts grumbling and chaos. Some people rush towards the speaker, many moves towards the well, several raise their fists in anger, one or two tangle with each other and there is no dearth who tear papers, throw missiles and fume in anger. Many meaningful people come to save the situation, a few stand in between agitated members and some persuade them to keep silent. The Speaker throws requests after requests, calls them by names to take their seats but all in vain. When situation further worsens, Marshals are called, few are shown the doors. If the situation continues to worsen the Speaker declares the Parliament or Assembly meetings adjourned *sine die* or for a few hours.

When they reassemble, session starts with seriousness. The concerned minister presents his or her ministry's performance record upon which there are showers of questions, objections, replies and counter replies. The budget session is very lively and full of vigour and curiosity so also the question hours. There is a tug of war between the ruling party and the Opposition members. Charges and counter-charges are levelled against each other. Majority of the people play the role of supporters, agitators and desk thumpers. They mostly keep quiet and watch the whole scene with rapt attention. There are some known faces that appear pro-active, meaningful and significant and they are the centers of attraction in Parliament or Assemblies. Mostly, they play their active role and the whole Parliament or Assemblies revolve around them. Many a time a few surprises can also play wonders so also the silent spectators. After the session is over many are found giving press briefings which too are full of charges and counter charges.

The scene becomes very tense at the time of special sessions particularly when the vote of confidence is sought or clarification of any policy matter is made or corruption charges are levelled against any dignitary or it is the question of the ratification of any treaty or deal. There is intense lobbying outside and inside the Parliament and Assemblies. Party spokesmen clarify their view points and it becomes clear who will support, who will oppose and who will be the neutrals and the surprises. Alas! When the final result comes to the notice of the people, it appears to so many that it was a stage managed show. Few raise fingers at the Opposition parties, several criticise the so-called idealists and multitude lament the way the ruling party of the country and the Opposition function in unison in India. It has been observed on several occasions that various political parties despite their ideological and other differences unite with the ruling government due to the weaknesses of their party bosses or fear of any CBI investigation in matters of unaccounted money or for other personal interests. The Opposition also does not lag behind. It too makes compromises with issues that are highly significant but suit them and their cadre.

There was a time when the ruling party mustered the support of two-third majority and it had no difficulty in appointing ministers, electing the President or Vice-President of India or conducting the functions of the government. For many years only one dominant party ran the government with substantial majority but these days it has become difficult for any party to have absolute majority at the Parliament. There is coalition politics in the country and it has created uncertainty and in-action. There are various political parties in the country that have different ideologies, different approaches towards socio-economic problems and different viewpoints. Similarly, their regional issues and problems are different and varied from the problems and issues of other parties. Over and above this, they are being headed by different bosses whose mindsets are at variance with each other. They want *quid pro quo*. Under such circumstances the politics of appeasement or give and take is played which mostly proves detrimental to the country.

Having known the present political climate of the country and the mind-sets of the politicians of the nation and the attitude of civil society one can safely conclude that all is not well with the affairs of the nation. Under such circumstances we cannot apportion blame solely on one segment since almost all the sections are equally responsible in one way or the other. People generally consider the political dynasties, political heavy weights and cast, class and religious leaders as well as the ideologists responsible for worsening the situation.

Despite the fact that the politicians are committing blunders and the masses are not satisfied with their workings and dislike the way they are elected violating all principles, they give them second and third chance and neither change them nor expose them nor do anything to bring necessary changes to make the whole system viable simply because the whole political scene of the country has been vitiated by the lack of true leaders and absence of genuine followers. The problem with the nation is that:

Firstly, those who are competent and can do something do not come in the picture. Secondly, the masses who select them also do not exercise their minds; thirdly, nobody is willing to bell the cat. Lastly, all of them have accepted the on-going situation as a pragmatic reality and left the destiny of the nation at the hands of those who can afford to garner votes. It is a fact that right type of people cannot dare to come forward to seek elections because they are sure that they cannot be elected. They know that huge amount of money; energy and time as well as better connections, muscle and tongue-power and tremendous amount of flexibility, dynamism and opportunism are needed to see the success in the field of politics which they do not possess. Being honest they cannot spend crores of rupees on electioneering knowing full well that they may or may not be elected and even if elected they cannot recoup the same through honest and genuine means. Besides, they cannot command large following and sincere workers to fight elections without spending money and support of the influential persons. Moreover, they cannot afford to go door to door and bluff people that they would help them rightly and wrongly in lieu of their votes. Thus, seeing all this they peacefully quit and leave the ground open for those who can afford all types of hum bucks. The entry of the conscientious, competent and honest people in Indian politics can be made possible only when the general public becomes proactive and conscientious. If the general public itself approaches the meaningful people and assures them of its complete support without involving their resources and allow them to work freely, impartially without expecting any untoward reward from them in lieu of the support, things can be improved dramatically. This type of situation appears difficult in near future because the Indian society is not homogeneous in nature. It is composed of various castes, belief systems and interest groups. The dichotomy of interests would not allow them to come on a common platform. Besides, the vested interests would take the advantage of the ignorance and backwardness of their sects and succeed in misleading them in their personal interests. However, if the general atmosphere changes across the country due to charismatic entry of a few leaders the solid foundation can be laid for the entry of honest and efficient persons in Indian politics which would go a long way in shaping the destiny of the people.

**Experience After Getting Democracy**

Indian democracy is functioning despite so many odds because there are countless people in the country who are neither aware of the niceties of the democratic functioning nor about the rights and duties of the elected representatives nor about the powers and responsibilities of civil society. Many of them do not find any fault seeing their several representatives accumulating huge amount of money illegally, moving with the caravans of cars and army of subordinates because in their daily lives they observe even ordinary officials of government enjoying similar facilities. They have also seen that several dishonest persons who got government jobs generally multiplied resources beyond their means and many rogues who became ministers mostly collected sufficient resources enough for the survival of two to three generations.

Similarly, when some of their MLAs and MPs took any money, resources or benefit from them to assist them or any party or group for bailing out at the time of no confidence motion or raising their issues in proper forums or in lieu of some work done by them or some favour shown by them, they found no fault in that because they confronted hardly any official obliging them without greasing his palms. Likewise, they found nothing wrong in floor crossing, distributing money, liquor etc., at the time of elections being the part and parcel of the game. In the same way, the dynasties or families or a few over Lords ruling the country directly or by remote controls is not a new thing for them since in business all these things happen. Moreover, they

never expect that their elected representatives would come to them for they know that they have to go to a *patwari* or SHO at his office for their work rather than calling them at their doorsteps. Besides, they cannot think in dreams that they can recall their leaders or terminate their membership for they never succeeded in getting any government official transferred or suspended due to his not serving them properly. Since they judge the functioning of our democracy in the light of their experiences they find it as good or bad as other government offices are.

The fact is that the masses being helpless and ignorant of many complexities of Indian democracy are confused. They are silently watching as spectators what is happening in the country around them without expressing their specific opinion and exerting pro-actively at the time of giving votes, a glimpse of which would be visible from the following observations. If we ask them their opinion about the nature of Indian democracy most of them would say that in real sense it is the monopoly of a few. They are convinced that they have observed no material difference in the life of millions of people after 1947. If there appears any change it is merely cosmetic in nature. They agree that their assemblies and Parliament do not have representatives from all the sections and segments of the society in proportion to their numerical strength. Instead they are the nominees of the selected few lords ruling the country due to their unfading influence. Likewise, they emphasise sincerely and honestly that their elected bodies do not serve all sections of the society from grassroots level to the high ups justly, equitably and conscientiously. In their opinion they are the properties of a few families and the last refuges of the vested interests. Similarly, the masses accept the fact that they do not have any power to compel their elected representatives to serve their constituencies nicely and behave properly in their day to day affairs save to watch helpless till the next election. Similarly, they watch silently the untoward activities of their representatives and know that they cannot recall them in case they feel that they are boycotting the assemblies and the Parliament and not performing their duties sincerely and honestly. They also believe that they cannot stop them from moving from one political party on whose symbol they were selected to other party in search of fresh pastures. Despite this apathy they have no action plan. Likewise, they have no objection in allowing politicians winning elections till death despite their age, health and other handicaps and do not want to put certain restrictions in election rules to check them winning elections time and again. They do not want to discourage family and dynastic inbreeding in Indian politics because they find nothing wrong in it. Over and above this, they believe in the *status quo* and do not want to restrict the number of political parties in the country. Essentially, they consider themselves non-entities and know that they cannot do anything in the matter but certainly take pride in the fact that the world calls their democracy as the largest functioning democracy of the world.

In the same way, many of them seldom doubt the integrity of the ruling party and Opposition but appear satisfied by their sincerity, integrity, commitment and devotion. They are least concerned whether their political parties are functioning on Gandhian principles or adopted glamorous ways. Since they have no caliber to judge the functioning of high offices they sincerely believe that their Prime Ministers, Ministers, leaders of opposition and parliamentarians performed satisfactorily and remained above board. They do not understand the difference between Presidential form of government and parliamentary democracy hence cannot answer whether the President of India should have more powers even in the parliamentary form of democracy or should be satisfied with existing ones. They certainly do not believe in making the affairs of the highest offices simplified since they are convinced that the offices of the President and the Vice-President of India really need an excellent super structure and magnificent paraphernalia. They have no opinion of their own in matter as to how the President and the Vice-President of India should be elected as to suit the dignity of these two highest offices of the country. However, since they adore all the former Presidents and the Vice-Presidents they are convinced that all the Presidents and Vice-Presidents of the country were chosen due to their integrity, geniuses, public image, popularity and suitability and no politics played any role anywhere. They believe that the Presidents and the Governors of the country acted mostly impartially at the time of forming governments, nominating people, providing mercy and doing important works and they had no leanings towards the ruling parties or opposition. They certainly believe that the pay structure of the public and private sectors should be so designed that nobody gets higher pay than the President. They never believe that the foreign journeys of our higher authorities were courtesy journeys but believe that the state benefitted from the foreign journeys of the Presidents, Vice-Presidents, Prime Ministers and Ministers to various countries of the world despite costing huge amount. They have no calibre to answer whether they are satisfied by the laws so far enacted by the Parliament but they do not approve laws that are contrary to Indian ethos, customs and traditions. Actually, they are simple-minded people and believe in what is told to them or what they hear in the speeches of their leaders. Instead of telling anything on their faces or showing their reactions they keep quiet. The perverted politicians consider their silence as their positive approval and use it in their favour which tends to perpetuate the evil of corruption in the country. Corruption in high offices and at lower levels too is surviving because the rogue people in the governing structure have taken it for granted. Nobody should take the dormant power of *Aam Aadmi* lightly. The history shows that when *Aam Aadmi* came on roads he ruined the careers of many stalwarts who took them lightly and ignored their interests time and again.

### The Problem of Corruption

If the Indian democracy has given anything to us in abundance, it has given us corruption, nepotism, red-tapism, bribery, commissions, cuts and what not. Corruption is India's biggest problem. Even Rajiv Gandhi, the former Prime Minster of India confessed that out of rupee one meant to spend on development and public projects, only 18 paisa's reached the grassroots level. The money which was provided for the construction of the roads, bridges, high ways, dams and buildings, schools, colleges, hospitals and scientific laboratories filled the pockets of the unscrupulous government servants, contractors, builders and mafia from top to the bottom. The resources which were allocated for providing jobs to the unemployed, in granting subsidised food grains to below poverty people and in helping the poor farmers through cooperative societies were usurped by fraudulent agents for buying their cars and building majestic mansions. The money that came for the mid-day meal of the children of the marginalised sections, in giving pensions to widows and aged and handicapped and in providing health care to the downtrodden was embezzled by anti-social elements for enjoying five star facilities in the world class hotels of the world. In short, whatever was provided for the development of different people, regions, segments, sections and sectors, was looted by the cheats and they used the bribed money lavishly in organising lavish marriage parties, purchasing gold, diamonds, costly properties, enjoying foreign trips, consuming imported liquor, educating their children in foreign countries and in depositing the surplus money in foreign banks.

**Corruption from Highest to the Lowest Level**

It is an admitted fact that India is facing corruption from the highest level to the lowest with some meaningful exceptions. There is tremendous corruption among few undesirable politicians on high positions. Scams after scams have been reported but without any result. The CBI filled cases against many Chief Ministers, Ministers, Members of Parliament, Members of Legislative Assemblies and other important dignitaries giving the impression as if the menace of corruption would be completely routed out from the country. For the time being the televisions and the print media cried foul but ultimately things subsided as the bubbles subside when they are punctured. Initially people were very enthusiastic and believed that the government, opposition and all the meaningful people of the country were sincere in their resolve to wipe out corruption from the face of the country but later on it appeared that it was perhaps stage-managed show. Many a time it looked to the people that cases were filed to pressurise their rivals and when they yielded to the pressing groups, the same were withdrawn. Fingers were also raised at some of the Chief Justices and Justices of the Supreme Court, Judges of the High Courts and others but ultimately nothing materially happened. It also happened that many IAS, IPS and secretary level government officials, bureaucrats, many Vice-Chancellors of the Universities and several army personnel of high ranks were targetted as the violators of country's rules and regulations but most of them too escaped unhurt. Besides, several businessmen, builders, exporters, importers and money launderers, batters, gamblers, smugglers too faced the music but finally the countrymen did not hear much about them. It is said with caution that many unscrupulous Central and State Ministers perhaps charge huge sums for transfers, promotions, purchasing material for the government and in performing their legal duties. Most of the people allege that many important government properties situated at prestigious positions were taken over by the politicians themselves or transferred on nominal payments to the vested interests in lieu of money. Several claim that there is a fixed rate for every task and interested people religiously pay the same in order to get work done from most of the functionaries both at the central and state levels.

It is generally the talk of the town that many irresponsible Members of Parliament and Members of State Legislative Assemblies misuse the development fund given to them for the development of their constituencies. It is also alleged that many took huge bribes at the time of protecting the government from falling from power, a few took money for raising certain questions in the Parliament or assemblies, many work as helper to the needy in getting their work done through ministries or governing structure in lieu of pecuniary benefits and some got lands and petrol pumps and other government facilities and benefits being in favourable positions. Every Indian hears every day that billions of rupees which should have gone to national exchequer have been kept by the corrupt politicians, businessmen, government officials and others in foreign banks. Likewise, huge money received in the shape of commissions, cuts and bribes in the purchase of equipment and materials for various ministries too is lying somewhere undetected.

It has been rightly said that just as water flows from higher level to the lower level similarly corruption too flows from higher offices and positions to the lower offices and positions. The impact of the corruption in high offices is that people in the lower offices and positions are boldly demanding money for performing their official work.

Previously, they were taking petty bribe but cautiously and fearfully but now they have become bold. They often impress that they come to the office since they are paid salaries but for doing work they need to be paid according to the nature of the work. They also say it in secret that all the money does not go to them but it is shared between different people including the people on the top. It has been rightly said that if the king snatches one egg from the public illegally and forcibly, its subordinates eat away all the fowls of the town. It is openly said by the general public that no paper moves in government offices without giving the bribe. People sincerely feel that Indian bureaucratic system is problem creating rather than problem solving. The babus are experts in creating problems for the people. Unless and until the fixed sums of money are paid no work is done in time. If you want license for the twelve bore gun or a rifle or a revolver or you want gas connection, ration card, passport, identification card you would be quoted amounts for each one of them. Likewise, if you want to establish a school, a college, a medical or dental or engineering college or a university in the state, people claim that it can be done provided the specified amount is paid to the concerned persons.

Similarly, for getting government contracts, quotas, facilities, grants or establishing factories, getting letters of registration, etc., one has to pay the prescribed money. It is alleged that people do not hesitate in demanding bribe as if they feel that it is their right. Once the prescribed money is paid, it is said that work is done as promised. It is an established fact that one cannot escape the boggy of corruption wherever one goes. The beauty of corruption is that those who have money and resources can get everything done through the boggy of corruption. If one could not get reservation in the train and wants reservation out of the way one has to oblige the ticket collector. If one wants to change the date of hearing in the court the experienced ones allege that one has to pay to the clerk certain sum of money for the favour. If one wants some favour in the sales tax office or in income tax department it is alleged that work cannot be done without pleasing the babus. People generally say that for getting any favour from police personnel money is the only alternative. It is also stressed that if one goes to registration department and wants to buy or sell the house or land one has to incur huge extra money to get the work accomplished. What to talk of big offices it is alleged that even *patwaris*, clerks and peons do not move if bribe is not paid to them.

**Corruption Institutionalised**

Corruption in the country has been institutionalised. Many honest, sincere and committed government officials are hard pressed. A few of them have resigned and many are facing the music. One Kerala cadre IAS officer who was IIT-graduate and had history of topping all his exams and who has written 25 books and who also succeeded in securing the All India first rank was transferred twenty four times in his twenty year career for working honestly, transparently and devotedly. Likewise, one IAS Jharkhand state administrative service officer known for his uprightness and fearlessness was transferred 56 times in a 36 years long career. There are many officers who are fighting even after retirement and there are many who are facing frequent transfers to odd areas yet they have not yielded. The misfortune of the country is that more or less every segment of India is infected by the virus of corruption. Several students claim that bogus teachers ask for money for showing them favours, the patients lament that the dirty physicians and surgeons want money in government hospital for consultation, operation and getting other facilities, the farmers complain that they have to pay money to get credit from the rogue Cooperative officials, the labourers agitate that they are not paid their full due when they work on government projects. Government contractors confess that they are compelled to do substandard work because they have to pay to the anti-social engineers.

Similarly, the licensees, quota holders and petrol pump owners whisper that they too are the victims of corrupt officials. Not only this, the private sector too cries that it has to pay to a number of government officials connected with their business concerns from the lowest to the highest positions so that hurdles are not created in their routine work. The limit is that if they ask for police help in the wake of some disturbance by their employees they generally have to grease the palms. Sometimes they are obliged to pay a fixed sum to irresponsible police officers every month to get their assured help. Besides, they have to spare their cars, arrange for hospitability in hotels, pay donations, present gifts and arrange parties occasionally. Many important businessmen including the foreign companies have made corruption as the part of their cost of production which is being paid by the general public in the form of higher prices. It is disgusting to note that corruption has taken various shapes most of which are dirty, immoral and lewd. Many anti-social people, mafia and international gangs do not hesitate using call girls, threats, murders, black mailing and kidnapping to achieve their objectives. Corruption has given impetus to anti-national activities, drug-trafficking, arms smuggling and such economic and criminal offences which have created instability at world level.

**Mark up Corruption**

It is the belief of the ordinary Indian that corruption is part and parcel of Indian life and no one can escape it. It is working like the mark up inflation. Since the washer man has to pay higher prices for the detergents and other soaps, he increases his washing charges. As the barber has to pay higher washing charges to washer man, he increases his cutting charges. Likewise, because the milkman has to pay higher cutting and higher washing charges, he increases the price of his milk. In this way with the increase in price in one segment, the prices are increased in all the segments. Similarly, corruption is prospering in every sector because when one person pays the bribe somewhere and if he is in a position to get the bribe elsewhere he would not miss the opportunity. For instance, if one pays extra money or bribe to get favour at customs department, he would charge for his services if he is an official in police department and in this way many segments of the society are involved in the boggy of corruption. It is boldly told by many at the road side that be it the agricultural department or forest, health, education, law, personnel or any one of them if one wants to get things done within reasonable time one usually has to pay some kind of convenience fee. It is an admitted fact that for spreading corruption one cannot place the blame entirely on the heads of the government officials. The general public is equally responsible. Many people try to take illegal and objectionable work by the government officials which they find difficult and cumbersome. Thus, to tempt them they offer bribe to which many succumb. For instance, if someone has committed murder the relatives would approach the police and request the police officials to impose minor clauses against him and not the section 302 *in lieu* of substantial money or when a thief is caught his relatives would try to get him free by greasing palms. Similarly, many contractors themselves offer bribes to the engineers to get the contract or the Indians coming from foreign countries too offer bribes to custom officials to get the contraband items cleared. Mostly the bribe is taken for giving out of turn favours.

The interesting thing is that rather than waiting for some time so that the government officials may properly look into their files and do the needful many Indians themselves offer the bribe to government officials for taking quick service for which they charge the so called convenience fee. People weigh paying the bribe to get prompt work rather than getting the work done in routine manner. If they are convinced that giving bribe would be more profitable than waiting for too long, they would prefer giving the bribe. In a sense, it can be concluded that it is the pro-active civilians who are also in some way responsible in corrupting government servants and perpetuating corrupt practices in the society. Besides, it has been seen that when many of us and our own kith and kin got the opportunities to serve the government departments we too did more or less the same thing. Many of us did not mind getting wealth from whatever source it came to us. Likewise, we never complained to the law enforcing agencies about those who accumulated resources beyond their means through bribes, never showed our disrespect towards them but agreed to marry our children and considered it as our good fortune to have contacts with them due to their brilliant financial positions. This shows that heart to heart many of us also relish bribe. It would not be wrong to say that many people could not take bribe either because they did not get the opportunity or got afraid due to fear of law. There are hardly a few glorious persons among us who desisted from corruption considering it as a legal and moral crime. Many of us who kept away from corruption considered corruption as a legal rather than a moral crime. If this state of affairs persists, corruption would continue for some more time.

**For How Long People will Remain Silent**

It is a fact that corruption has broken the backbone of the country and the whole atmosphere of the nation is in flux and turmoil. All the intellectuals, meaningful people and the well-wishers of the country are highly perturbed. The way corruption is being detected in every segment, the manner in which people at highest level are being booked everyday puzzle every citizen. The mode in which the Indian democracy is functioning and the style in which the country is drifting towards inaction and stagnation is causing alarm.

Foreign investors are eying on India's resources, the Indian businessmen are complaining about the lack of direction on the part of state, the legislators are playing the game of chess to force the general election upon the public. The prices of food stuffs are sky rocketing, the exports are falling, Stock Exchanges are crashing, value of the rupee is dwindling, growth of the country is declining and unemployment is mounting. Black money is creating hoarding and smuggling and forests are being mercilessly destroyed, environment is badly polluted and there is practically no control over terrorism and lawlessness.

Think for a moment for how long the masses would remain silent especially when they would see the foundations of democracy shaking? How far they would not react when they would observe that the Parliament and the Assemblies are disturbed again and again, no work is done on the floors of the houses, politicians get busy in infighting and there is frequent floor crossing. They are bound to agitate when they would notice that the work is done at snails rate, decisions are not taken timely and the rate of failures far exceeds expectations. They would surely cry foul when the bureaucracy would become supreme, law-makers would become defunct and the judiciary would be the talk of the town. Their blood would boil when the press would become business minded, televisions would show pro-government and pro-businessmen programmes in lieu of money, the news correspondents would lose their sharpness and the sanctity of media would be dented. They would certainly lament when the policemen would lose their grace, the security personnel would shy away, the authority of the state would be at the stake and government officials would be questioned. They would be shocked when businessmen and profiteers would be interrogated, builders and commission agents would be challenged and corrupt officials would be investigated and criminals and anti-social elements would be dealt with by the masses. They would cry when strikes would take place, lockouts would be very frequent, foreign investment would move out of the country, exports would cease, growth would miserably decline and unemployment would mount. They would explode when most of the people would lose jobs and would be hard pressed by inflation and their buying capacity would be exhausted and it would become difficult for them to meet two ends. At that time efforts would be made to set things right but it would be too late.

Seeing these conditions no sensible person who has slightest respect for the country would keep quiet. A time may come soon when some group of hot-headed politicians may ask people to rise against those irresponsible leaders, elected representatives and petty bosses who are enjoying all facilities of governing structure for decades without caring for their electorates and general public. Some frustrated reformers might incite citizens against the corrupt government officials who have minted money and enjoyed seven star facilities from public exchequer in connivance with the dishonest bosses. A few hot blooded statesmen may arise the sentiments of general public against those anti-social businessmen who have evaded taxes, adulterated goods, hoarded the commodities and collected uncountable black money and illegally transferred the same in foreign banks. Some pro-active people might even provoke people to teach lesson to those that are involved in foreign exchange bungling, big scams and mighty frauds. It is also possible that some misguided one might jump up from among the mob to persuade the public to take law in its own hands against those licensers and commission agents that have illegally built splendid mansions, accumulated hoards of wealth, bought luxury cars and are leading kingly lives through bribed money. It may also happen that a large segment of conscientious *Aam Aadmi* might arise on the Indian horizon under the able-bodied guidance of distinguish people and completely change the destiny of the people and the future of the country.

We know this much that nothing like Middle East is going to happen in the country of Mahatma Gandhi which believes in non-violence and peaceful co-existence. Whatever would happen would happen through the power of ballets peacefully, democratically and constitutionally and not through bullets. It appears that the peaceful *Aam Aadmi* Revolution is at the corner. Its symptoms are visible on Indian horizon. The rise of *Aam Aadmi* in the country after the victory of *Aam Aadmi* Party has created a new mind-set in the country as a consequence of which people are now terribly fed-up of muscle men, mafia, smugglers, hoarders, adulterators, unscrupulous builders, fraudulent politicians, crooked professionals, deceitful bureaucrats, devious NGO's and dishonest commission agents. They neither want the heavy weights, nor political dynasties nor those who are rich and famous to rule the country but want those who are associated with grassroots and *Aam Aadmi.*

They do not want highly idealist people or saints in politics but want sensible, practical and moderate people. The general public would have no objection if they keep reasonable security for their safety and use government buildings and offices for their uses equipped with necessary modern amenities and get reasonable perks and salaries and servant and vehicle, travelling and other facilities required to perform their duties. Basically people want a change in the mindset of the ruling class. They want a different set of people who do not make false promises with them. Never deceive them and dare not to consider them trivial. They are trustworthy in their words, sincere in their deeds, honest in their practices, committed in their objectives and transparent in their dealings. They want those politicians who can provide them safety of life, honour, property and possessions, who can make their homes, neighbourhood and cities safe and secure for them, who can make them safe in trains, buses, market places and during evenings and nights when they are out of their houses. They also want such persons who can protect them from kidnappers, land grabbers, criminals and cheaters. They want cheap and speedy justice and criminals behind the bars. They would prefer those who would help them in getting regular supply of clean water, uninterrupted electricity and cooking gas at reasonable prices. They desire adulteration free eatables, fruits and vegetables and adequate control over weights and measures. They would support those who would help them in getting a clean environment, all-weather pakka roads, dirt and refuge free by-lanes and efficient drainage system. They would patronise such beings who would assist them in fighting the rogue policemen, corrupt officials, shady ration suppliers, sinister vendors, questionable moneylenders and fishy satta and lottery agents. They would welcome those who would bring schools, poly-techniques, training centers, hospitals, banks, post offices, parks, recreation facilities in their vicinity. They would respect those who would help them in getting reasonably sized *pucca* houses at affordable costs, education to their children within their means and cheep health care in government and private hospitals. They would expect from their governments controls over the prices of life saving drugs and adequate supervision over the specialty centers so that ordinary people may get affordable treatment in time. They would expect from their leaders employment to their children, social security, and old age pension and unemployment benefits to their destitute. They would like to see to it that nobody sleeps on the foot path, railway plat forms, bus stands and isolated places, no one suffers due to scorching heat and crumbling cold and none among the unfortunates is without shelter home. They desire that there is no exploitation of women, children, orphans, widows, destitute and others in the country and the country looks after them with compassion and care. They would cherish that their cities are free from beggars, patients with dreaded diseases, *Ghettos* and slums. They want to make it sure that if they wish to travel by trains, roadways, or other modes they get the facilities without any inconvenience at reasonable prices. Besides, they may get reasonable hotel and restaurant facilities in important towns and cities at affordable prices. Likewise, they also aspire that their goods and service are transferred to them without any pilferage. They would like that their children are educated and married without any difficulty and their elders get respectable farewell to their last abodes.

The *Aam Aadmi* would not support those political parties which would have no vision about the heritage of the country and follow divisive policies and divide people on the basis of caste, region, religion, sex and place of birth. Common man would abhor those who commit scams on high and low places, who take the help of criminals and anti social elements and who are men of dubious character. Besides, those people who would not follow economy drive and would not keep away from pomp and show would get beating at the hands of public. Masses would not tolerate those ministers who would have no control over law and order, bureaucracy, police, judiciary, media, prices, terrorism and over all condition of the country and who would unnecessarily interfere in the working of the governing machinery. A man on the street would not allow those persons to rule the country whose economic policies would be growth dampening, who would fail to eradicate, hunger, diseases, poverty and ignorance from the country and also fail to check the irrational entry of FDI's and other goods and services of high mass consumption. People want adequate taxation policy at the levels of the centre, states and municipal corporations as well as a healthy import and export policy for the country. They do not want extreme gaps between rich and poor, urbanites and rural people. Similarly, those who would not protect rivers from pollution, forests from devastations would not be tolerated by people. In the same way people will have zero tolerance about those leaders who would dare to destroy wild life and country's flora and fauna. They would discard those legislators who would frame laws contravening the age old and glorious traditions of the country, who would follow shabby foreign policies and who would be unmindful of the defense of the country and fail to protect country's borders, high seas and the sky.

From what is happening in the country it is certain that a mighty movement of cleansing Indian system would take some definite shape from 2019 onwards and the reign of the government and economics, social and cultural organisations will be in the hands of those who would be sincere, committed, honest and morally sound. They would be honest, competent, committed, and large-hearted, and non-communal. They would belong to every segment of the society and represent every corner of the country and would have country's interest uppermost in their minds. They would be compassionate to poor and downtrodden, soft towards honest and efficient officers but harsh to corrupt and the rogues. Their acts would be generally just, transparent and equitable. They would have strong cadre of men of integrities in which it would be difficult for the dishonest to enter. They would not be idealists or *sadhus* and saints but pragmatic and practical people. They would follow a sensible, middle-of-the-road achievable vision but would be bold, aggressive, dynamic and decisive. People will see in them their Saviour or *Messiah* and they would see in the people their helpers, sympathisers and friends.

**Our Last Submission**

We have dwelt upon various aspects of the country which have affected different segments of the society. We have highlighted our expectations and realisations as well as our omissions and commissions. We have identified our strengths and weaknesses. We have emphasised at what we were and what we have become. We have stressed where we succeeded and where we failed. We have exhibited where we should have gone and where we are going. We have pointed out our priorities and our goals. We have showed our glorious heritage and hinted at how we have become rootless. We have cautioned how we are blowing with the wind and how are we losing our age old institutions. We have cajoled the whole society by saying that we are not confronting the realities of the world dauntlessly but timidly making compromises with them. We have also warned our intellectuals of the dangers of the new world order and cautioned that if we did not awake to face the dreaded monster it would flatten our social, cultural and spiritual principles. We have forewarned that the *Aam Aadmi* has waited for too long and his patience has been completely exhausted. If some concrete measures to salvage his problems are not taken, a significant portion of the conscientious *Aam Aadmi* would rise to the occasion and snatch the reigns of the country from the hands of the unscrupulous persons through a peaceful and constitutional *Aam Aadmi* movement based on ethics, values and morality. If the people in the governing structure, the responsible people in the country, and the civil society act constructively and favourably and salvage the problems of the country and the country men especially that of the *Aam Aadmi* within a meaningful time horizon, the author would feel rewarded.

# Index